FREE VIDEO      FREE VIDEO

ASVAB Essential Test Tips Video from Trivium Test Prep!

Dear Customer,

Thank you for purchasing from Trivium Test Prep! We're honored to help you prepare for your ASVAB exam.

To show our appreciation, we're offering a **FREE** *ASVAB Essential Test Tips* **Video by Trivium Test Prep.*** Our video includes 35 test preparation strategies that will make you successful on the ASVAB. All we ask is that you email us your feedback and describe your experience with our product. Amazing, awful, or just so-so: we want to hear what you have to say!

To receive your **FREE** *ASVAB Essential Test Tips* **Video**, please email us at 5star@ triviumtestprep.com. Include "Free 5 Star" in the subject line and the following information in your email:

1. The title of the product you purchased.
2. Your rating from 1 – 5 (with 5 being the best).
3. Your feedback about the product, including how our materials helped you meet your goals and ways in which we can improve our products.
4. Your full name and shipping address so we can send your **FREE** *ASVAB Essential Test Tips* **Video**.

If you have any questions or concerns please feel free to contact us directly at 5star@trivium-testprep.com.

Thank you!

- Trivium Test Prep Team

*To get access to the free video please email us at 5star@triviumtestprep.com, and please follow the instructions above.

ASVAB Study Guide 2021–2022

Test Prep Book with Practice Questions for the Armed Services Vocational Aptitude Battery Exam

TABLE OF CONTENTS

ONLINE RESOURCES

To help you fully prepare for your ASVAB exam, Trivium includes online resources with the purchase of this study guide.

Practice Test

In addition to the practice test included in this book, we also offer an online exam. Since many exams today are computer based, getting to practice your test-taking skills on the computer is a great way to prepare.

Flash Cards

A convenient supplement to this study guide, Trivium flash cards enable you to review important terms easily on your computer or smartphone.

Cheat Sheets

Review the core skills you need to master the exam with easy-to-read Cheat Sheets.

From Stress to Success

Watch From Stress to Success, a brief but insightful YouTube video that offers the tips, tricks, and secrets experts use to score higher on the exam.

Reviews

Leave a review, send us helpful feedback, or sign up for Trivium promotions—including free books!

Access these materials at:

www.triviumtestprep.com/asvab-online-resources

INTRODUCTION

Congratulations on choosing to take the Armed Services Vocational Aptitude Battery (ASVAB) exam! By purchasing this book, you've taken an important step on your path to joining the military.

This guide will provide you with a detailed overview of the ASVAB, so you know exactly what to expect on exam day. We'll take you through all the concepts covered on the exam and give you the opportunity to test your knowledge with practice questions. Even if it's been a while since you last took a major exam, don't worry; we'll make sure you're more than ready!

WHAT IS THE ASVAB?

The ASVAB exam is designed to assess the aptitude of individuals aspiring to gain entrance into any of the five branches of the US Armed Forces. All applicants must pass the ASVAB as one of the qualifications to join the military. The ASVAB testing program is under the purview of the Department of Defense and is administered at regional Military Entrance Processing Stations (MEPS) or local satellite offices called Military Entrance Test (MET) sites. Military personnel administer the exam at MEPS locations, while typically civilian contractors or government employees administer the exam at the MET sites.

High school students in grades 11 and 12 are eligible to take the exam as well as students in postsecondary schools. In order for your exam score to be considered for enlistment, you must have attained the age of seventeen when you take the oath to join the military, and your exam score must be no more than two years old. Adults who wish to take the ASVAB and join the military must be no older than the maximum age accepted by their desired branch of service at the time of enlistment.

There are two versions of the ASVAB applicants may take—the computerized (CAT-ASVAB) and the paper-and-pencil ASVAB exam. Please note that current military members who wish to increase their score to qualify for certain advanced schooling should take the Armed Forces Classification Exam (AFCT).

COMPUTER ADAPTIVE TESTING

Computer adaptive testing (CAT) allows the test administrators to get a more complete view of your skills in less time and with fewer questions. These tests start with a question of average difficulty. If you answer this question correctly, the next question will be harder; if you answer it incorrectly, the next question will be easier. This continues as you go through the section, with questions getting harder or easier based on how well you perform. Once you've answered enough questions for the computer to determine your score, that section of the test will end.

Often you will be able to immediately see your score after taking a CAT exam. You will also probably answer fewer questions than if you'd taken a paper-and-pencil test, and the section will take less time. However, you will not be able to go back and check or change your answers.

The ASVAB is offered in both CAT and paper-and-pencil form. The paper-and-pencil ASVAB exams are typically administered at MET sites where the CAT-ASVAB exam computer stations or military testing personnel are not available, such as high schools or at the National Guard Armory.

Retaking the ASVAB

If you are not satisfied with your ASVAB score, you may retake the ASVAB exam. The first two retake exams must be completed at least one calendar month from the date of the initial exam. After the second retake, applicants must wait at least six calendar months to retake the exam. ASVAB exam results are valid for two years.

WHAT'S ON THE ASVAB?

The ASVAB consists of ten subtests. In the following table, each subtest is listed with the approximate number of questions and the time limit allowed. Once you finish a subtest (or time runs out), you cannot return to that section. All questions are in a multiple-choice format. Applicants use the computer keyboard and mouse to select answers for the CAT-ASVAB and bubble answer sheets to select answers for the paper-and-pencil ASVAB.

What's on the ASVAB?

Subject	CAT-ASVAB		PAPER-AND-PENCIL ASVAB	
	Approximate Number of Questions	Time Limit	Approximate Number of Questions	Time Limit
General Science	16	8 minutes	25	11 minutes
Arithmetic Reasoning	16	39 minutes	30	36 minutes
Word Knowledge	16	8 minutes	35	11 minutes
Paragraph Comprehension	11	22 minutes	15	13 minutes
Mathematics Knowledge	16	20 minutes	25	24 minutes
Electronics	16	8 minutes	20	9 minutes
Auto Information	11	7 minutes	25	11 minutes
Shop Information	11	6 minutes	This subtest is combined with the Auto Information subtest.	
Mechanical Comprehension	16	20 minutes	25	19 minutes
Assembling Objects	16	16 minutes	25	15 minutes
Total	145 questions	2 hours, 34 minutes	225 questions	2 hours, 29 minutes

Breakdown of the Subtests

General Science (GS): tests your knowledge and application of Earth and physical sciences, biology, chemistry, and physics.

Arithmetic Reasoning (AR)*: tests your ability to calculate mathematical word problems using basic addition, subtraction, multiplication, division, percentages, ratio, and proportions.

Word Knowledge (WK)*: identifies the breadth of your vocabulary by asking you to select the correct meaning of a word, synonyms, and antonyms.

Paragraph Comprehension (PC)*: tests your reading comprehension through analysis of reading passages.

Mathematics Knowledge (MK)*: asks you to solve secondary-level math problems involving algebra, geometry, and converting fractions.

Electronics Information (EI): tests your ability to employ electrical circuits and formulas, identify their components, and use terminology.

Auto Information (AI)**: tests your knowledge of vehicle systems (e.g., engines, transmissions, and brakes) and repair techniques.

Shop Information (SI)**: tests your knowledge of correct tool use, shop terminology, and wood and metal shop practices.

Mechanical Comprehension (MC): asks you about basic mechanical principles surrounding levers and pulleys, complex machinery, force, mass, and kinetic energy.

Assembling Objects (AO): tests your spatial orientation skills by asking you to identify how objects fit together.

*Indicates the subtests used to compose the AFQT score.

**For the paper-and-pencil ASVAB exam, the Auto Information and Shop Information subtests are combined into one subtest. The score received for this subtest is listed as AS.

HOW IS THE ASVAB SCORED?

The ASVAB Score

Raw scores (number of correct answers) from four of the ten ASVAB subtests (Word Knowledge [WK], Paragraph Comprehension [PC], Arithmetic Reasoning [AR], and Mathematic Knowledge [MK]) are computed and weighted to make up the Armed Forces Qualification Exam (AFQT) score.

To calculate the AFQT score, the WK and PC scores are added together and compared to a Verbal Expression chart to get the Verbal Expression (VE) value. This new VE value is doubled. Add to the VE value the MK and AR weighted scores to get the overall AFQT score.

For example, suppose you received the following points for each of the categories:
- WK—15; PC—11; MK—32; AR—42
- Add 15 + 11 = 26. The score 26 equates to 40 for a VE value.
- Double the VE value = 80.
- Add 80 + 32 + 42 = 154.
- The total of 154 equates to 38 as an AFQT score.

Please note that the MK and AR raw scores are not used in computing the overall AFQT score. Applicants receive additional points for correctly answering more difficult questions in these two subtests, thus resulting in a weighted score.

The Standard Score

The Standard Score compares your raw scores (number of correct answers) combining the WK, PC, AR, and MK subtests to those of other applicants between the ages of eighteen and twenty-three. It is displayed as a percentile ranking (1–99 percent).

The Service Composite Score

Together with their recruiter, applicants may select a certain career field or military occupational specialty (MOS) depending on their ASVAB score. This score not only determines eligibility for entry into the military; it is also an indicator of which career field would best suit the individual. The score you receive may qualify or disqualify you for certain MOS within your chosen career field. Selection for assignment to some MOS requires higher scores than others. This is important to know if you wish to enter into a technical MOS. Ask your recruiter for qualifying scores of MOS that you may be interested in pursuing.

The Service Composite Score is the score the services use to determine if an applicant meets the qualifications for a specific MOS. The US Army, Air Force, and Marine Corps determine the Service Composite Score by calculating the raw scores from a combination of ALL subtests, not just the four subtests making up the AFQT score. These scores are known as line (or composite) scores. The Air Force uses the Numerical Operations (NO) and Coding Speed (CS) line scores in addition to the Standard Scores. Examples of the line (composite) scores needed for certain MOSs are as follows:

- Army AVENGER System repairer job: Add GS + AS + MK + EI. The total score must be 98 or above.
- Air Force in-flight refueler job: Add AR + VE. The total score must be 53 or above.
- Marine intelligence specialist job: Add VE + AR. The total score must be 100 or above.
- Navy aviation boatswain mate job: Add VE + AR + MK + AS. The total score must be 184 or above.
- Coast Guard: Add VE +AR. The total score must be 109 or above.

The Career Exploration Score

The Career Exploration Program is a tool for recruiters to identify aptitude and career interest in high school and postsecondary students. Students take the ASVAB and combine it with an interest inventory. Together these documents and results help pave the path for students with an interest in joining the military. This program is marketed specifically in select high schools and colleges. Students interested in this program should contact their local recruiter or high school counselor.

Qualifying Scores

Being fully qualified for military service requires applicants to achieve many benchmarks. To qualify for military service, applicants who possess a high school diploma must achieve different scores on the ASVAB than applicants with a General Education Development (GED). The Department of Defense places applicants in one of three tiers.

- Tier 1 applicants possess a high school diploma or some college.
- Tier 2 applicants possess a GED.
- Tier 3 applicants do not possess an educational certificate or diploma.

Tier 3 applicants must score higher on the AFQT than a Tier 2 applicant. Likewise, a Tier 2 applicant must score higher on the AFQT than a Tier 1 applicant.

Recruitment goals always change, so an applicant who is Tier 3 may not qualify at all despite the AFQT score. Contact your recruiter for eligibility requirements.

Additionally, one qualifying score for the Army may not qualify that same individual for the Air Force.

The minimum ASVAB scores required for each service for applicants with at least a high school diploma or GED are as follows:

- US Air Force—36 with a diploma; 65 with a GED
- US Army—31 with a diploma; 50 with a GED
- Coast Guard—40 with a diploma; 50 with a GED
- Marine Corps—32 with a diploma; 50 with a GED
- National Guard—31 with a diploma; 50 with a GED
- US Navy—35 with a diploma; 50 with a GED

HOW IS THE ASVAB ADMINISTERED?

If you are ready to take the ASVAB, contact your local recruiter. Your recruiter will determine your initial qualifications and schedule you for the ASVAB. The location where you take the ASVAB will decide when a test seat is available.

On the day of the exam, you will need to bring valid photo identification to verify your identity. Testing materials are provided by the test proctor. Calculators are not allowed. If your recruiter drives you to the testing location, the recruiter cannot be in the testing room. Personal breaks are scheduled by the proctor, so be prepared to remain in the testing seat until dismissed.

GETTING TO KNOW THE UNITED STATES MILITARY

Joining the greatest and strongest military force in the world is an honor for which only a few qualify. If you have not decided on a specific branch of service, research all branches, as they offer a wide array of careers to choose from. Each branch of service has unique missions that it is commonly known for; for instance, the Army is known for land mission operations, Air Force is primarily jet aviation, Navy for sea operations, Coast Guard for sea border patrolling, and the Marines for worldwide security. To support these unique missions, all branches share certain identical career fields (e.g., administrative, pilots, and maintenance specialists) to choose from.

The rank structure of the military branches is broken down into three categories: enlisted, warrant officers, and commissioned officers. Enlisted members may join straight out of high school, and the military provides job training after basic training. Warrant officers are current military members who apply and qualify for advanced specialized training in certain technical career fields. They are considered technical experts in their career fields. As warrant officers, they are saluted by enlisted personnel. Commissioned officers enter the service after earning a four-year college degree or successful completion at a military academy or Reserve Officer Training Corp (ROTC) program. Commissioned officers are trained in tactics and leadership courses to lead the enlisted members assigned to them.

THE MILITARY RECRUITMENT PROCESS

As stated before, passing the ASVAB is just one requirement for military service qualification. You may contact your local recruiter through your high school counselor or college adviser, or visit your local military recruitment center.

Once you contact your local recruiter, he or she will meet with you at the recruiting office, your school, or your home. During this meeting, the recruiter will conduct an interview to initiate the recruitment process. This process begins with the recruiter determining if you meet the basic qualification requirements. Expect a review of your education level, financial record, background investigation, interests, criminal record or drug history, height and weight, age, and citizenship. Once basic qualifications have been established, the recruiter schedules you to take the ASVAB exam and a physical exam. After these, you will meet with your recruiter to discuss your ASVAB scores and any medical issue that may preclude your enlistment. During this meeting, the recruiter will discuss which branch(es) of service you qualify for and possible career options for you to choose from.

After selecting an MOS, you and your recruiter can discuss entry dates for your basic training and enroll you in online training courses to introduce you to the military and prepare you for basic training. While going through the testing and online training, your recruiter is your main contact until the date you take the oath of enlistment. Your recruiter can answer any concerns or questions you have along the way.

ABOUT THIS GUIDE

This guide will help you master the most important exam topics and also develop critical exam-taking skills. We have built features into our books to prepare you for your exams and increase your score. Along with a detailed summary of the exam's format, content, and scoring, we offer an in-depth overview of the content knowledge required to pass the exam. In the review you'll find sidebars that provide interesting information, highlight key concepts, and review content so that you can solidify your understanding of the exam's concepts. You can also test your knowledge with sample questions throughout the text and practice questions that reflect the content and format of the ASVAB. We're pleased you've chosen Trivium Test Prep to be a part of your military journey!

GENERAL SCIENCE

CHEMISTRY

Atoms and Elements

An ATOM is the smallest particle of an element that is still identifiable as a part of that element; if you break down an atom any further, it is no longer an identifiable element.

An atom is made up of several subatomic particles. The three most important are PROTONS; which have a positive charge; ELECTRONS, which have a negative charge; and NEUTRONS, which are neutral. The protons and neutrons of an atom are located at its center in the nucleus; the electrons move in orbitals around the nucleus. Protons and neutrons both have mass that is measured in atomic mass units (amu); the mass of an electron is so negligible that it is usually not considered.

Electrons orbit the nucleus in increasing energy levels called SHELLS. Only the electrons in the outermost, or VALENCE, shell are involved in chemical reactions. Atoms that are close to having a completely full or empty shell will be the most reactive and will easily give electrons (if the shell is almost empty) or receive electrons (if the shell is almost full). Atoms with full valence shells, which include the noble gases, are nonreactive. The space taken up by orbiting electrons is large relative to the size of the nucleus. Thus, the nucleus

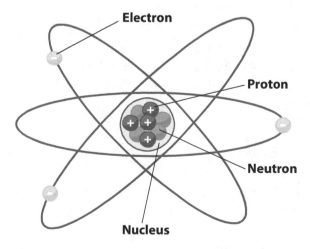

Figure 1.1. Atomic Structure

is only a small portion of the total amount of space an atom takes up, even though it contains most of an atom's mass.

All atoms of the same **ELEMENT** have the same number of protons (called that element's **ATOMIC NUMBER**). For example, all carbon atoms have four protons. There are approximately 109 known elements; eighty-eight of these occur naturally on the earth, while the others are synthesized (manufactured). The elements are grouped together on the periodic table, and each has its own one- or two-letter symbol.

The **PERIODIC TABLE OF ELEMENTS** is a chart that arranges the chemical elements in an easy-to-understand way. Each element is listed in order of increasing atomic number and aligned so that the elements exhibit similar qualities. Each row in the table is known as a period, and each column is called a group.

1	2		3	4	5	6	7	8	9	10	11	12	13	14	15	16	17	18
1 H 1.0079																		2 He 4.0026
3 Li 6.9411	4 Be 9.0122												5 B 10.811	6 C 12.011	7 N 14.007	8 O 15.999	9 F 18.998	10 Ne 20.180
11 Na 22.990	12 Mg 24.305												13 Al 26.982	14 Si 28.086	15 P 30.974	16 S 32.065	17 Cl 35.453	18 Ar 39.948
19 K 39.098	20 Ca 40.078	21 Sc 44.956	22 Ti 47.867	23 V 50.942	24 Cr 51.996	25 Mn 54.938	26 Fe 55.845	27 Co 58.933	28 Ni 58.693	29 Cu 63.546	30 Zn 65.39	31 Ga 69.723	32 Ge 72.61	33 As 74.922	34 Se 78.96	35 Br 79.904	36 Kr 83.80
37 Rb 85.468	38 Sr 87.62	39 Y 88.906	40 Zr 91.224	41 Nb 92.906	42 Mo 95.94	43 Tc [98]	44 Ru 101.07	45 Rh 102.91	46 Pd 106.42	47 Ag 107.87	48 Cd 112.41	49 In 114.82	50 Sn 118.71	51 Sb 121.76	52 Te 127.60	53 I 126.90	54 Xe 131.29
55 Cs 132.91	56 Ba 137.33	57-70 *	71 Lu 174.97	72 Hf 178.49	73 Ta 180.95	74 W 183.84	75 Re 186.21	76 Os 190.23	77 Ir 192.22	78 Pt 195.08	79 Au 196.97	80 Hg 200.59	81 Tl 204.38	82 Pb 207.2	83 Bi 208.98	84 Po [209]	85 At [210]	86 Rn [222]
87 Fr [223]	88 Ra [226]	89-102 **	103 Lr [262]	104 Rf [261]	105 Db [262]	106 Sg [266]	107 Bh [264]	108 Hs [269]	109 Mt [268]	110 Uun [271]	111 Uuu [272]	112 Uub [277]	114 Uuq [289]					

* Lanthanide Series	57 La 138.91	58 Ce 140.12	59 Pr 140.91	60 Nd 144.24	61 Pm [145]	62 Sm 150.36	63 Eu 151.96	64 Gd 157.25	65 Tb 158.93	66 Dy 162.50	67 Ho 164.93	68 Er 167.26	69 Tm 168.93	70 Yb 173.04
** Actinide Series	89 Ac [227]	90 Th 232.04	91 Pa 231.04	92 U 238.03	93 Np [237]	94 Pu [244]	95 Am [243]	96 Cm [247]	97 Bk [247]	98 Cf [251]	99 Es [252]	100 Fm [257]	101 Md [258]	102 No [259]

Figure 1.2. The Periodic Table

Elements in the periodic table exhibit trends across periods and groups:

- Elements within a group have the same outer electron arrangement. The number of the main group corresponds to the number of valence electrons in those elements; however, most of the transition elements contain two electrons in their valence shells.
- The horizontal rows correspond to the number of occupied electron shells of the atom.
- The elements set below the main table are the lanthanides (upper row) and actinides. They also usually have two electrons in their outer shells.
- In general, the elements increase in mass from left to right and from top to bottom.

While all atoms in an element have the same number of protons, they can have different numbers of neutrons and electrons. Atoms of the same element with different numbers of neutrons are called **ISOTOPES** and can have different masses. Atoms of the same element that have different numbers of electrons are called **IONS** and will have a charge. Positive ions are called cations, and negative ions are called anions. If an atom has the same number of protons and electrons, it is neutral.

When two or more atoms join together they form a **MOLECULE**. For example, O_3 (ozone) contains three oxygen atoms bound together, and H_2O (water) contains two hydrogen atoms and one oxygen. Water is considered a **COMPOUND** because it is made by combining two or more different elements. Atoms can be joined together by different types of bonds. In a **COVALENT BOND**, the atoms share electrons. In an **IONIC BOND**, two ions with opposite charges are attracted to each other and bind together. Chemical formulas are used to represent the atomic composition of a molecule. For example, one molecule of water contains two hydrogen atoms (H) and one oxygen atom (O), so its chemical formula is H_2O.

Examples

1. Which term describes the smallest unit of an element?

   (A) molecule

   (B) atom

   (C) proton

   (D) ion

   Answers:

   (A) is incorrect. A molecule is the simplest form of a compound, consisting of two or more atoms.

   (B) is correct. An atom is the smallest unit of an element.

   (C) is incorrect. A proton is a positively charged particle in the nucleus of an atom.

   (D) is incorrect. An ion is an electrically charged atom or group of atoms.

2. The identity of an element is determined by

   (A) the number of its protons.

   (B) the number of its electrons.

   (C) its charge.

   (D) its atomic mass.

   Answers:

   (A) is correct. The number of protons in an atom determines which element it is.

   (B) is incorrect. The number of electrons determines the charge of an atom but not its element. Atoms with the same number of electrons can be different elements.

   (C) is incorrect. An atom may carry a charge, but it does not determine what element it is.

   (D) is incorrect. Atomic mass is the sum of the mass of an atom's protons and neutrons. Atoms with the same atomic mass may be different elements.

Compounds and Mixtures

Substances that contain more than one type of element are called **COMPOUNDS** (so, a molecule that contains more than one element is also a compound). Compounds made up of identical molecules are called pure substances. Water, for example, is a pure substance made up only of identical water molecules.

A **MIXTURE** consists of two or more substances that are not chemically bonded. Mixtures are generally placed in one of two categories. The components in a **HOMOGENEOUS MIXTURE** are uniformly distributed; examples include salt water and air. In a **HETEROGENEOUS MIXTURE**, the components are not uniformly distributed. Vegetable soup, for example, is heterogeneous, as are rocks and soil.

A uniform, or homogenous, mixture of different molecules is called a **SOLUTION**. If the solution is a liquid, the material being dissolved is the **SOLUTE**, and the liquid it is being dissolved in is called the **SOLVENT**. Both solids and gases can dissolve in liquids. A **SATURATED SOLUTION** has reached a point of maximum concentration; no more solute will dissolve in it.

Example

A coffee solution is produced when a teaspoon of dry coffee crystals is dissolved in a cup of hot water. The original crystals are classified as a

(A) reactant.

(B) product.

(C) solute.

(D) solvent.

Answers:

(A) is incorrect. Reactants are the molecules that react in a chemical reaction.

(B) is incorrect. Products are formed after a chemical reaction.

(C) is correct. The solute is the material that dissolves in a solution.

(D) is incorrect. The solvent is the material the solute dissolves into. In this example, the hot water is the solvent.

States of Matter

The physical states of matter are generally grouped into three main **STATES**:

SOLIDS are rigid; they maintain their shape and have strong intermolecular forces. In solids, the molecules are closely packed together, and solid materials usually have a high density. In the majority of solids, called crystalline solids, the ions or molecules are packed into a crystal structure that is highly ordered.

LIQUIDS cannot maintain their own shape; they conform to their containers but contain forces strong enough to keep molecules from dispersing into spaces.

GASES have indefinite shape; they disperse rapidly through space due to random movement of particles and are able to occupy any volume. They are held together by weak forces.

Two other states of matter include **LIQUID CRYSTALS**, which can maintain their shape as well as be made to flow, and **PLASMAS**, gases in which electrons have been stripped from their nuclei.

Changes in temperature and pressure can cause matter to change states. Generally, adding energy (in the form of heat) changes a substance to a higher energy state (e.g., solid to liquid). Transitions from a high to lower energy state (e.g., liquid to solid) release energy. Each of these changes has a specific name:

- solid to liquid: melting
- liquid to solid: freezing
- liquid to gas: evaporation
- gas to liquid: condensation
- solid to gas: sublimation
- gas to solid: deposition

Example

Which of the following describes the process that causes water droplets to form on the outside of a cold glass of water on a hot day?

(A) melting

(B) deposition

(C) evaporation

(D) condensation

Answers:

(A) is incorrect. Melting is the process of solids becoming liquid.

(B) is incorrect. Deposition is the process of gasses becoming solid.

(C) is incorrect. Evaporation is the process of liquids becoming gas.

(D) is correct. The water droplets form when gaseous water in the air comes in contact with the cold glass and condenses into liquid water.

Chemical Reactions

A **CHEMICAL REACTION** occurs when there is a conversion of one set of chemical substances to another set. Chemical reactions are caused primarily by a change in bonding structure in these substances due to the exchange of electrons.

In a chemical reaction, the starting substances are called the **REAGENTS** or **REACTANTS**, and the ending substances are called the **PRODUCTS**. In the reaction below, the reactants sodium hydroxide ($NaOH$) and iron sulfate ($FeSO_4$) react to form the products sodium sulfate (Na_2SO_4) and iron hydroxide ($Fe(OH)_2$). Note the **COEFFICIENT** of 2 in front of the sodium hydroxide reactant: for every one mole of the other reactants and products, the reaction requires two moles of sodium hydroxide.

$$2NaOH + FeSO_4 \rightarrow Na_2SO_4 + Fe(OH)_2$$

This reaction is known as a **DOUBLE DISPLACEMENT REACTION** because the ions in each reagent are displaced and trade places to form two new products. In a **SINGLE DISPLACEMENT REACTION**, a lone atom or molecule displaces an ion in the second reagent, creating two new products, as shown below:

$$MgCl_2 + 2Na \rightarrow Mg + 2NaCl$$

In a **SYNTHESIS REACTION**, two compounds combine to form a single product:

$$C + O_2 \rightarrow CO_2$$

The opposite reaction, when a single reactant breaks down into two or more products, is called a DECOMPOSITION REACTION.

Finally, a COMBUSTION REACTION occurs when oxygen is reacted in the presence of heat to a combustible compound, usually an organic compound. The products of a combustion reaction are always water and carbon dioxide. For example, the reaction of methane with oxygen will proceed as follows:

$$CH_4 + 2O_2 \rightarrow CO_2 + 2H_2O$$

In OXIDATION/REDUCTION REACTIONS (also called redox reactions), electrons are transferred between atoms. In a redox reaction, the total number of electrons shared by the reactants does not change—they are simply shifted around. An element is OXIDIZED when it loses its electrons, and the element that gains those electrons is now REDUCED. Therefore, the element that does the oxidizing is known as the REDUCING AGENT because it has given electrons, or has reduced, a different element in the reaction. The same thing happens with the reduced element. It is called the OXIDIZING AGENT because it has taken electrons from a different element. In the reaction below, copper is reduced and silver is oxidized.

Oxidation Is Losing
Reduction Is Gaining

Example

Which type of chemical reaction takes place when kerosene reacts with oxygen to light a lamp?

(A) oxidation

(B) neutralization

(C) combustion

(D) sublimation

Answers:

(A) is incorrect. Oxidation is a chemical change in which a substance loses electrons, as happens when iron is exposed to oxygen and rusts.

(B) is incorrect. Neutralization is a chemical reaction that occurs when an acid and a base react to form a salt and water.

(**C**) **is correct.** Combustion is a chemical reaction that produces carbon dioxide and water. Burning lamp oil (fuel) is combustion.

(D) is incorrect. Sublimation is a physical change that takes place when matter transitions from a solid to a gas.

Properties of Matter

MATTER is commonly defined as anything that takes up space and has mass. MASS is the quantity of matter something possesses (e.g., how much of something there is); it is usually measured in grams (g) or kilograms (kg). In addition to mass, it is possible to measure many other properties of matter, including weight, volume, density, and reactivity. These properties fall into one of two categories: EXTRINSIC PROPERTIES are directly related to the amount of material being measured (e.g., mass and volume), while INTRINSIC PROPERTIES are those that are independent of the quantity of matter present (e.g., density and specific gravity).

Matter can undergo two types of change: chemical and physical. A CHEMICAL CHANGE occurs when an original substance is transformed into a new substance with different properties. An example would be the burning of wood, which produces ash and smoke. Transformations that do not produce new substances, such as cutting a piece of wood or melting ice, are called PHYSICAL CHANGES.

Example

Which of the following is not a physical change?

(A) melting of aspirin

(B) lighting a match

(C) putting sugar in tea

(D) boiling antifreeze

Answers:

(A) is incorrect. Melting is a change in state, which is a physical change.

(B) is correct. Lighting a match results in combustion, a chemical reaction.

(C) is incorrect. Putting sugar in tea forms a solution, which is a physical change.

(D) is incorrect. Boiling is a change in state, which is a physical change.

Acids and Bases

There are a number of different technical definitions for acids and bases. In general, an ACID can be defined as a substance that produces hydrogen ions (H^+) in solution, while a BASE produces hydroxide ions (OH^-). Acidic solutions, which include common liquids like orange juice and vinegar, share a set of distinct characteristics: they have a sour taste and react strongly with metals. Bases, such as bleach and detergents, will taste bitter and have a slippery texture.

The acidity or basicity of a solution is described using its **pH** value, which is the negative log of the concentration of hydrogen ions. A neutral solution, which has the same concentration of hydrogen and hydroxide ions, has a pH of 7. Bases have a pH between 7

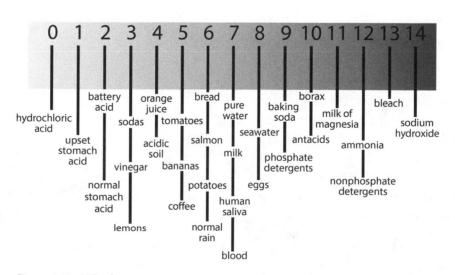

Figure 1.3. pH Scale

and 14, and acids have a pH between 0 and 7. Note that the pH scale is exponential, so a solution with a pH of 2 has 100 times more hydrogen ions than one with a pH of 4. A **STRONG ACID** ionizes completely in solution, meaning it releases all of its H^+ ions and will have a pH close to 1.

A **BUFFER** is any solution that exhibits very little change in its pH when small amounts of an acid or base are added to it. An acidic buffer solution is simply one with a pH of less than 7. Often a weak acid and one of its salts are combined to create an acidic buffer. Other times a weak base can be combined with one of its salts to create an alkaline buffer. Any solution with a pH greater than 7 would be known as an alkaline buffer solution.

Example

Which substance can be used to neutralize an acid spill?

(A) sodium bicarbonate

(B) citric acid

(C) cat litter

(D) water

Answers:

(A) is correct. Sodium bicarbonate, which is a base, will neutralize an acid.

(B) is incorrect. Citric acid neutralizes a base spill.

(C) is incorrect. Cat litter may absorb an acid, but it will not neutralize it.

(D) is incorrect. Water is neutral and therefore will not neutralize an acid.

PHYSICS

Force and Motion

To study motion, it is necessary to understand the concept of scalars and vectors. **SCALARS** are measurements that have a quantity but no direction. **VECTORS**, in contrast, have both a quantity and a direction. **DISTANCE** is a scalar: it describes how far an object has traveled along a path. Distance can have values such as 54 m or 16 miles. **DISPLACEMENT** is a vector: it describes how far an object has traveled from its starting position. A displacement value will indicate direction, such as 54 m east or –16 miles.

SPEED describes how quickly something is moving. It is found by dividing distance by time, and so it is a scalar value. **VELOCITY** is the rate at which an object changes position. Velocity is found by dividing displacement by time, meaning it is a vector value. An object that travels a certain distance and then returns to its starting point has a velocity of zero because its final position did not change. Its speed, however, can be found by dividing the

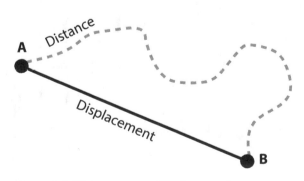

Figure 1.4. Distance versus Displacement

total distance it traveled by the time it took to make the trip. ACCELERATION is how quickly an object changes velocity.

A push or pull that causes an object to move or change direction is called a FORCE. Forces can arise from a number of different sources. GRAVITY is the attraction of one mass to another mass. For example, the earth's gravitational field pulls objects toward it, and the sun's gravitational field keeps planets in motion around it. Electrically charged objects will also create a field that will cause other charged objects in that field to move. Other forces include TENSION, which is found in ropes pulling or holding up an object; FRICTION, which is created by two objects moving against each other; and the NORMAL FORCE, which occurs when an object is resting on another object. The BUOYANT force is the upward force experienced by floating objects.

The normal force balances out gravity in resting objects. When a book rests on a table, gravity pulls down on it, and the normal force pushes up, canceling each other out and holding the book still.

An object that is at rest or moving with a constant speed has a net force of zero, meaning all the forces acting on it cancel each other out. Such an object is said to be at EQUILIBRIUM. Isaac Newton proposed three LAWS OF MOTION that govern forces:

- NEWTON'S FIRST LAW: An object at rest stays at rest, and an object in motion stays in motion, unless acted on by a force.
- NEWTON'S SECOND LAW: Force is equal to the mass of an object multiplied by its acceleration ($F = ma$).
- NEWTON'S THIRD LAW: For every action, there is an equal and opposite reaction.

The laws of motion have made it possible to build SIMPLE MACHINES, which take advantage of the rules of motion to make work easier to perform. Simple machines include the inclined plane, wheel and axle, pulley, screw, wedge, and lever.

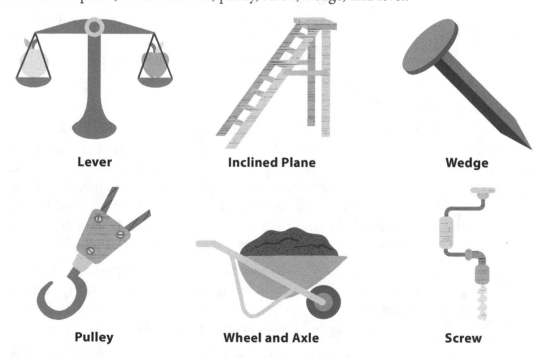

Figure 1.5. Simple Machines

Examples

1. What term describes the speed and direction of a moving soccer ball?

   (A) velocity

   (B) acceleration

   (C) mass

   (D) force

   Answers:

   (A) is correct. Velocity is the speed of an object in a certain direction.

   (B) is incorrect. Acceleration describes how quickly an object's velocity is changing.

   (C) is incorrect. Mass refers to the amount of matter in an object.

   (D) is incorrect. A force causes an object to change speed or direction.

2. What term describes the resistance to motion caused by one object rubbing against another object?

   (A) inertia

   (B) friction

   (C) velocity

   (D) gravity

   Answers:

   (A) is incorrect. Inertia is an object's tendency not to change position or direction unless an outside force acts upon it.

   (B) is correct. Friction occurs when motion is impeded because one object is rubbing against another object.

   (C) is incorrect. Velocity is the rate at which an object is displaced from its original position.

   (D) is incorrect. Gravity is a force that attracts objects to one another.

Energy and Matter

ENERGY is the capacity of an object to do work. In other words, it is the capacity of an object to cause some sort of movement or change. There are two kinds of energy: kinetic and potential. KINETIC ENERGY is the energy possessed by objects in motion, and POTENTIAL ENERGY is possessed by objects that have the potential to be in motion due to their position. Potential energy is defined in relation to a specific point. For example, a book held 10 feet off the ground has more potential energy than a book held 5 feet off the ground, because it has the potential to fall farther (i.e., to do more work).

Kinetic energy can be turned into potential energy, and vice versa. In the example above, dropping one of the books turns potential energy into kinetic energy. Conversely, picking up a book and placing it on a table turns kinetic energy into potential energy.

> ⚠️ Like matter, energy is always conserved. It can be changed from one form to another, but it can never be created or destroyed.

There are several types of potential energy. The energy stored in a book placed on a table is GRAVITATIONAL POTENTIAL ENERGY; it is derived from the pull of the earth's gravity on the book. ELECTRIC POTENTIAL ENERGY is derived from the interaction between positive and negative charges. Because opposite charges attract each other, and like charges repel, energy can be stored when opposite charges are moved apart or when like charges are pushed together. Similarly, compressing a spring stores ELASTIC POTENTIAL ENERGY. Energy is also stored in chemical bonds as CHEMICAL POTENTIAL ENERGY.

TEMPERATURE is the special name given to the kinetic energy of all the atoms or molecules in a substance. While it might look like a substance is not in motion, in fact, its atoms are constantly spinning and vibrating. The more energy the atoms have, the higher the substance's temperature. HEAT is the movement of energy from one substance to another. Energy will spontaneously move from high-energy (high-temperature) substances to low-energy (low-temperature) substances.

This energy can be transferred by radiation, convection, or conduction. RADIATION does not need a medium; the sun radiates energy to the earth through the vacuum of space. CONDUCTION occurs when two substances are in contact with each other. When a pan is placed on a hot stove, the heat energy is conducted from the stove to the pan and then to the food in the pan. CONVECTION transfers energy through circular movement of air or liquids. For example, a convection oven transfers heat through circular movement caused by hot air rising and cold air sinking.

Example

Which example has the least amount of kinetic energy?

(A) a plane flying through the sky

(B) a plane sitting on the runway

(C) a ladybug flying toward a flower

(D) a meteorite falling to the earth

Answers:

(A) is incorrect. A plane flying through the sky would have kinetic energy because of its mass and velocity.

(B) is correct. Something that is not moving has zero velocity; therefore, it has no kinetic energy.

(C) is incorrect. Even though it has a low mass and a low velocity, a ladybug does have a small amount of kinetic energy.

(D) is incorrect. A meteorite falling toward the earth would have a large amount of kinetic energy because of its mass and velocity.

Waves

Energy can also be transferred through WAVES, which are repeating pulses of energy. Waves that travel through a medium, like ripples on a pond or compressions in a Slinky, are called MECHANICAL WAVES. Waves that vibrate up and down (like the ripples on a pond) are TRANSVERSE WAVES, and those that travel through compression (like the Slinky) are LONGITUDINAL WAVES. Mechanical waves will travel faster through denser mediums; for example, sound waves will move faster through water than through air.

Waves can be described using a number of different properties. A wave's highest point is called its CREST, and its lowest point is the TROUGH. A wave's midline is halfway between the crest and trough; the AMPLITUDE describes the distance between the midline and the crest (or trough). The distance between crests (or troughs) is the WAVELENGTH. A wave's

PERIOD is the time it takes for a wave to go through one complete cycle, and the number of cycles a wave goes through in a specific period of time is its FREQUENCY.

SOUND is a special type of longitudinal wave created by vibrations. Our ears are able to interpret these waves as particular sounds. The frequency, or rate, of the vibration determines the sound's PITCH. LOUDNESS depends on the amplitude, or height, of a sound wave.

The **DOPPLER EFFECT** is the difference in perceived pitch caused by the motion of the object creating the wave. For example, as an ambulance approaches, the siren's pitch will appear to increase to the observer and then to decrease as the ambulance moves away. This occurs because sound waves are compressed as the ambulance approaches an observer and are spread out as the ambulance moves away from the observer.

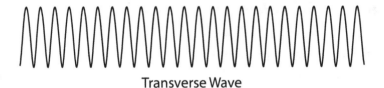

Longitudinal Wave

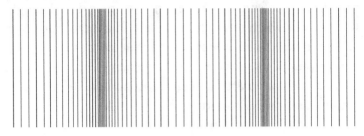

Transverse Wave

Figure 1.6. Types of Waves

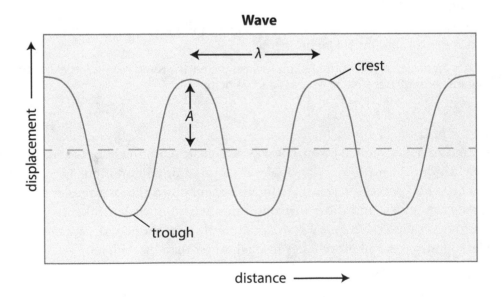

λ = wavelength
A = amplitude

Figure 1.7. Parts of a Wave

ELECTROMAGNETIC WAVES are composed of oscillating electric and magnetic fields and thus do not require a medium to travel through. The electromagnetic spectrum classifies the types of electromagnetic waves based on their frequency. These include radio waves, microwaves, X-rays, and visible light.

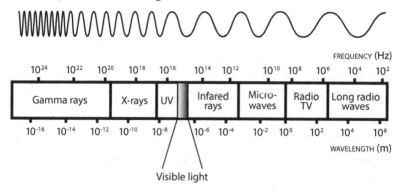

Figure 1.8. The Electromagnetic Spectrum

The study of light is called OPTICS. Because visible light is a wave, it will display similar properties to other waves. It will REFLECT, or bounce off, surfaces, which can be observed by shining a flashlight on a mirror. Light will also REFRACT, or bend, when it travels between substances. This effect can be seen by placing a pencil in water and observing the apparent bend in the pencil.

Curved pieces of glass called LENSES can be used to bend light in a way that affects how an image is perceived. Some microscopes, for example, make objects appear larger through the use of specific types of lenses. Eyeglasses also use lenses to correct poor vision.

The frequency of a light wave is responsible for its COLOR, with red/orange colors having a lower frequency than blue/violet colors. White light is a blend of all the frequencies of visible light. Passing white light through a prism will bend each frequency at a slightly different angle, separating the colors and creating a RAINBOW. Sunlight passing through raindrops can undergo this effect, creating large rainbows in the sky.

 The order of the colors in the spectrum of light can be remembered using **ROY G. BIV**: Red – Orange – Yellow – Green – Blue – Indigo – Violet.

Examples

1. Which type of wave is a longitudinal wave?

   (A) ocean wave

   (B) light wave

   (C) sound wave

   (D) X-ray wave

Answers:

(A) is incorrect. Waves on the surface of the ocean are transverse waves.

(B) is incorrect. Light waves are transverse waves.

(C) is correct. Sound waves are longitudinal waves because the vibrations travel in the same direction as the energy.

(D) is incorrect. X-rays are electromagnetic waves, which are transverse.

2. Which example demonstrates refraction?

   (A) a rainbow during a rainstorm

   (B) an echo in a cave

   (C) a candle appearing in a mirror

   (D) the Doppler effect

Answers:

(A) is correct. The light of the sun hits rain droplets and bends into a band of colors. The bending of waves is refraction.

(B) is incorrect. Echo is an example of sound reflection.

(C) is incorrect. A mirror is used to show light reflection.

(D) is incorrect. The Doppler effect describes the change in pitch caused by moving sources of sound waves.

Electricity and Magnetism

ELECTRIC CHARGE is created by a difference in the balance of protons and electrons, which creates a positively or negatively charged object. Charged objects create an electric field that spreads outward from the object. Other charged objects in that field will experience a force: objects that have opposite charges will be ATTRACTED to each other, and objects with the same charge will be REPELLED, or pushed away, from each other.

Because protons cannot leave the nucleus, charge is created by the movement of electrons. Static electricity, or ELECTROSTATIC charge, occurs when a surface has a buildup of charges. For example, if a student rubs a balloon on her head, the friction will cause electrons to move from her hair to the balloon. This creates a negative charge on the balloon and a positive charge on her hair; the resulting attraction will cause her hair to move toward the balloon.

ELECTRICITY is the movement of electrons through a conductor, and an electric circuit is a closed loop through which electricity moves. Circuits include a VOLTAGE source, which powers the movement of electrons known as CURRENT. Sources of voltage include batteries, generators, and wall outlets (which are in turn powered by electric power stations). Other elements, such as lights, computers, and microwaves, can then be connected to the circuit to be powered by its electricity.

MAGNETS are created by the alignment of spinning electrons within a substance. This alignment will occur naturally in some substances, including iron, nickel, and cobalt, all of which can be used to produce PERMANENT MAGNETS. The alignment of electrons creates a MAGNETIC FIELD, which, like an electric or grav-

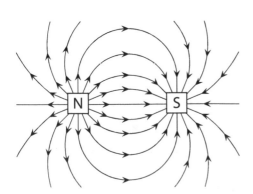

Figure 1.9. Magnetic Field Lines

itational field, can act on other objects. Magnetic fields have a north and a south pole that act similarly to electric charges: opposite poles will attract, and same poles will repel each other. However, unlike electric charge, which can be either positive or negative, a magnetic field ALWAYS has two poles. If a magnet is cut in half, the result is two magnets, each with a north and a south pole.

Electricity and magnetism are closely related. A moving magnet creates an electric field, and a moving charged particle will create a magnetic field. A specific kind of TEMPORARY MAGNET known as an electromagnet can be made by coiling a wire around a metal object and running electricity through it. A magnetic field will be created when the wire contains a current but will disappear when the flow of electricity is stopped.

Examples

1. What part of the atom flows through a circuit to power a light bulb?

   (A) protons

   (B) neutrons

   (C) electrons

   (D) nucleus

   Answers:

   (A) is incorrect. Protons remain in the nucleus of an atom.

   (B) is incorrect. Neutrons remain in the nucleus of an atom.

   (C) is correct. Electrons are negatively charged subatomic particles that exist outside the nucleus of an atom. A power source forces moving electrons through a circuit.

   (D) is incorrect. The nucleus is the part of an atom that contains protons and neutrons.

2. Which metal attracts magnets?

   (A) iron

   (B) copper

   (C) silver

   (D) gold

   Answers:

   (A) is correct. Magnets readily attract iron.

   (B) is incorrect. Not all metals are attracted to magnets; copper is not.

   (C) is incorrect. Silver is not attracted to magnets.

   (D) is incorrect. Gold is not attracted to magnets.

LIFE SCIENCE

Biological Molecules

The cells and bodies of all living organisms contain many different kinds of molecules. These molecules are usually held together by covalent bonds and often consist of carbon atoms in rings or long chains. Other atoms—such as hydrogen, oxygen, and nitrogen—can attach to these carbon atoms. If a molecule contains carbon and hydrogen atoms, it is called an ORGANIC MOLECULE. Large organic molecules that contain many atoms and repeating units are often called MACROMOLECULES. The covalent bonds that join each subunit of a macromolecule form when one subunit loses a hydroxyl group (OH), while the other subunit loses an atom of hydrogen (H). Since water is lost to form the bond, this process is called DEHYDRATION SYNTHESIS. Life is built from four main macromolecules: proteins, lipids, nucleic acids, and carbohydrates.

Dehydration synthesis is easily distinguished from hydrolysis (when water reacts with a molecule and chemical bonds are broken), because the prefix *de–* means removal, loss, or separation; *hydro* means water. Loss of water creates a bond between two atoms; the addition of water breaks a bond between two atoms.

PROTEINS are built from amino acids; enzymes are important proteins that catalyze the chemical reactions of a cell. CARBOHYDRATES are polymers made of carbon, hydrogen, and oxygen atoms; they are also known as sugars, and one of their most important functions is to store energy. LIPIDS are built from fatty acids and glycerol and play important roles in the cell, including in energy storage and in the structure of membranes. Long chains of nucleotides form the two types of NUCLEIC ACIDS—DNA (deoxyribonucleic acid) and RNA (ribonucleic acid)—which store the genetic information of a cell.

In contrast, INORGANIC MOLECULES usually contain a small number of atoms held together by ionic bonds. These molecules often contain metals and nonmetals, and although most inorganic molecules are not as common in living organisms as organic molecules, organisms still require certain inorganic molecules for survival. Water, for instance, does not contain carbon, so it is not classified as an organic molecule. Yet, to persist, all life needs water.

Example

Macromolecules are formed from small subunits called monomers. The monomers that make up a protein are called

(A) monosaccharides.

(B) nucleotides.

(C) amino acids.

(D) fatty acids.

Answers:

(A) is incorrect. Monosaccharide monomers make up a polysaccharide.

(B) is incorrect. Nucleotide monomers make up nucleic acids.

(C) is correct. Amino acid monomers are the building blocks of proteins.

(D) is incorrect. Fatty acid monomers are the subunits of lipids.

Nucleic Acids

All cells carry genetic information that is replicated and passed on to daughter cells when the parent cell divides. The macromolecule that carries this hereditary information is **DNA** (deoxyribonucleic acid). DNA is a type of nucleic acid, a complex molecule built from subunits called NUCLEOTIDES. Certain sequences of nucleotides direct the synthesis of proteins. **RNA** (ribonucleic acid) is the second type of nucleic acid. RNA plays a key role in deciphering the information stored in DNA.

Although DNA and RNA are structurally and functionally different, at their most basic level, both DNA and RNA are built from nucleotides, which consist of three parts: a single or two-ringed organic molecule containing nitrogen, a sugar containing five carbon atoms, and a phosphate group.

Nucleotides are joined through dehydration reactions that bind the sugar molecule of one nucleotide to the phosphate group of another nucleic acid. In this way, a long, SINGLE-STRAND structure with a SUGAR-PHOSPHATE BACKBONE forms. The nitrogen-containing organic molecule (called a nitrogenous base) attached to each nucleotide extends from the sugar-phosphate backbone. Nitrogenous bases pair in specific ways called COMPLEMENTARY BASE PAIRING. There are four nitrogenous bases found in DNA: ADENINE (**A**), THYMINE (**T**), GUANINE (**G**), and CYTOSINE (**C**).

In DNA, two strands of nucleotides wrap around each other to form a DOUBLE HELIX, or twisted structure. The sugar-phosphate backbone lies on the outside of this structure, and the nitrogenous bases of each strand are joined by hydrogen bonds on the inside of the double helix.

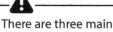

There are three main differences between DNA and RNA:
1. DNA contains the nucleotide thymine; RNA contains the nucleotide uracil.
2. DNA is double-stranded; RNA is single-stranded.
3. DNA is made from the sugar deoxyribose; RNA is made from the sugar ribose.

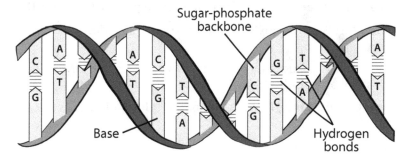

Figure 1.10. The Double Helix of DNA

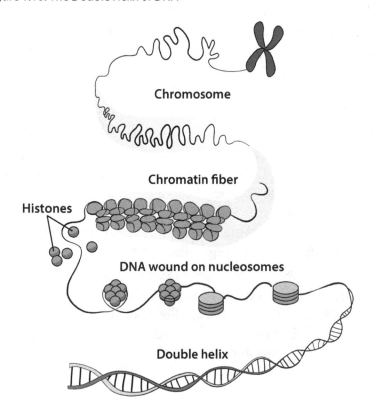

Figure 1.11. DNA, Chromatin, and Chromosomes

When it is not being transcribed, DNA is tightly wound around proteins called HISTONES into packages called CHROMATIN. The structure of chromatin allows large amounts of DNA to be stored in a very small space and helps regulate transcription by controlling access to specific sections of DNA. Tightly folding the DNA also helps prevent damage to the genetic code. Chromatin is further bundled into packages of DNA called CHROMOSOMES. During cell division, DNA is replicated to create two identical copies of each chromosome called CHROMATIDS.

Example

Which of the following is NOT true of RNA?

(A) Hydrogen bonds form between A – T and G – C bases.

(B) A sequence of RNA will not contain T bases but will contain U bases.

(C) RNA is single stranded.

(D) RNA stores genetic information.

Answers:

(A) is correct. These are the complementary base pairs that form in DNA.

(B) is incorrect. This is true; RNA does not carry thymine bases but does carry uracil bases.

(C) is incorrect. This is true; a molecule of RNA exists as one long chain of nucleotides, not as a double helix.

(D) is incorrect. This is true; RNA stores genetic information in its nucleotide sequence.

Structure and Function of Cells

The word *cell* comes from the Latin word *cella*, which means a small room or chamber. A cell, therefore, is the smallest unit of life. The cells of some organisms contain special compartments that carry out specific functions of the cell. These compartments are called ORGANELLES. Not all cells, however, carry organelles. Organelles are typically found in EUKARYOTIC CELLS (complex cells with a membrane-bound nucleus) but not in PROKARYOTIC CELLS (relatively simple cells that do not possess a membrane-bound nucleus).

Most organelles are membrane-bound structures, and each performs an important cellular process. The NUCLEUS, for instance, is a spherical structure that houses the genetic information of an organism. The GOLGI APPARATUS collects, packages, and distributes the proteins produced by ribosomes, which are found either free in the cytoplasm or attached to the ENDOPLASMIC RETICULUM. The Krebs cycle and electron transport chain are carried out in various parts of MITOCHONDRIA; therefore, much of the energy-producing metabolism of a cell takes place in these organelles. A LYSOSOME is an organelle that contains enzymes that degrade other molecules; these enzymes often catalyze hydrolytic reactions.

CHLOROPLASTS are plant organelles; the reactions of photosynthesis are catalyzed in these compartments. A chloroplast is a kind of PLASTID; plastids are organelles that synthesize or store sugars. VACUOLES are also typically found in plant cells; these organelles carry water and collect the metabolic waste products of a cell.

Together, all the material within a cell, excluding the nucleus, is called the CYTOPLASM of all cells. The cytoplasm, whether prokaryotic or eukaryotic, is surrounded by a CELL MEMBRANE—or plasma membrane—made of two layers of phospholipids.

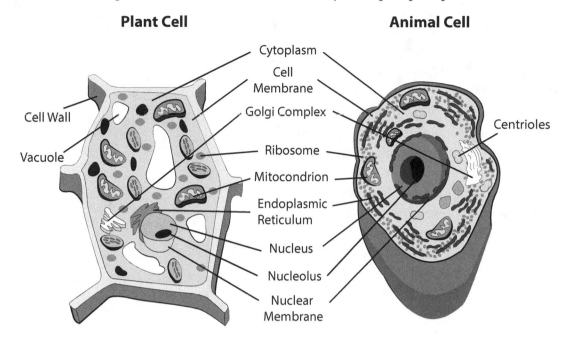

Figure 1.12. Cell Organelles

Example

Which structure listed above is NOT bound by a cellular membrane?

(A) nucleus

(B) chloroplast

(C) ribosome

(D) lysosome

Answers:

(A) is incorrect. Like many organelles, the nucleus is bound by a cellular membrane.

(B) is incorrect. Chloroplasts have an outer membrane, inner membrane, and internal sacs called thylakoids that are also bounded by membranes.

(C) is correct. Ribosomes consist of two subunits built from ribosomal RNA and protein. They are not bound by a membrane.

(D) is incorrect. The degradative enzymes of a lysosome are held in place by a cellular membrane.

Cell Division

The DNA of a eukaryotic cell divides in one of two ways: nonreproductive cells divide by MITOSIS, while reproductive cells divide by MEIOSIS. INTERPHASE is the first stage of the cell cycle in a eukaryotic cell. There are three phases of interphase: In the G_1 phase, where G stands for *Gap*, the cell is growing, transcribing genes into messenger RNA (mRNA) and translating mRNA into protein. In the S, or *synthesis*, phase of interphase, two copies of each chromosome are produced. In the G_2 phase of interphase, chromosomes condense, mitochondria replicate, and microtubules are synthesized. The four stages of mitosis (or M phase)—PROPHASE, METAPHASE, ANAPHASE, and TELOPHASE—follow interphase. The final stage of cell division is CYTOKINESIS, which is also referred to as C phase.

In contrast to mitosis, MEIOSIS describes the process of sexual reproduction, or the formation of GAMETES (EGG and SPERM cells) and the fusion of these gametes to form a new cell called a zygote. Gamete-forming cells are diploid, or 2n, cells. Gametes, however, are haploid cells; an egg cell (1n) and a sperm cell (1n) fuse to form a diploid (2n) zygote. Meiosis, therefore, is a cell division process that results in gametes that carry a reduced set of chromosomes. Meiosis is divided into two phases. In phase I, DNA is replicated and the cell divides to create two 2n daughter cells. Each daughter cell then divides again to create four 1n daughter cells.

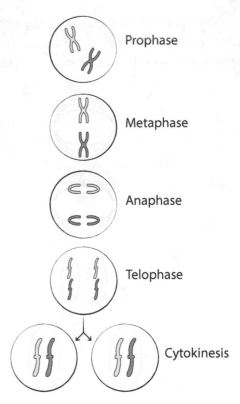

Figure 1.13. Phases of Mitosis

Example

A cell spends most of its life in the

(A) G_1 phase.

(B) S phase.

(C) G_2 phase.

(D) M phase.

Answers:

(A) **Correct.** In this phase, cells do much of their growing, carrying out processes like metabolism and gene expression.

(B) Incorrect. A cell gears up for cell division in the S phase by synthesizing new DNA.

(C) Incorrect. Chromosomes condense in the G_2 phase; mitochondria are replicated and microtubules are produced.

(D) Incorrect. The M phase stands for *mitosis*, which is a small part of the cell's life cycle.

Genetics

Genetics is the study of heredity—how characteristics are passed from parents to offspring. These characteristics, or TRAITS, are determined by genes, which are located on chromosomes and are the basic units of heredity. Each individual has two versions of the same gene, called ALLELES. Parents each contribute one set of alleles to their offspring. The combination of genes that make up individual traits are known as GENOTYPES. A genotype is a full set of genetic material and differs from an organism's **PHENOTYPE**, which is the set of observable traits in an organism. An example of a phenotype is brown hair; the genotype of this trait is a set of alleles that contain the genetic information for brown hair.

SEGREGATION of genes occurs as cells undergo meiosis. These cells are **DIPLOID**, meaning that each contains a full set of DNA, or genetic information, from both parents. This information is found on genes in the cell's chromosomes. The process of meiosis creates a **HAPLOID** reproductive cell, or gamete. These cells each contain one half of a cell's genetic information. As a result, each gamete contains one allele for each gene.

When writing the genetic information for a genotype, the dominant allele is written as a capital letter (B) while the recessive is written in a lowercase (b). A genotype that is homozygous can be written as (BB) or (bb), and a genotype that is heterozygous can be written as (Bb).

Different combinations of alleles result in different traits that are expressed in offspring. If an individual has identical alleles from each parent for a given trait, he or she is considered to be **HOMOZYGOUS**. The resulting phenotype is straightforward. For example, if an individual inherits the same blood type from each parent, then he or she will express that same blood type.

If the individual inherits one type of allele for a given trait from one parent but a different allele from the other parent, then he or she is considered to be **HETEROZYGOUS**. The resulting phenotype is more complicated for heterozygous traits. In this case, the more **DOMINANT** allele will be expressed, while the **RECESSIVE** (less dominant) allele will not be expressed.

The rare but permanent changes in the DNA sequences of genes are known as **MUTATIONS**. Some mutations cause harm to a cell and may lead to the death of that cell; some mutations have no effect on the cell. Other mutations, however, are beneficial to a cell, and if these changes are **GERM-LINE MUTATIONS**, or mutations that occur in a cell that will become a gamete, then these mutations can be passed on to the **OFFSPRING** of an organism. These are the changes in a cell or organism that are inherited. These are also the changes that, through natural selection, might result in the evolution of an organism.

If the mutation in the DNA sequence of an organism occurs in a cell other than a germ-line cell, then this change is called a **SOMATIC MUTATION** because it happens to a somatic cell, which is a body cell, not a germ-line cell. Somatic mutations cannot be passed on to the offspring of an organism.

Example

Which of the following is NOT a scenario in which the dominant allele will be expressed as a trait?

(A) a recessive allele from the father paired with a recessive allele from the mother

(B) a dominant allele from the father paired with a dominant allele from the mother

(C) a dominant allele from the father paired with a recessive allele from the mother

(D) a recessive allele from the father paired with a dominant allele from the mother

Answers:

(A) is correct. This genotype is homozygous, and the recessive trait is the only trait that can be expressed.

(B) is incorrect. This genotype is homozygous, and the dominant trait is the only trait that can be expressed.

(C) is incorrect. This dominant allele will be expressed over the recessive allele in this heterozygous combination.

(D) is incorrect. This dominant allele will be expressed over the recessive allele in this heterozygous combination.

Evolution

The simple definition of EVOLUTION is the gradual genetic change in species over time. Upon a closer look, however, the process is quite complex. Multiple mechanisms of change are at play during this process. These mechanisms include natural and artificial selection, genetic drift, coevolution, and adaptive radiation. These mechanisms alter the variation and frequency of certain alleles and phenotypes within a population. This increased variation and frequency leads to varying reproductive success, in which individuals with certain traits survive over others. Combined, these mechanisms lead to a gradual change to individual populations of animals that, over time, can result in the creation of a new species.

NATURAL SELECTION is a process in which only the members of a population best adapted to their environment tend to survive and reproduce, which ensures that their favorable traits will be passed on in future generations of the species. There are four basic conditions that must be met in order for natural selection to occur:

1. inherited variation
2. overproduction of offspring
3. fitness to environment
4. differential reproduction

The offspring with inherited variations best suited for their environment will be more likely to survive than others and are therefore more likely to pass on their successful genes to future populations through reproduction. This is referred to as FITNESS. An organism that is considered biologically "fit" will be more successful passing on its genes through reproduction compared to other members of the population. The frequency of certain alleles in a gene pool will change as a result.

> ⚠️ **Intersexual selection** is a type of sexual selection in which one mate, usually the female, actively selects a mate based on many visual cues. The selection of male peacocks by peahens is a classic example of this type of selection.

ARTIFICIAL SELECTION occurs in a species when humans get involved in the reproductive process. Over the course of time, humans have intentionally bred together organisms with the same desirable traits in a process called SELECTIVE BREEDING. This has led to the evolution of many common crops and farm animals that are bred specifically for human consumption, as well as among domesticated animals, such as horses or dogs. Although the mechanisms of evolution are different, the end result is the same as natural selection: the change in a population over time.

Example

Which of the following is not an example of natural selection?

(A) peahens selecting the most brightly colored peacocks as mates

(B) large bears chasing smaller rivals away from food sources

(C) sparrows with a certain beak shape reaching plentiful food sources

(D) farmers planting seeds only from the most productive corn plants

Classification of Organisms

Scientists use the characteristics of organisms to sort them into a variety of CLASSIFICATIONS using a system called taxonomy. The highest level of taxonomic classification is the KINGDOM, and each kingdom is then broken down into smaller categories. The smallest level of classification is a SPECIES, which includes individuals with similar genetics that are capable of breeding. The entire system is given below:

- kingdom
- phylum
- class
- order
- family
- genus
- species

All organisms are sorted into one of five kingdoms: Monera, Protista, Fungi, Plantae, and Animalia. The kingdom MONERA includes bacteria, which are unicellular organisms that have no nucleus. PROTISTS are also unicellular organisms, but they have a nucleus. Both Monera and Protists reproduce asexually by cellular division.

FUNGI are a group of unicellular and multicellular organisms that have unique cell walls and reproduction strategies. This kingdom includes common organisms like mushrooms and molds. Fungi can reproduce both asexually by cellular division and sexually through spores. Many species of fungi are decomposers and attain energy by breaking down organic matter in the environment.

PLANTS are a kingdom of organisms that use the energy from sunlight to make food (the sugar glucose) through the process of photosynthesis. A plant has ROOTS that anchor the plant to the ground and absorb water and nutrients from the soil. The STEM transports nutrients and water from the roots to other parts of the plant, including the LEAVES, where photosynthesis occurs.

Plants can reproduce asexually when a part of the plant (e.g., a cut branch) buds to create a new, identical plant. Plants can also reproduce sexually. Seed plants produce POLLEN (male sex cells) and eggs (female sex cells). When the pollen fertilizes the egg, an embryo is formed. This embryo is protected and nourished by the SEED. In angiosperms (flowering plants), seeds are contained within fruit. In gymnosperms, such as spruce and pines, seeds are contained within cones.

The kingdom Animalia contains multicellular organisms that can move around and must consume other organisms for energy. The kingdom includes several notable classes that divide organisms based on a number of important features. These include whether the organism has a backbone or spine: VERTEBRATES do, while INVERTEBRATES do not. Animals are also classified based on whether they are EXOTHERMIC, meaning their source of body heat comes from the environment, or ENDOTHERMIC, meaning their body heat is derived from metabolic processes within the body. Exothermic animals are sometimes known as cold-blooded, and endothermic animals as warm-blooded. Animal classification also looks at animal reproduction: some animals lay eggs, while others give birth to live young.

AMPHIBIANS are exothermic vertebrate animals that have gills when they hatch from eggs but develop lungs as adults. Examples of amphibians include frogs, toads, newts, and salamanders. REPTILES, such as snakes, lizards, crocodiles, turtles, and tortoises, are cold-blooded vertebrates that have scales and lay eggs on land. MAMMALS are endothermic vertebrate animals that have hair, give live birth, and produce milk for the nourishment of their young.

All organisms have a LIFE CYCLE, the stages of life for that organism. For example, when a frog lays eggs in water, the eggs hatch to become tadpoles with gills. The tadpoles eventually grow legs and develop lungs, and the tail is absorbed into the body. At this point, a tadpole has become an adult frog.

Example

Organisms in the same class are also in the same

(A) phylum.

(B) order.

(C) genus.

(D) species.

Answers:

(A) is correct. Living things are subdivided into progressively smaller groups in the following order: kingdom, phylum, class, order, family, genus, and species.

(B) is incorrect. An order is a smaller group than a class.

(C) is incorrect. A genus is a smaller group than a class.

(D) is incorrect. A species is a smaller group than a class.

Ecology

ECOLOGY is the study of organisms' interactions with each other and the environment. As with the study of organisms, ecology includes a classification hierarchy. Groups of organisms of the same species living in the same geographic area are called POPULATIONS. These organisms will COMPETE with each other for resources and mates and will display characteristic patterns in growth related to their interactions with the environment. For example, many populations exhibit a CARRYING CAPACITY, which is the highest number of individuals the resources in a given environment can support. Populations that outgrow their carrying capacity are likely to experience increased death rates until the population reaches a stable level again.

Populations of different species living together in the same geographic region are called COMMUNITIES. Within a community there are many different interactions among individuals of different species. PREDATORS consume PREY for food, and some species are in COMPETITION for the same limited pool of resources. In a SYMBIOTIC relationship, two species have evolved to share a close relationship. Two species may also have a **parasitic** relationship in which one organism benefits to the detriment of the other, such as ticks feeding off a dog. Both species benefit in a **MUTUALISTIC** relationship, and in a **COMMEN-SALISTIC** relationship, one species benefits and the other feels the effects.

Within a community, a species exists in a **FOOD WEB**: every species either consumes or is consumed by another (or others). The lowest trophic level in the web is occupied by **PRODUCERS**, which include plants and algae that produce energy directly from the sun. The next level are **PRIMARY CONSUMERS** (herbivores), which consume plant matter. The next trophic level includes **SECONDARY CONSUMERS** (carnivores), which consume herbivores. A food web may also contain another level of **TERTIARY CONSUMERS** (carnivores that consume other carnivores). In a real community, these webs can be extremely complex, with species existing on multiple trophic levels. Communities also include **DECOMPOSERS**, which are organisms that break down dead matter.

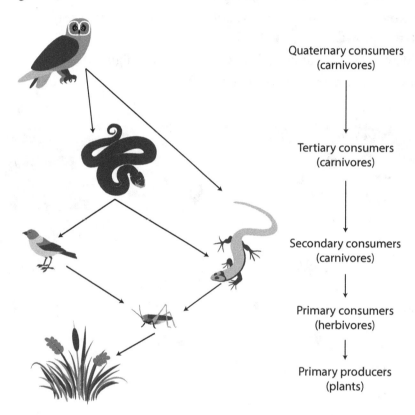

Figure 1.14. Food Web

The collection of **BIOTIC** (living) and **ABIOTIC** (nonliving) features in a geographic area is called an **ECOSYSTEM**. For example, in a forest, the ecosystem consists of all the organisms (animals, plants, fungi, bacteria, etc.), in addition to the soil, groundwater, rocks, and other abiotic features.

BIOMES are collections of plant and animal communities that exist within specific climates. They are similar to ecosystems, but they do not include abiotic components and can exist within and across continents. For example, the Amazon rainforest is a specific ecosystem, while tropical rainforests in general are considered a biome that includes a set of similar communities across the world. Together, all the living and nonliving parts of the earth are known as the **BIOSPHERE**.

Terrestrial biomes are usually defined by distinctive patterns in temperature and rainfall, and aquatic biomes are defined by the type of water and organisms found there. Examples of biomes include:

- **DESERTS**: extreme temperatures and very low rainfall with specialized vegetation and small mammals
- **TROPICAL RAINFORESTS**: hot and wet with an extremely high diversity of species
- **TEMPERATE GRASSLANDS**: moderate precipitation and distinct seasons with grasses and shrubs dominating
- **TEMPERATE BROADLEAF FORESTS**: moderate precipitation and temperatures with deciduous trees dominating
- **TUNDRA**: extremely low temperatures and short growing seasons with little or no tree growth
- **CORAL REEFS**: a marine (saltwater) system with high levels of diversity
- **LAKE**: an enclosed body of fresh water

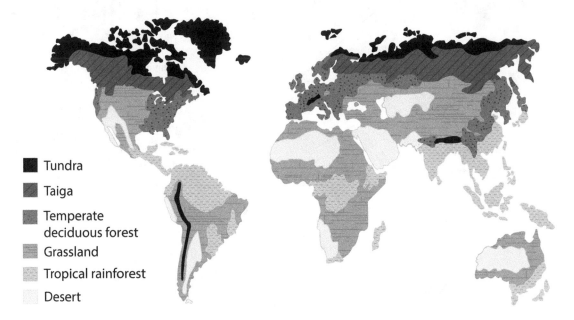

Figure 1.15. The World's Biomes

If the delicate balance of an ecosystem is disrupted, the system may not function properly. For example, if all the secondary consumers disappear, the population of primary consumers would increase, causing the primary consumers to overeat the producers and eventually starve. Species called **KEYSTONE SPECIES** are especially important in a particular community, and removing them decreases the overall diversity of the ecosystem.

Example

Which of the following is an example of an abiotic environmental factor that influences population size?

(A) food availability

(B) rate of precipitation

(C) interspecific competition

(D) competition

ANATOMY AND PHYSIOLOGY

ANATOMY is the study of the structure of organisms, and **PHYSIOLOGY** is the study of how the structures of an organism function. Both disciplines study the systems that allow organisms to perform a number of crucial functions, including the exchange of energy, nutrients, and waste products with the environment. This exchange allows organisms to maintain **HOMEOSTASIS**, or the stabilization of internal conditions.

Humans have a number of body systems that allow us to perform these vital functions, including the digestive, excretory, respiratory, circulatory, skeletal, muscular, immune, nervous, endocrine, and reproductive systems.

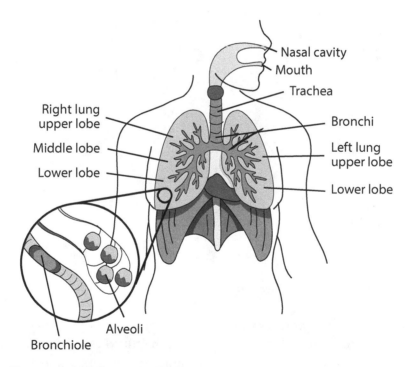

Figure 1.16. The Respiratory System

The **RESPIRATORY SYSTEM** takes in oxygen (which is needed for cellular functioning) and expels carbon dioxide. Humans take in air primarily through the nose but also through the mouth. This air travels down the **TRACHEA**, **BRONCHI**, and **BRONCHIOLES** into the **LUNGS**, which are further broken down into **LOBES**. The lungs are composed of millions of small structures called **ALVEOLI** that allow for the exchange of gases between the blood and the air.

The **DIGESTIVE SYSTEM** breaks down food into nutrients for use by the body's cells. Food enters through the **MOUTH** and moves through the **ESOPHAGUS** to the **STOMACH**, where it is physically and chemically broken down. The food particles then move into the **SMALL INTESTINE**, where the majority of nutrients are absorbed. Finally, the remaining particles enter the **LARGE INTESTINE**, which mostly absorbs water, and waste exits through the **RECTUM** and **ANUS**. This system also includes other organs, including the **LIVER**, **GALLBLADDER**, and **PANCREAS**, that manufacture substances needed for digestion.

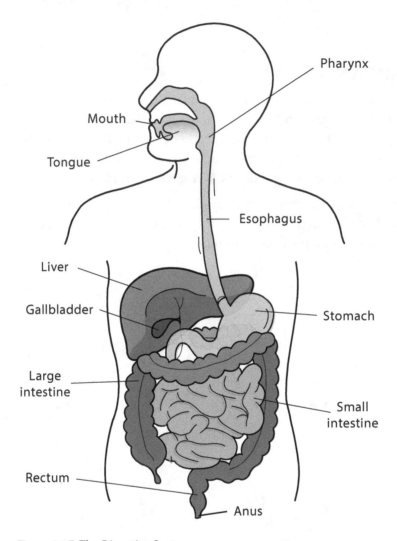

Figure 1.17. The Digestive System

The **EXCRETORY SYSTEM** removes waste products from the body. Its organs include the liver, which breaks down harmful substances, and the **KIDNEYS**, which filter waste from the bloodstream. The excretory system also includes the **BLADDER** and **URINARY TRACT**, which expel the waste filtered by the kidneys; the lungs, which expel the carbon dioxide created by cellular metabolism; and the skin, which secretes salt in the form of perspiration.

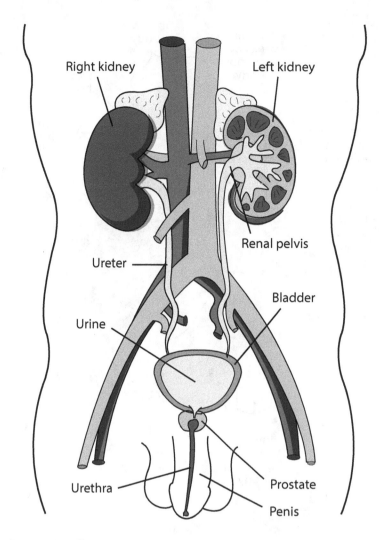

Figure 1.18. The Urinary System

The circulatory system carries oxygen, nutrients, and waste products in the blood to and from all the cells of the body. The **HEART** is a four-chambered muscle that pumps blood throughout the body. Deoxygenated blood (blood from which all the oxygen has been extracted and used) enters the heart in the right side and then is sent by the heart to the lungs, where it collects oxygen. The oxygen-rich blood then returns to the left side of the heart and is pumped out to the rest of the body.

Blood travels through a system of vessels. The largest of these are the **ARTERIES**, which branch directly off the heart. The vessels then branch into smaller and smaller vessels until they become **CAPILLARIES**, which are the smallest vessels and the site where gas exchange occurs. Deoxygenated blood travels back to the heart in **VEINS**.

The **SKELETAL SYSTEM**, which is composed of the body's **BONES** and **JOINTS**, provides support for the body and helps with movement. Bones are composed primarily of calcium, and include a rigid outer layer and a softer inner layer called **MARROW**. The marrow produces specific types of cells, including many immune cells and blood cells. Humans are born with **237** bones. However, many of these bones fuse during childhood, and adults will have only **206** bones.

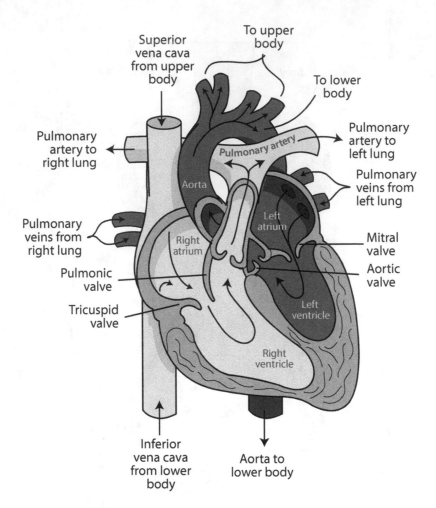

Figure 1.19. The Heart

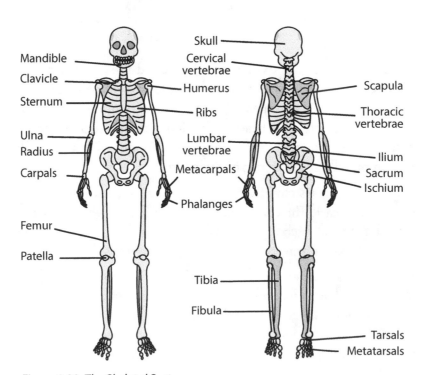

Figure 1.20. The Skeletal System

Bones are divided into four main categories. **LONG BONES**, such as the femur and humerus, are longer than they are wide. **SHORT BONES**, in contrast, are wider than they are long. These include the clavicle and carpals. **FLAT BONES** are wide and flat, and usually provide protection. Examples of flat bones include the bones of the skull, pelvis, and rib cage. **IRREGULAR BONES**, as the name suggests, have an irregular shape that does not fit into the other categories. These bones include the vertebrae and bones of the jaw.

The **MUSCULAR SYSTEM** allows the body to move and also moves blood and other substances through the body. The human body has three types of muscles. **SKELETAL MUSCLES** are voluntary muscles (meaning they can be controlled) that are attached to bones and move the body. **SMOOTH MUSCLES** are involuntary muscles (meaning they cannot be controlled) that create movement in parts of the digestive tract, blood vessels, and reproduction system. Finally, **CARDIAC MUSCLE** is the involuntary muscle that contracts the heart, allowing it to pump blood throughout the body.

Muscle is composed of two proteins: **ACTIN** (thin filaments) and **MYOSIN** (thick filaments). These proteins are arranged in a lattice structure. When the muscle receives a signal from a motor neuron, the actin and myosin slide past each other to **CONTRACT**, or shorten, the muscle. When they return to their resting position, the muscle is **RELAXED**. The process of contraction requires the energy molecule ATP. In skeletal and cardiac muscle, actin and myosin are bundled into **SARCOMERES**, which are the building blocks of the tubular muscle fibers called **MYOFIBRILS**. The sarcomeres appear as alternating dark and light bands under a light microscope.

Some skeletal muscles, such as the diaphragm and those that control blinking, can be voluntarily controlled but usually operate involuntarily.

The **IMMUNE SYSTEM** protects the body from infection by foreign particles and organisms. It includes the **SKIN** and mucous membranes, which act as physical barriers, and a number of specialized cells that destroy foreign substances in the body. The body's innate response includes cells that respond to nonspecific threats. The human body also has an adaptive immune system that can recognize and respond to specific foreign substances once it has been exposed to them. (This is the underlying mechanism behind vaccines.)

Table 1.1. Lines of Defense in the Immune System

1. external barriers	skin, enzymes, mucus, earwax, native bacteria
2. the innate response	inflammation, eukocytes (white blood cells), antimicrobial peptides, natural killer lymphocytes, interferon
3. the adaptive response	helper T-cells, cytotoxic T-cells, B-cells, memory B-cells

The **NERVOUS SYSTEM** processes external stimuli and sends signals throughout the body. It is made up of two parts. The **CENTRAL NERVOUS SYSTEM** (CNS) includes the brain and spinal cord and is where information is processed and stored. In general, the brain is organized into lobes that each carry out a broad, common function. For example, the processing of visual information occurs in the **OCCIPITAL LOBE**, and the **TEMPORAL LOBE** is involved in language comprehension and emotional associations. Brain structures in the **CEREBRAL CORTEX** (the outermost brain layer) form a convoluted pattern of gyri (ridges) and sulci (valleys) that maximize the ratio of surface area to volume.

The **PERIPHERAL NERVOUS SYSTEM** (PNS) includes cells called **NEURONS** that transmit information throughout the body using electrical signals. These cells typically contain an **AXON**, a long projection from the cell that sends information over a distance. These cells also have **DENDRITES**, which are long, branching extensions of the cell that receive information from neighboring cells. Most neurons are surrounded by a fatty layer called the **MYELIN SHEATH**, which insulates the axon and increases the efficiency of the electrical signals carried by the neurons.

The peripheral nervous system is further divided into two systems. The **AUTOMATIC NERVOUS SYSTEM** (ANS) is the part of the peripheral nervous system that controls involuntary bodily functions such as digestion, respiration, and heart rate. These aspects of the automatic nervous system are controlled by the hypothalamus. The adrenal glands control the "fight or flight" bodily response that is also part of the automatic nervous system. The second part of the peripheral nervous system, called the **SOMATIC NERVOUS SYSTEM**, controls sensory information and motor control.

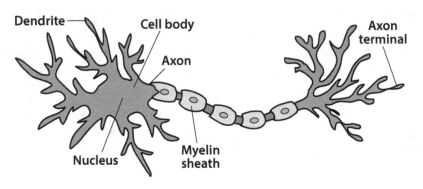

Figure 1.21. Neuron

The **ENDOCRINE SYSTEM** is a collection of organs that produce **HORMONES**, which are chemicals that regulate bodily processes. These organs include the pituitary gland, hypothalamus, pineal gland, thyroid gland, parathyroid glands, adrenal glands, testes (in males), ovaries (in females), and the placenta (in pregnant females). Together, the hormones produced by these organs regulate a wide variety of bodily functions, including hunger, sleep, mood, reproduction, and body temperature. Some organs that are part of other systems can also act as endocrine organs, including the pancreas and liver.

Table 1.2. Endocrine System Glands and Hormones

GLAND	REGULATES	HORMONES PRODUCED
pineal gland	circadian rhythms (the sleep/wake cycle)	melatonin
pituitary gland	growth, blood pressure, reabsorption of water by the kidneys, temperature, pain relief, and some reproductive functions related to pregnancy and childbirth	human growth hormone (HGH), thyroid-stimulating hormone (TSH), prolactin (PRL), luteinizing hormone (LH), follicle-stimulating hormone (FSH), oxytocin, antidiuretic hormone (ADH)

GLAND	REGULATES	HORMONES PRODUCED
hypothalamus	pituitary function and metabolic processes including body temperature, hunger, thirst, and circadian rhythms	thyrotropin-releasing hormone (TRH), dopamine, growth-hormone-releasing hormone (GHRH), gonadotropin-releasing hormone (GnRH), oxytocin, vasopressin
thyroid gland	energy use and protein synthesis	thyroxine (T4), triiodothyronine (T3), calcitonin
parathyroid	calcium and phosphate levels	parathyroid hormone (PTH), calcitonin
adrenal glands	"fight or flight" response, regulation of salt and blood volume	epinephrine, norepinephrine, cortisol, androgens
pancreas	blood sugar levels and metabolism	insulin, glucagon, somatostatin
testes	maturation of sex organs, secondary sex characteristics	androgens (e.g., testosterone)
ovaries	maturation of sex organs, secondary sex characteristics, pregnancy, childbirth, and lactation	progesterone, estrogens
placenta	gestation and childbirth	progesterone, estrogens, human chorionic gonadotropin, human placental lactogen

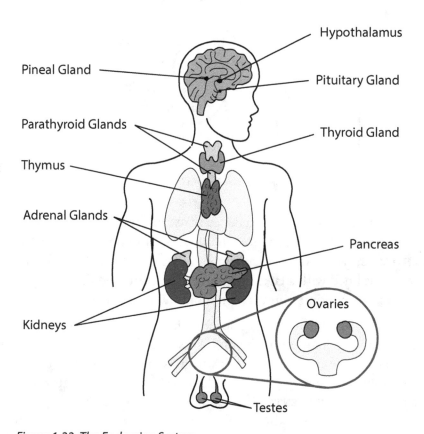

Figure 1.22. The Endocrine System

The male reproductive system produces SPERM, or male gametes, and passes them to the female reproductive system. Sperm are produced in the TESTES (also called testicles), which are housed externally in a sac-like structure called the SCROTUM. The scrotum contracts and relaxes to move the testes closer or farther from the body. This process keeps the testes at the appropriate temperature for sperm production, which is slightly lower than regular body temperature. Mature sperm are stored in the EPIDIDYMIS. During sexual stimulation, sperm travel from the epididymis through a long, thin tube called the VAS DEFERENS. Along the way, the sperm is joined by fluids from three glands to form SEMEN. The SEMINAL VESICLES secrete the bulk of the fluid that makes up semen, which is composed of various proteins, sugars, and enzymes. The PROSTATE contributes an alkaline fluid that counteracts the acidity of the vaginal tract. Finally, the COWPER GLAND secretes a protein-rich fluid that acts as a lubricant. Semen travels through the URETHRA and exits the body through the PENIS, which becomes rigid during sexual arousal.

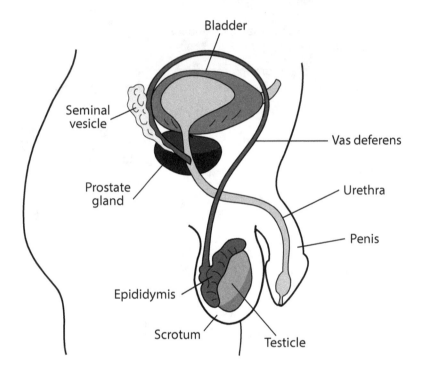

Figure 1.23. The Male Reproductive System

The female reproductive system produces EGGS, or female gametes, and gestates the fetus during pregnancy. Eggs are produced in the OVARIES and travel through the FALLOPIAN TUBES to the UTERUS, which is a muscular organ that houses the fetus during pregnancy. The uterine cavity is lined with a layer of blood-rich tissue called the ENDOMETRIUM. If no pregnancy occurs, the endometrium is shed monthly during MENSTRUATION.

FERTILIZATION occurs when the egg absorbs the sperm; it usually takes place in the fallopian tubes but may happen in the uterus itself. After fertilization the new zygote implants itself in the endometrium, where it will grow and develop over thirty-eight weeks (roughly nine months). During gestation, the developing fetus acquires nutrients and passes waste through the PLACENTA. This temporary organ is attached to the wall of the uterus and is connected to the baby by the UMBILICAL CORD. When the fetus is mature, powerful muscle contractions occur in the myometrium, the muscular layer next to the endometrium. These contractions push the fetus through an opening called the CERVIX into the vagina, from which it exits the body. The placenta and umbilical cords are also expelled through the vagina shortly after birth.

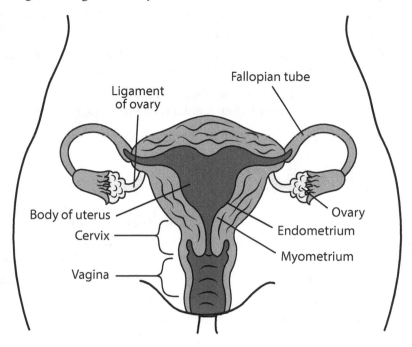

Figure 1.24. The Female Reproductive System

Examples

1. Solid waste is stored and then excreted from the body in which of the following organs?

   (A) stomach

   (B) pancreas

   (C) colon

   (D) rectum

   Answers:

   (A) is incorrect. The stomach is the organ where food is physically and chemically broken down.

   (B) is incorrect. The pancreas is an accessory organ of the digestive tract that produces digestive enzymes.

   (C) is incorrect. The colon is a large portion of the large intestine where water and nutrient absorption take place.

   (D) is correct. The rectum is located at the end of the digestive tract and is the final storage space for wastes before they are defecated through the anus.

2. Which of the following structures are small air sacs that function as the site of external respiration and gas exchange in the lungs?

   (A) capillaries

   (B) bronchi

   (C) alveoli

   (D) cilia

EARTH AND SPACE SCIENCE

Astronomy

Astronomy is the study of space. Our **PLANET**, Earth, is just one out of a group of planets that orbit the **SUN**, which is the star at the center of our **SOLAR SYSTEM**. Other planets in our solar system include Mercury, Venus, Mars, Jupiter, Saturn, Uranus, and Neptune. Every planet, except Mercury and Venus, has **MOONS**, or naturally occurring satellites that orbit a planet. Our solar system also includes **ASTEROIDS** and **COMETS**, small rocky or icy objects that orbit the Sun. Many of these are clustered in the asteroid belt, which is located between the orbits of Mars and Jupiter.

Figure 1.25. Solar System

Our solar system is a small part of a bigger star system called a galaxy. (Our galaxy is called the Milky Way.) **GALAXIES** consist of stars, gas, and dust held together by gravity and contain millions of **STARS**, which are hot balls of plasma and gasses. The universe includes many types of stars, including supergiant stars, white dwarfs, giant stars, and neutron stars. Stars form in nebulas, which are large clouds of dust and gas. When very large stars collapse, they create **BLACK HOLES**, which have a gravitational force so strong that light cannot escape.

Earth, the moon, and the sun interact in a number of ways that impact life on our planet. When the positions of the three align, eclipses occur. A **LUNAR ECLIPSE** occurs when Earth lines up between the moon and the sun; the moon moves into the shadow of Earth and appears dark in color. A **SOLAR ECLIPSE** occurs when the moon lines up between Earth and the sun; the moon covers the sun, blocking sunlight.

The cycle of day and night and the seasonal cycle are determined by the earth's motion. It takes approximately 365 days, or one year, for Earth to revolve around the sun. While Earth is revolving around the sun, it is also rotating on its axis, which takes approximately twenty-four hours, or one day. As the planet rotates, different areas alternately face toward the sun and away from the sun, creating night and day.

> ⚠ The phrase *My Very Educated Mother Just Served Us Noodles* can help students remember the order of the planets: Mercury – Venus – Earth – Mars – Jupiter – Saturn – Uranus – Neptune.

The earth's axis is not directly perpendicular to its orbit, meaning the planet tilts on its axis. The seasons are caused by this tilt. When the Northern Hemisphere is tilted toward the sun, it receives more sunlight and experiences summer. At the same time that the Northern Hemisphere experiences summer, the Southern Hemisphere, which receives less direct sunlight, experiences winter. As the earth revolves, the Northern Hemisphere will tilt away from the sun and move into winter, while the Southern Hemisphere tilts toward the sun and moves into summer.

Example

What term describes what occurs when the moon moves between the earth and the sun?

(A) aurora

(B) lunar eclipse

(C) black hole

(D) solar eclipse

Answers:

(A) is incorrect. An aurora occurs when particles from the solar wind are trapped in the earth's magnetic field.

(B) is incorrect. A lunar eclipse is when the earth moves between the moon and the sun, blocking moonlight.

(C) is incorrect. A black hole is a massive star with a gravitational field so strong that light cannot escape.

(D) is correct. When the moon moves between the earth and the sun, a solar eclipse occurs, blocking sunlight from the planet.

Geology

GEOLOGY is the study of the minerals and rocks that make up the earth. A **MINERAL** is a naturally occurring, solid, inorganic substance with a crystalline structure. There are several properties that help identify a mineral, including color, luster, hardness, and density. Examples of minerals include talc, diamonds, and topaz.

> ⚠ Luster describes how light reflects off the surface of a mineral. Terms to describe luster include dull, metallic, pearly, and waxy.

Although a **ROCK** is also a naturally occurring solid, it can be either organic or inorganic and is composed of one or more minerals. Rocks are classified based on their method of formation. The three types of rocks are igneous, sedimentary, and metamorphic. IGNEOUS rocks are the result of tectonic processes that bring MAGMA, or melted rock, to the earth's surface; they can form either above or below the surface. SEDIMENTARY rocks are formed from the compaction of rock fragments that results from weathering and erosion. Lastly, METAMORPHIC ROCKS form when extreme temperature and pressure cause the structure of pre-existing rocks to change.

The rock cycle describes how rocks form and break down. Typically, the cooling and solidification of magma as it rises to the surface creates igneous rocks. These rocks are then subject to WEATHERING, the mechanical and/or chemical processes by which rocks break down. During EROSION the resulting sediment is deposited in a new location. As sediment is deposited, the resulting compaction creates new sedimentary rocks. As new layers are added, rocks and minerals are forced closer to the earth's core where they are subjected to heat and pressure, resulting in metamorphic rock. Eventually, they will reach their melting point and return to magma, starting the cycle over again. This process takes place over hundreds of thousands or even millions of years.

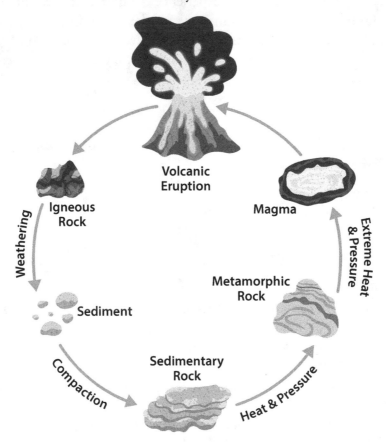

Figure 1.26. The Rock Cycle

PALEONTOLOGY, the study of the history of life on Earth, is sometimes also considered part of geology. Paleontologists study the ROCK RECORD, which retains biological history through FOSSILS, the preserved remains and traces of ancient life. Fossils can be used to learn about the evolution of life on the planet, particularly bacteria, plants, and animals that have gone extinct. Throughout Earth's history, there have been five documented catastrophic events that caused major extinctions. For each mass extinction, there are several theories about the cause but no definitive answers. Theories about what triggered mass extinctions include climate change, ice ages, asteroid and comet impacts, and volcanic activity.

The surface of the earth is made of large plates that float on the less dense layer beneath them. These TECTONIC PLATES make up the lithosphere, the planet's surface layer. Over 200 million years ago, the continents were joined together in one giant landmass called Pangea. Due to continental drift, or the slow movement of tectonic plates, the continents gradually shifted to their current positions.

The boundaries where plates meet are the locations for many geologic features and events. Mountains are formed when plates collide and push land upward, and trenches form when one plate is pushed beneath another. In addition, the friction created by plates sliding past each other is responsible for most EARTHQUAKES.

VOLCANOES, which are vents in the earth's crust that allow molten rock to reach the surface, frequently occur along the edges of tectonic plates. However, they can also occur at hotspots located far from plate boundaries.

The outermost layer of the earth, which includes tectonic plates, is called the LITHOSPHERE. Beneath the lithosphere are, in order, the ASTHENOSPHERE, MESOSPHERE, and core. The CORE includes two parts: the outer core is a liquid layer, and the inner core is composed of solid iron. It is believed the inner core spins at a rate slightly different than the rest of the planet, which creates the earth's magnetic field.

Example

Which type of rock forms when lava cools and solidifies?

(A) igneous

(B) sedimentary

(C) metamorphic

(D) sandstone

Answers:

(A) is correct. Igneous rocks form when liquid rock cools and solidifies.

(B) is incorrect. Sedimentary rocks form when sediments are cemented together.

(C) is incorrect. Metamorphic rocks form when igneous or sedimentary rocks are exposed to extreme temperature and/or pressure to the point that the rocks are changed physically or chemically.

(D) is incorrect. Sandstone is a type of sedimentary rock.

Hydrology

The earth's surface includes many bodies of water that together form the HYDROSPHERE. The largest of these are the bodies of salt water called OCEANS. There are five oceans: the Arctic, Atlantic, Indian, Pacific, and Southern. Together, the oceans account for 71 percent of the earth's surface and 97 percent of the earth's water.

Oceans are subject to cyclic rising and falling water levels at shorelines called TIDES, which are the result of the gravitational pull of the moon and sun. The oceans also experience WAVES, which are caused by the movement of energy through the water.

Other bodies of water include LAKES, which are usually freshwater, and SEAS, which are usually saltwater. RIVERS and STREAMS are moving bodies of water that flow into lakes, seas, and oceans. The earth also contains GROUNDWATER, or water that is stored underground in rock formations called aquifers.

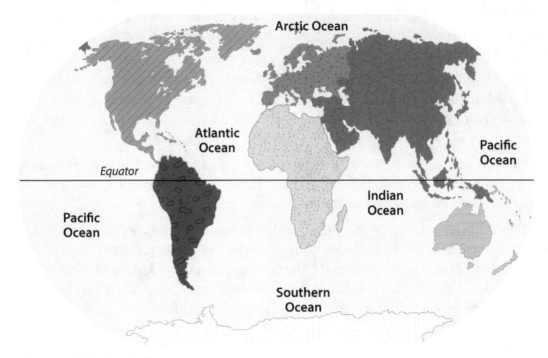

Figure 1.27. The Earth's Oceans

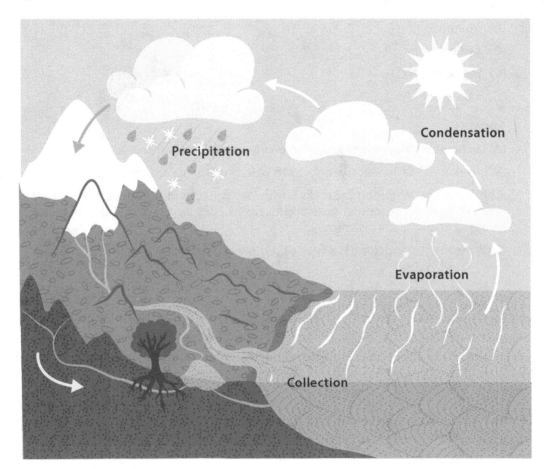

Figure 1.28. The Water Cycle

Much of the earth's water is stored as ice. The North and South Poles are usually covered in large sheets of ice called POLAR ICE. GLACIERS are large masses of ice and snow that move. Over long periods of time, they scour Earth's surface, creating features such as lakes and valleys. Large chunks of ice that break off from glaciers are called ICEBERGS.

The WATER CYCLE is the circulation of water throughout the earth's surface, atmosphere, and hydrosphere. Water on the earth's surface EVAPORATES, or changes from a liquid to a gas, and becomes water vapor. Plants also release water vapor through TRANSPIRATION. Water vapor in the air then comes together to form CLOUDS. When it cools, this water vapor condenses into a liquid and falls from the sky as PRECIPITATION, which includes rain, sleet, snow, and hail. Precipitation replenishes groundwater and the water found in features such as lakes and rivers, thus starting the cycle over again.

Example

During the water cycle, groundwater is replenished by

(A) transpiration.

(B) glaciers.

(C) lakes.

(D) precipitation.

Answers:

(A) is incorrect. Transpiration is the process through which water is released by plants as vapor.

(B) is incorrect. Glaciers are large masses of ice; they do not contribute to the groundwater supply.

(C) is incorrect. Lakes are large bodies of water; they do not contribute to the groundwater supply.

(D) is correct. Precipitation such as rain and snow seep into the ground to add to the groundwater supply.

Meteorology

Above the surface of Earth is the mass of gasses called the ATMOSPHERE. The atmosphere includes the troposphere, which is closest to the earth, followed by the stratosphere, mesosphere, and thermosphere. The outermost layer of the atmosphere is the exosphere, which is located 6,200 miles above the surface. Generally, temperature in the atmosphere decreases with altitude. The OZONE LAYER, which captures harmful radiation from the sun, is located in the stratosphere.

 Between each layer, a boundary exists where conditions change. This boundary takes the first part of the name of the previous layer followed by "pause." For example, the boundary between the troposphere and stratosphere is called the tropopause.

The humidity, or amount of water vapor in the air, and the temperature are two major atmospheric conditions that determine WEATHER, the day-to-day changes in atmospheric conditions. A warm front occurs when warm air moves over a cold air mass, causing the air to feel warmer and more humid. A cold front occurs when cold air moves under a warm air mass, causing a drop in temperature.

Sometimes, weather turns violent. Tropical cyclones, or HURRICANES, originate over warm ocean water. Hurricanes have destructive winds of more than 74 miles per hour and create large storm surges that can cause extensive damage along coastlines. Hurricanes, typhoons, and cyclones are all the same type of storm; they just have different names based on where the storm is located. Hurricanes originate in the Atlantic or Eastern Pacific Ocean, typhoons in the Western Pacific Ocean, and cyclones in the Indian Ocean. TORNADOES occur when unstable warm and cold air masses collide and a rotation is created by fast-moving winds.

> Most of Earth's atmosphere is composed of nitrogen (78 percent) and oxygen (21 percent). Other elements and compounds including argon, water, carbon dioxide, and methane make up the remaining 1 percent.

The long-term weather conditions in a geographic location are called CLIMATE. A CLIMATE ZONE is a large area that experiences similar average temperature and precipitation. The three major climate zones, based on temperature, are the polar, temperate, and tropical zones. Each climate zone is subdivided into subclimates that have unique characteristics. The tropical climate zone (warm temperatures) can be subdivided into tropical wet, tropical wet and dry, semiarid, and arid. The temperate climate zones (moderate temperatures) include Mediterranean, humid subtropical, marine West Coast, humid continental, and subarctic. The polar climate zones (cold temperatures) include tundra, highlands, nonpermanent ice, and ice cap. Polar climates are cold and experience prolonged, dark winters due to the tilt of the earth's axis.

Example

Which gas is found in large quantities in Earth's atmosphere?

(A) carbon monoxide

(B) bromine

(C) nitrogen

(D) fluorine

Answers:

(A) is incorrect. Carbon monoxide is a rare gas.

(B) is incorrect. Bromine is a rare gas.

(C) is correct. Nitrogen makes up 78 percent of Earth's atmosphere.

(D) is incorrect. Fluorine is a rare gas.

2

ARITHMETIC REASONING

The Arithmetic Reasoning section on the CAT-ASVAB includes 16 questions to be answered in 39 minutes. The pen-and-paper ASVAB has 30 questions to be answered in 36 minutes. The questions test candidates' ability to solve word problems using basic mathematical principles such as ratios, percentages, and probability. These problems will not require the use of algebra or other advanced math topics. Instead, the focus will be on interpreting written scenarios and applying the correct mathematical operations.

TYPES OF NUMBERS

Numbers are placed in categories based on their properties.

- A **NATURAL NUMBER** is greater than 0 and has no decimal or fraction attached. These are also sometimes called counting numbers {1, 2, 3, 4, ...}.

- **WHOLE NUMBERS** are natural numbers and the number 0 {0, 1, 2, 3, 4, ...}.

- **INTEGERS** include positive and negative natural numbers and 0 {..., –4, –3, –2, –1, 0, 1, 2, 3, 4, ...}.

- A **RATIONAL NUMBER** can be represented as a fraction. Any decimal part must terminate or resolve into a repeating pattern. Examples include –12, $-\frac{4}{5}$, 0.36, $7.\bar{7}$, $26\frac{1}{2}$, etc.

- An **IRRATIONAL NUMBER** cannot be represented as a fraction. An irrational decimal number never ends and never resolves into a repeating pattern. Examples include –R7, π, and 0.34567989135...

- A **REAL NUMBER** is a number that can be represented by a point on a number line. Real numbers include all the rational and irrational numbers.

- An **IMAGINARY NUMBER** includes the imaginary unit i, where $i = \sqrt{-1}$ Because $i^2 = -1$, imaginary numbers produce a negative value when squared. Examples of imaginary numbers include $-4i$, $0.75i$, $i\sqrt{2}$ and $\frac{8}{3}i$.

- A **COMPLEX NUMBER** is in the form $a + bi$, where a and b are real numbers.

Examples of complex numbers include $3 + 2i$, $-4 + i$, $\sqrt{3} - i^3\sqrt{5}$ and $\frac{5}{8} - \frac{7i}{8}$. All imaginary numbers are also complex.

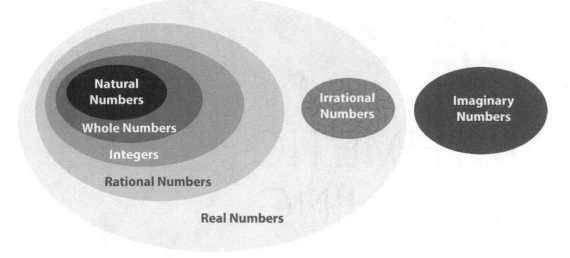

Figure 2.1. Types of Numbers

The **FACTORS** of a natural number are all the numbers that can multiply together to make the number. For example, the factors of 24 are 1, 2, 3, 4, 6, 8, 12, and 24. Every natural number is either prime or composite. A **PRIME NUMBER** is a number that is only divisible by itself and 1. (The number 1 is not considered prime.) Examples of prime numbers are 2, 3, 7, and 29. The number 2 is the only even prime number. A **COMPOSITE NUMBER** has more than two factors. For example, 6 is composite because its factors are 1, 6, 2, and 3. Every composite number can be written as a unique product of prime numbers, called the **PRIME FACTORIZATION** of the number. For example, the prime factorization of 90 is $90 = 2 \times 3^2 \times 5$. All integers are either even or odd. An even number is divisible by 2; an odd number is not.

> ⚠️ If a real number is a natural number (e.g., 50), then it is also a whole number, an integer, and a rational number.

Properties of Number Systems

A system is **CLOSED** under an operation if performing that operation on two elements of the system results in another element of that system. For example, the integers are closed under the operations of addition, subtraction, and multiplication but not division. Adding, subtracting, or multiplying two integers results in another integer. However, dividing two integers could result in a rational number that is not an integer $(-2 \div 3 = \frac{-2}{3})$.

- The rational numbers are closed under all four operations (except for division by 0).
- The real numbers are closed under all four operations.
- The complex numbers are closed under all four operations.
- The irrational numbers are NOT closed under ANY of the four operations.

The **COMMUTATIVE PROPERTY** holds for an operation if order does not matter when performing the operation. For example, multiplication is commutative for integers: $(-2)(3) = (3)(-2)$.

The **ASSOCIATIVE PROPERTY** holds for an operation if elements can be regrouped without changing the result. For example, addition is associative for real numbers: $-3 + (-5 + 4) = (-3 + -5) + 4$.

The **DISTRIBUTIVE PROPERTY** of multiplication over addition allows a product of sums to be written as a sum of products: $a(b + c) = ab + ac$. The value a is distributed over the sum $(b + c)$. The acronym FOIL (First, Outer, Inner, Last) is a useful way to remember the distributive property.

When an operation is performed with an **IDENTITY ELEMENT** and another element a, the result is a. The identity element for multiplication on real numbers is 1 ($a \times 1 = a$), and for addition is 0 ($a + 0 = a$).

An operation of a system has an **INVERSE ELEMENT** if applying that operation with the inverse element results in the identity element. For example, the inverse element of a for addition is $-a$ because $a + (-a) = 0$. The inverse element of a for multiplication is $\frac{1}{a}$ because $a \times \frac{1}{a} = 1$.

Examples

1. Classify the following numbers as natural, whole, integer, rational, or irrational. (The numbers may have more than one classification.)

   (A) 72

   (B) $-\frac{2}{3}$

   (C) $\sqrt{5}$

   Answers:

   (A) The number is **natural**, **whole**, an **integer**, and **rational**.

   (B) The fraction is **rational**.

   (C) The number is **irrational**. (It cannot be written as a fraction, and written as a decimal is approximately 2.2360679...)

2. Determine the real and imaginary parts of the following complex numbers.

   (A) 20

   (B) $10 - i$

   (C) $15i$

   Answers:

   A complex number is in the form of $a + bi$, where a is the real part and bi is the imaginary part.

   (A) $20 = 20 + 0i$ **The real part is 20, and there is no imaginary part.**

   (B) $10 - i = 10 - 1i$ **The real part is 10, and $-1i$ is the imaginary part.**

   (C) $15i = 0 + 15i$ **The real part is 0, and the imaginary part is 15i.**

3. Answer True or False for each statement:

   (A) The natural numbers are closed under subtraction.

   (B) The sum of two irrational numbers is irrational.

   (C) The sum of a rational number and an irrational number is irrational.

Answers:

(A) **False**. Subtracting the natural number 7 from 2 results in 2 − 7 = −5, which is an integer, but not a natural number.

(B) **False**. For example, $(5 - 2\sqrt{3}) + (2 + 2\sqrt{3}) = 7$. The sum of two irrational numbers in this example is a whole number, which is not irrational. The sum of a rational number and an irrational number is sometimes rational and sometimes irrational.

(C) **True**. Because irrational numbers have decimal parts that are unending and with no pattern, adding a repeating or terminating decimal will still result in an unending decimal without a pattern.

4. Answer True or False for each statement:

(A) The associative property applies for multiplication in the real numbers.

(B) The commutative property applies to all real numbers and all operations.

Answers:

(A) **True**. For all real numbers, $a \times (b \times c) = (a \times b) \times c$. Order of multiplication does not change the result.

(B) **False**. The commutative property does not work for subtraction or division on real numbers. For example, 12 − 5 = 7, but 5 − 12 = −7 and 10 ÷ 2 = 5, but $2 \div 10 = \frac{1}{5}$.

POSITIVE AND NEGATIVE NUMBERS

POSITIVE NUMBERS are greater than 0, and **NEGATIVE NUMBERS** are less than 0. Both positive and negative numbers can be shown on a **NUMBER LINE**.

Figure 2.2. Number Line

The **ABSOLUTE VALUE** of a number is the distance the number is from 0. Since distance is always positive, the absolute value of a number is always positive. The absolute value of a is denoted $|a|$. For example, $|-2| = 2$ since −2 is two units away from 0.

Positive and negative numbers can be added, subtracted, multiplied, and divided. The sign of the resulting number is governed by a specific set of rules shown in the table below.

Table 2.1. Operations with Positive and Negative Numbers

ADDING REAL NUMBERS		SUBTRACTING REAL NUMBERS	
Positive + Positive = Positive	7 + 8 = 15	Negative − Positive = Negative	−7 − 8 = −7 + (−8) = −15
Negative + Negative = Negative	−7 + (−8) = −15	Positive − Negative = Positive	7 − (−8) = 7 + 8 = 15

ADDING REAL NUMBERS		SUBTRACTING REAL NUMBERS*	
Negative + Positive OR Positive + Negative = Keep the sign of the number with larger absolute value	$-7 + 8 = 1$ $7 + -8 = -1$	Negative – Negative = Change the subtraction to addition and change the sign of the second number; then use addition rules.	$-7 - (-8) =$ $-7 + 8 = 1$ $-8 - (-7) = -8$ $+ 7 = -1$

MULTIPLYING REAL NUMBERS		DIVIDING REAL NUMBERS	
Positive × Positive = Positive	$8 \times 4 = 32$	Positive ÷ Positive = Positive	$8 \div 4 = 2$
Negative × Negative = Positive	$-8 \times (-4) = 32$	Negative ÷ Negative = Positive	$-8 \div (-4) = 2$
Positive × Negative OR Negative × Positive = Negative	$8 \times (-4) = -32$ $-8 \times 4 = -32$	Positive ÷ Negative OR Negative ÷ Positive = Negative	$8 \div (-4) = -2$ $-8 \div 4 = -2$

Examples

1. Add or subtract the following real numbers:

(A) $-18 + 12$

(B) $-3.64 + (-2.18)$

(C) $9.37 - 4.25$

(D) $86 - (-20)$

Answers:

(A) Since $|-18| > |12|$, the answer is negative: $|-18| - |12| = 6$. So the answer is **−6**.

(B) Adding two negative numbers results in a negative number. Add the values: **−5.82**.

(C) The first number is larger than the second, so the final answer is positive: **5.12**.

(D) Change the subtraction to addition, change the sign of the second number, and then add: $86 - (-20) = 86 + (+20) =$ **106**.

2. Multiply or divide the following real numbers:

(A) $\left(\frac{10}{3}\right)\left(-\frac{9}{5}\right)$

(B) $\frac{-64}{-10}$

(C) $(2.2)(3.3)$

(D) $-52 \div 13$

Answers:

(A) Multiply the numerators, multiply the denominators, and simplify: $\frac{-90}{15} =$ **−6**.

(B) A negative divided by a negative is a positive number: **6.4**.

(C) Multiplying positive numbers gives a positive answer: **7.26**.

(D) Dividing a negative by a positive number gives a negative answer: **−4**.

ORDER OF OPERATIONS

The ORDER OF OPERATIONS is simply the order in which operations are performed. **PEMDAS** is a common way to remember the order of operations:

1.	Parentheses	4.	Division
2.	Exponents	5.	Addition
3.	Multiplication	6.	Subtraction

Multiplication and division, and addition and subtraction, are performed together from left to right. So, performing multiple operations on a set of numbers is a four-step process:

1. P: Calculate expressions inside parentheses, brackets, braces, etc.
2. E: Calculate exponents and square roots.
3. MD: Calculate any remaining multiplication and division in order from left to right.
4. AS: Calculate any remaining addition and subtraction in order from left to right.

Always work from left to right within each step when simplifying expressions.

Examples

1. Simplify: $2(21 - 14) + 6 \div (-2) \times 3 - 10$

Answer:

$2(21 - 14) + 6 \div (-2) \times 3 - 10$	
$= 2(7) + 6 \div (-2) \times 3 - 10$	Calculate expressions inside parentheses.
$= 14 + 6 \div (-2) \times 3 - 10$ $= 14 + (-3) \times 3 - 10$ $= 14 + (-9) - 10$	There are no exponents or radicals, so perform multiplication and division from left to right.
$= 5 - 10$ $= \mathbf{-5}$	Perform addition and subtraction from left to right.

2. Simplify: $-(3)^2 + 4(5) + (5 - 6)^2 - 8$

Answer:

$-(3)^2 + 4(5) + (5 - 6)^2 - 8$	
$= -(3)^2 + 4(5) + (-1)^2 - 8$	Calculate expressions inside parentheses.
$= -9 + 4(5) + 1 - 8$	Simplify exponents and radicals.
$= -9 + 20 + 1 - 8$	Perform multiplication and division from left to right.
$= 11 + 1 - 8$ $= 12 - 8$ $= \mathbf{4}$	Perform addition and subtraction from left to right.

3. Simplify: $\dfrac{(7 - 9)^3 + 8(10 - 12)}{4^2 - 5^2}$

Answer:

$\dfrac{(7-9)^3 + 8(10-12)}{4^2 - 5^2}$	
$= \dfrac{(-2)^3 + 8(-2)}{4^2 - 5^2}$	Calculate expressions inside parentheses.
$= \dfrac{-8 + (-16)}{16 - 25}$	Simplify exponents and radicals.
$= \dfrac{-24}{-9}$	Perform addition and subtraction from left to right.
$= \dfrac{8}{3}$	Simplify.

UNITS OF MEASUREMENT

The standard units for the metric and American systems are shown below, along with the prefixes used to express metric units.

Table 2.2. Units and Conversion Factors

DIMENSION	AMERICAN	SI
length	inch/foot/yard/mile	meter
mass	ounce/pound/ton	gram
volume	cup/pint/quart/gallon	liter
force	pound-force	newton
pressure	pound-force per square inch	pascal
work and energy	cal/British thermal unit	joule
temperature	Fahrenheit	kelvin
charge	faraday	coulomb

Table 2.3. Metric Prefixes

PREFIX	SYMBOL	MULTIPLICATION FACTOR
tera	T	1,000,000,000,000
giga	G	1,000,000,000
mega	M	1,000,000
kilo	k	1,000
hecto	h	100
deca	da	10
base unit	--	--
deci	d	0.1
centi	c	0.01
milli	m	0.001
micro	μ	0.000001
nano	n	0.000000001
pico	p	0.000000000001

Units can be converted within a single system or between systems. When converting from one unit to another unit, a conversion factor (a numeric multiplier used to convert a value with a unit to another unit) is used. The process of converting between units using a conversion factor is sometimes known as dimensional analysis.

⚠️

A mnemonic device to help remember the metric system is *King Henry Drinks Under Dark Chocolate Moon* (KHDUDCM).

Table 2.4. Conversion Factors

1 in. = 2.54 cm	1 lb. = 0.454 kg
1 yd. = 0.914 m	1 cal = 4.19 J
1 mi. = 1.61 km	$1 °F = \frac{9}{5} °C + 32 °C$
1 gal. = 3.785 L	$1 cm^3 = 1 mL$
1 oz. = 28.35 g	1 hr = 3600 s

Examples

1. Convert the following measurements in the metric system.

   (A) 4.25 kilometers to meters

   (B) $8 m^2$ to mm^2

   Answers:

   (A) $4.25 \text{ km} \left(\frac{1000 \text{ m}}{1 \text{ km}}\right) = \textbf{4250 m}$

   (B) $\frac{8 m^2}{1} \times \frac{1000 \text{ mm}}{1 \text{ m}} \times \frac{1000 \text{ mm}}{1 \text{ m}} = \textbf{8,000,000 mm}^2$

   Since the units are square units (m^2), multiply by the conversion factor twice, so that both meters cancel.

2. Convert the following measurements in the American system.

   (A) 12 feet to inches

   (B) $7 yd^2$ to ft^2

   Answers:

   (A) $12 \text{ ft} \left(\frac{12 \text{ in}}{1 \text{ ft}}\right) = \textbf{144 in}$

   (B) $7 yd^2 \left(\frac{3ft}{1yd}\right)\left(\frac{3ft}{1yd}\right) = \textbf{63 ft}^2$

   Since the units are square units (yd^2), multiply by the conversion factor twice.

3. Convert the following measurements in the metric system to the American system.

   (A) 23 meters to feet

   (B) $10 m^2$ to yd^2

   Answers:

   (A) $23 \text{ m} \left(\frac{3.28 \text{ ft}}{1 \text{ m}}\right) = \textbf{75.44 ft}$

   (B) $\frac{10 m^2}{1} \times \frac{1.094 \text{ yd}}{1 \text{ m}} \times \frac{1.094 \text{ yd}}{1 \text{ m}} = \textbf{11.97 yd}^2$

4. Convert the following measurements in the American system to the metric system.

(A) 8 in³ to milliliters

(B) 16 kilograms to pounds

Answers:

(A) $8 \text{ in}^3 \left(\dfrac{16.39 \text{ ml}}{1 \text{ in}^3}\right) = \textbf{131.12 mL}$

(B) $16 \text{ kg}\left(\dfrac{2.2 \text{ lb}}{1 \text{ kg}}\right) = \textbf{35.2 lb}$

DECIMALS AND FRACTIONS

Decimals

A **DECIMAL** is a number that contains a decimal point. A decimal number is an alternative way of writing a fraction. The place value for a decimal includes **TENTHS** (one place after the decimal), **HUNDREDTHS** (two places after the decimal), **THOUSANDTHS** (three places after the decimal), etc.

To determine which way to move the decimal after multiplying, remember that changing the decimal should always make the final answer smaller.

Table 2.5. Place Values

1,000,000	10^6	millions
100,000	10^5	hundred thousands
10,000	10^4	ten thousands
1,000	10^3	thousands
100	10^2	hundreds
10	10^1	tens
1	10^0	ones
.		decimal
$\frac{1}{10}$	10^{-1}	tenths
$\frac{1}{100}$	10^{-2}	hundredths
$\frac{1}{1000}$	10^{-3}	thousandths

Decimals can be added, subtracted, multiplied, and divided:

- To add or subtract decimals, line up the decimal point and perform the operation, keeping the decimal point in the same place in the answer.

- To multiply decimals, first multiply the numbers without the decimal points. Then, sum the number of decimal places to the right of the decimal point in the original numbers and place the decimal point in the answer so that there are that many places to the right of the decimal.

- When dividing decimals move the decimal point to the right in order to make the divisor a whole number and move the decimal the same number of places

$$4.2 \leftarrow \text{quotient}$$
$$2.5\overline{)10.5} \leftarrow \text{dividend}$$
$$\uparrow$$
$$\text{divisor}$$

Figure 2.3. Division Terms

in the dividend. Divide the numbers without regard to the decimal. Then, place the decimal point of the quotient directly above the decimal point of the dividend.

Examples

1. Simplify: 24.38 + 16.51 − 29.87

Answer:

24.38 + 16.51 − 29.87	
24.38 + 16.51 = 40.89	Align the decimals and apply the order of operations left to right.
40.89 − 29.87 = **11.02**	

2. Simplify: (10.4)(18.2)

Answer:

(10.4)(18.2)	
104 × 182 = 18,928	Multiply the numbers ignoring the decimals.
18,928 → 189.28	The original problem includes two decimal places (one in each number), so move the decimal point in the answer so that there are two places after the decimal point.

Estimating is a good way to check the answer: $10.4 \approx 10$, $18.2 \approx 18$, and $10 \times 18 = 180$.

3. Simplify: 80 ÷ 2.5

Answer:

80 ÷ 2.5	
80 → 800 2.5 → 25	Move both decimals one place to the right (multiply by 10) so that the divisor is a whole number.
800 ÷ 25 = 32	Divide normally.

Fractions

A **FRACTION** is a number that can be written in the form $\frac{a}{b}$, where b is not equal to 0. The a part of the fraction is the **NUMERATOR** (top number) and the b part of the fraction is the **DENOMINATOR** (bottom number).

If the denominator of a fraction is greater than the numerator, the value of the fraction is less than 1 and it is called a **PROPER FRACTION** (for example, $\frac{3}{5}$ is a proper fraction). In an **IMPROPER FRACTION**, the denominator is less than the numerator and the value of the fraction is greater than 1 ($\frac{8}{3}$ is an improper fraction). An improper fraction can be written as a **MIXED NUMBER**, which has a whole number part and a proper fraction part. Improper fractions can be converted to mixed numbers by dividing the numerator by the denominator, which gives the whole number part, and the remainder becomes the numerator of the proper fraction part. (For example, the improper fraction $\frac{25}{9}$ is equal to mixed number $2\frac{7}{9}$ because 9 divides into 25 two times, with a remainder of 7.)

Conversely, mixed numbers can be converted to improper fractions. To do so, determine the numerator of the improper fraction by multiplying the denominator by the whole number, and then adding the numerator. The final number is written as the (now larger) numerator over the original denominator.

Fractions with the same denominator can be added or subtracted by simply adding or subtracting the numerators; the denominator will remain unchanged. To add or subtract fractions with different denominators, find the **LEAST COMMON DENOMINATOR (LCD)** of all the fractions. The LCD is the smallest number exactly divisible by each denominator. (For example, the least common denominator of the numbers 2, 3, and 8 is 24.) Once the LCD has been found, each fraction should be written in an equivalent form with the LCD as the denominator.

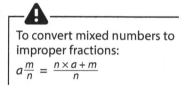

To convert mixed numbers to improper fractions:
$$a\frac{m}{n} = \frac{n \times a + m}{n}$$

To multiply fractions, the numerators are multiplied together and denominators are multiplied together. If there are any mixed numbers, they should first be changed to improper fractions. Then, the numerators are multiplied together and the denominators are multiplied together. The fraction can then be reduced if necessary. To divide fractions, multiply the first fraction by the reciprocal of the second.

$$\frac{a}{b} \pm \frac{c}{b} = \frac{a \pm c}{b}$$
$$\frac{a}{b} \times \frac{c}{d} = \frac{ac}{bd}$$
$$\frac{a}{b} \div \frac{c}{d} = \frac{a}{b} \times \frac{d}{c} = \frac{ad}{bc}$$

Any common denominator can be used to add or subtract fractions. The quickest way to find a common denominator of a set of values is simply to multiply all the values together. The result might not be the least common denominator, but it will allow the problem to be worked.

Examples

1. Simplify: $2\frac{3}{5} + 3\frac{1}{4} - 1\frac{1}{2}$

Answer:

$2\frac{3}{5} + 3\frac{1}{4} - 1\frac{1}{2}$	
$= 2\frac{12}{20} + 3\frac{5}{20} - 1\frac{10}{20}$	Change each fraction so it has a denominator of 20, which is the LCD of 5, 4, and 2.
$2 + 3 - 1 = 4$ $\frac{12}{20} + \frac{5}{20} - \frac{10}{20} = \frac{7}{20}$	Add and subtract the whole numbers together and the fractions together.
$4\frac{7}{20}$	Combine to get the final answer (a mixed number).

2. Simplify: $\frac{7}{8} \times 3\frac{1}{3}$

Answer:

$\frac{7}{8} \times 3\frac{1}{3}$	
$3\frac{1}{3} = \frac{10}{3}$	Change the mixed number to an improper fraction.
$\frac{7}{8}\left(\frac{10}{3}\right) = \frac{7 \times 10}{8 \times 3}$ $= \frac{70}{24}$	Multiply the numerators together and the denominators together.
$= \frac{35}{12}$ $= 2\frac{11}{12}$	Reduce the fraction.

3. Simplify: $4\frac{1}{2} \div \frac{2}{3}$

Answer:

$4\frac{1}{2} \div \frac{2}{3}$	
$4\frac{1}{2} = \frac{9}{2}$	Change the mixed number to an improper fraction.
$\frac{9}{2} \div \frac{2}{3}$ $= \frac{9}{2} \times \frac{3}{2}$ $= \frac{27}{4}$	Multiply the first fraction by the reciprocal of the second fraction.
$= 6\frac{3}{4}$	Simplify.

Converting Between Fractions and Decimals

A fraction is converted to a decimal by using long division until there is no remainder and no pattern of repeating numbers occurs.

A decimal is converted to a fraction using the following steps:

- Place the decimal value as the numerator in a fraction with a denominator of 1.
- Multiply the fraction by $\frac{10}{10}$ for every digit in the decimal value, so that there is no longer a decimal in the numerator.
- Reduce the fraction.

Examples

1. Write the fraction $\frac{7}{8}$ as a decimal.

Answer:

$$\begin{array}{r} 0.875 \\ 8\overline{)7000} \\ \underline{-64}\downarrow \\ 60 \\ \underline{-56}\downarrow \\ 40 \end{array}$$	Divide the denominator into the numerator using long division.

2. Write the fraction $\frac{5}{11}$ as a decimal.

Answer:

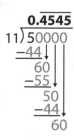

	Dividing using long division yields a repeating decimal.

3. Write the decimal 0.125 as a fraction.

Answer:

0.125

$= \frac{0.125}{1}$	Create a fraction with 0.125 as the numerator and 1 as the denominator.
$\frac{0.125}{1} \times \frac{10}{10} \times \frac{10}{10} \times \frac{10}{10} = \frac{125}{1000}$	Multiply by $\frac{10}{10}$ three times (one for each numeral after the decimal).
$= \frac{1}{8}$	Simplify.

Alternatively, recognize that 0.125 is read "one hundred twenty-five thousandths" and can therefore be written in fraction form as $\frac{125}{1000}$.

FACTORIALS

A **FACTORIAL** of a number n is denoted by $n!$ and is equal to $1 \times 2 \times 3 \times 4 \times \dots \times n$. Both $0!$ and $1!$ are equal to 1 by definition. Fractions containing factorials can often be simplified by crossing out the portions of the factorials that occur in both the numerator and denominator.

Examples

1. Simplify: 8!

Answer:

8!

$= 8 \times 7 \times 6 \times 5 \times 4 \times 3 \times 2 \times 1$ $= \mathbf{40,320}$	Expand the factorial and multiply.

2. Simplify: $\frac{10!}{7!3!}$

Answer:

$\frac{10!}{7!3!}$

$= \frac{10 \times 9 \times 8 \times 7!}{7! \times 3 \times 2 \times 1}$	Expand the factorial.
$= \frac{10 \times 9 \times 8}{3 \times 2 \times 1}$	Cross out values that occur in both the numerator and denominator.
$= \frac{720}{6}$ $= \mathbf{120}$	Multiply and simplify.

RATIOS

A **RATIO** is a comparison of two numbers and can be represented as $\frac{a}{b}$, $a{:}b$, or a to b. The two numbers represent a constant relationship, not a specific value: for every a number of items in the first group, there will be b number of items in the second. For example, if the ratio of blue to red candies in a bag is 3:5, the bag will contain 3 blue candies for every 5 red candies. So, the bag might contain 3 blue candies and 5 red candies, or it might contain 30 blue candies and 50 red candies, or 36 blue candies and 60 red candies. All of these values are representative of the ratio 3:5 (which is the ratio in its lowest, or simplest, terms).

To find the "whole" when working with ratios, simply add the values in the ratio. For example, if the ratio of boys to girls in a class is 2:3, the "whole" is five: 2 out of every 5 students are boys, and 3 out of every 5 students are girls.

Examples

1. There are 10 boys and 12 girls in a first-grade class. What is the ratio of boys to the total number of students? What is the ratio of girls to boys?

    Answer:

number of boys: 10 number of girls: 12 number of students: 22	Identify the variables.
number of boys : number of students $= 10 : 22$ $= \frac{10}{22}$ $= \frac{5}{11}$	Write out and simplify the ratio of boys to total students.
number of girls : number of boys $= 12 : 10$ $= \frac{12}{10}$ $= \frac{6}{5}$	Write out and simplify the ratio of girls to boys.

2. A family spends $600 a month on rent, $400 on utilities, $750 on groceries, and $550 on miscellaneous expenses. What is the ratio of the family's rent to their total expenses?

Answer:

rent = 600 utilities = 400 groceries = 750 miscellaneous = 550 total expenses = 600 + 400 + 750 + 550 = 2300	Identify the variables.
rent : total expenses = 600 : 2300 = $\frac{600}{2300}$ = $\frac{6}{23}$	Write out and simplify the ratio of rent to total expenses.

PROPORTIONS

A **PROPORTION** is an equation which states that two ratios are equal. A proportion is given in the form $\frac{a}{b} = \frac{c}{d}$, where the a and d terms are the extremes and the b and c terms are the means. A proportion is solved using cross-multiplication ($ad = bc$) to create an equation with no fractional components. A proportion must have the same units in both numerators and both denominators.

Examples

1. Solve the proportion for x: $\frac{3x-5}{2} = \frac{x-8}{3}$.

Answer:

$\frac{(3x-5)}{2} = \frac{(x-8)}{3}$	
$3(3x-5) = 2(x-8)$	Cross-multiply.
$9x - 15 = 2x - 16$ $7x - 15 = -16$ $7x = -1$ $x = -\frac{1}{7}$	Solve the equation for x.

2. A map is drawn such that 2.5 inches on the map equates to an actual distance of 40 miles. If the distance measured on the map between two cities is 17.25 inches, what is the actual distance between them in miles?

Answer:

$\frac{2.5}{40} = \frac{17.25}{x}$	Write a proportion where x equals the actual distance and each ratio is written as inches : miles.
$2.5x = 690$ $x = 276$ The two cities are **276 miles apart**.	Cross-multiply and divide to solve for x.

3. A factory knows that 4 out of 1000 parts made will be defective. If in a month there are 125,000 parts made, how many of these parts will be defective?

Answer:

$$\frac{4}{1000} = \frac{x}{125,000}$$

Write a proportion where x is the number of defective parts made and both ratios are written as defective : total.

$1000x = 500,000$

$x = 500$

There are **500 defective parts** for the month.

Cross-multiply and divide to solve for x.

PERCENTAGES

A **PERCENT** (or percentage) means per hundred and is expressed with a percent symbol (%). For example, 54% means 54 out of every 100. A percent can be converted to a decimal by removing the % symbol and moving the decimal point two places to the left, while a decimal can be converted to a percent by moving the decimal point two places to the right and attaching the % sign. A percent can be converted to a fraction by writing the percent as a fraction with 100 as the denominator and reducing. A fraction can be converted to a percent by performing the indicated division, multiplying the result by 100, and attaching the % sign.

The equation for finding percentages has three variables: the part, the whole, and the percent (which is expressed in the equation as a decimal). The equation, as shown below, can be rearranged to solve for any of these variables.

- part = whole × percent
- percent = $\frac{\text{part}}{\text{whole}}$
- whole = $\frac{\text{part}}{\text{percent}}$

This set of equations can be used to solve percent word problems. All that's needed is to identify the part, whole, and/or percent, and then to plug those values into the appropriate equation and solve.

Examples

1. Change the following values to the indicated form:

(A) 18% to a fraction

(B) $\frac{3}{5}$ to a percent

(C) 1.125 to a percent

(D) 84% to a decimal

Answers:

(A) The percent is written as a fraction over 100 and reduced: $\frac{18}{100} = \frac{9}{50}$.

(B) Dividing 5 by 3 gives the value 0.6, which is then multiplied by 100: **60%.**

(C)   The decimal point is moved two places to the right:
       $1.125 \times 100 = \textbf{112.5\%}$.

D.   The decimal point is moved two places to the left: $84 \div 100 = \textbf{0.84}$.

2. In a school of 650 students, 54% of the students are boys. How many students are girls?

Answer:

Percent of students who are girls = 100% − 54% = 46% percent = 46% = 0.46 whole = 650 students part = ?	Identify the variables.
part = whole × percent = 0.46 × 650 = 299 **There are 299 girls.**	Plug the variables into the appropriate equation.

Percent Change

Percent change problems involve a change from an original amount. Often percent change problems appear as word problems that include discounts, growth, or markups. In order to solve percent change problems, it's necessary to identify the percent change (as a decimal), the amount of change, and the original amount. (Keep in mind that one of these will be the value being solved for.) These values can then be plugged into the equations below:

Key terms associated with percent change problems include discount, sales tax, and markup.

- amount of change = original amount × percent change

- $\text{percent change} = \dfrac{\text{amount of change}}{\text{original amount}}$

- $\text{original amount} = \dfrac{\text{amount of change}}{\text{percent change}}$

Examples

1. An HDTV that originally cost $1,500 is on sale for 45% off. What is the sale price for the item?

Answer:

original amount =$1,500 percent change = 45% = 0.45 amount of change = ?	Identify the variables.
amount of change = original amount × percent change = 1500 × 0.45 = 675	Plug the variables into the appropriate equation.
1500 − 675 = 825 **The final price is $825.**	To find the new price, subtract the amount of change from the original price.

2. A house was bought in 2000 for $100,000 and sold in 2015 for $120,000. What was the percent growth in the value of the house from 2000 to 2015?

Answer:

original amount = \$100,000 amount of change = 120,000 − 100,000 = 20,000 percent change = ?	Identify the variables.
percent change = $\frac{\text{amount of change}}{\text{original amount}}$ = $\frac{20,000}{100,000}$ = 0.20	Plug the variables into the appropriate equation.
$0.20 \times 100 = \mathbf{20\%}$	To find the percent growth, multiply by 100.

EXPONENTS AND RADICALS

Exponents

An expression in the form b^n is in an exponential notation where b is the BASE and n is an EXPONENT. To perform the operation, multiply the base by itself the number of times indicated by the exponent. For example, 2^3 is equal to $2 \times 2 \times 2$ or 8.

Table 2.6. Operations with Exponents

RULE	EXAMPLE	EXPLANATION
$a^0 = 1$	$5^0 = 1$	Any base (except 0) to the 0 power is 1.
$a^{-n} = \frac{1}{a^n}$	$5^3 = \frac{1}{5^3}$	A negative exponent becomes positive when moved from numerator to denominator (or vice versa).
$a^m a^n = a^{m+n}$	$5^3 5^4 = 5^{3+4} = 5^7$	Add the exponents to multiply two powers with the same base.
$(a^m)^n = a^{mn}$	$(5^3)^4 = 5^{3(4)} = 5^{12}$	Multiply the exponents to raise a power to a power.
$\frac{a^m}{a^n} = a^{m-n}$	$\frac{5^4}{5^3} = 5^{4-3} = 5^1$	Subtract the exponents to divide two powers with the same base.
$(ab)^n = a^n b^n$	$(5 \times 6)^3 = 5^3 6^3$	Apply the exponent to each base to raise a product to a power.
$\frac{a}{b}^n = \frac{a^n}{b^n}$	$\frac{5}{6}^3 = \frac{5^3}{6^3}$	Apply the exponent to each base to raise a quotient to a power.
$\frac{a}{b}^{-n} = \frac{b}{a}^n$	$\frac{5}{6}^{-3} = \frac{6^3}{5}$	Invert the fraction and change the sign of the exponent to raise a fraction to a negative power.
$\frac{a^m}{b^n} = \frac{b^{-n}}{a^{-m}}$	$\frac{5^3}{6^4} = \frac{6^{-4}}{5^{-3}}$	Change the sign of the exponent when moving a number from the numerator to denominator (or vice versa).

Examples

1. Simplify: $\dfrac{(10^2)^3}{(10^2)^{-2}}$

Answer:

$\dfrac{(10^2)^3}{(10^2)^{-2}}$	
$= \dfrac{10^6}{10^{-4}}$	Multiply the exponents raised to a power.
$= 10^{6-(-4)}$	Subtract the exponent in the denominator from the one in the numerator.
$= 10^{10}$ $= \mathbf{10,000,000,000}$	Simplify.

2. Simplify: $\dfrac{(x^{-2}y^2)^2}{x^3y}$

Answer:

$\dfrac{(x^{-2}y^2)^2}{x^3y}$	
$= \dfrac{x^{-4}y^4}{x^3y}$	Multiply the exponents raised to a power.
$= x^{-4-3}y^{4-1}$ $= x^{-7}y^3$	Subtract the exponent in the denominator from the one in the numerator.
$= \dfrac{\boldsymbol{y^3}}{\boldsymbol{x^7}}$	Move negative exponents to the denominator.

Radicals

RADICALS are expressed as $\sqrt[b]{a}$, where b is called the INDEX and a is the RADICAND. A radical is used to indicate the inverse operation of an exponent: finding the base which can be raised to b to yield a. For example, $\sqrt[3]{125}$ is equal to 5 because $5 \times 5 \times 5$ equals 125. The same operation can be expressed using a fraction exponent, so $\sqrt[b]{a} = a^{\frac{1}{b}}$. Note that when no value is indicated for b, it is assumed to be 2 (square root).

When b is even and a is positive, $\sqrt[b]{a}$ is defined to be the positive real value n such that $n^b = a$ (example: $\sqrt{16} = 4$ only, and not –4, even though $(-4)(-4) = 16$). If b is even and a is negative, $\sqrt[b]{a}$ will be a complex number (example: $\sqrt{-9} = 3i$). Finally if b is odd, $\sqrt[b]{a}$ will always be a real number regardless of the sign of a. If a is negative, $\sqrt[b]{a}$ will be negative since a number to an odd power is negative (example: $\sqrt[5]{-32} = -2$ since $(-2)^5 = -32$).

$\sqrt[n]{x}$ is referred to as the nth root of x.

- $n = 2$ is the square root
- $n = 3$ is the cube root
- $n = 4$ is the fourth root
- $n = 5$ is the fifth root

The following table of operations with radicals holds for all cases EXCEPT the case where b is even and a is negative (the complex case).

Table 2.7. Operations with Radicals

RULE	EXAMPLE	EXPLANATION
$\sqrt[b]{ac} = \sqrt[b]{a}\sqrt[b]{c}$	$\sqrt[3]{81} = \sqrt[3]{27}\sqrt[3]{3} = 3\sqrt[3]{3}$	The values under the radical sign can be separated into values that multiply to the original value.
$\sqrt[b]{\frac{a}{c}} = \frac{\sqrt[b]{a}}{\sqrt[b]{c}}$	$\sqrt{\frac{4}{81}} = \frac{\sqrt{4}}{\sqrt{81}} = \frac{2}{9}$	The b-root of the numerator and denominator can be calculated when there is a fraction under a radical sign.
$\sqrt[b]{a^c} = (\sqrt[b]{a})^c = a^{\frac{c}{b}}$	$\sqrt[3]{6^2} = (\sqrt[3]{6})^2 = 6^{\frac{2}{3}}$	The b-root can be written as a fractional exponent. If there is a power under the radical sign, it will be the numerator of the fraction.
$\frac{c}{\sqrt[b]{a}} \times \frac{\sqrt[b]{a}}{\sqrt[b]{a}} = \frac{c\sqrt[b]{a}}{a}$	$\frac{5}{\sqrt{2}}\frac{\sqrt{2}}{\sqrt{2}} = \frac{5\sqrt{2}}{2}$	To rationalize the denominator, multiply the numerator and denominator by the radical in the denominator until the radical has been canceled out.
$\frac{c}{b-\sqrt{a}} \times \frac{b+\sqrt{a}}{b+\sqrt{a}}$ $= \frac{c(b+\sqrt{a})}{b^2-a}$	$\frac{4}{3-\sqrt{2}}\frac{3+\sqrt{2}}{3+\sqrt{2}}$ $= \frac{4(3+\sqrt{2})}{9-2} = \frac{12+4\sqrt{2}}{7}$	To rationalize the denominator, the numerator and denominator are multiplied by the conjugate of the denominator.

Examples

1. Simplify: $\sqrt{48}$

Answer:

$\sqrt{48}$	
$= \sqrt{16 \times 3}$	Determine the largest square number that is a factor of the radicand (48) and write the radicand as a product using that square number as a factor.
$= \sqrt{16}\sqrt{3}$ $= \mathbf{4\sqrt{3}}$	Apply the rules of radicals to simplify.

2. Simplify: $\frac{6}{\sqrt{8}}$

Answer:

$\frac{6}{\sqrt{8}}$	
$= \frac{6}{\sqrt{4}\sqrt{2}}$ $= \frac{6}{2\sqrt{2}}$	Apply the rules of radicals to simplify.
$= \frac{6}{2\sqrt{2}}(\frac{\sqrt{2}}{\sqrt{2}})$ $= \mathbf{\frac{3\sqrt{2}}{2}}$	Multiply by $\frac{\sqrt{2}}{\sqrt{2}}$ to rationalize the denominator.

ABSOLUTE VALUE

The **ABSOLUTE VALUE** of a number means the distance between that number and zero. The absolute value of any number is positive since distance is always positive. The notation for absolute value of a number is two vertical bars:

$|-27| = 27$ The distance from –27 to 0 is 27.

$|27| = 27$ The distance from 27 to 0 is 27.

Solving equations and simplifying inequalities with absolute values usually requires writing two equations or inequalities, which are then solved separately using the usual methods of solving equations. To write the two equations, set one equation equal to the positive value of the expression inside the absolute value and the other equal to the negative value. Two inequalities can be written in the same manner. However, the inequality symbol should be flipped for the negative value.

The formal definition of the absolute value is

$$|x| = \begin{cases} -x, & x < 0 \\ x, & x \geq 0 \end{cases}$$

This is true because whenever x is negative, the opposite of x is the answer (for example, $|-5| = -(-5) = 5$, but when x is positive, the answer is just x. This type of function is called a **PIECE-WISE FUNCTION**. It is defined in two (or more) distinct pieces. To graph the absolute value function, graph each piece separately. When $x < 0$ (that is, when it is negative), graph the line $y = -x$. When $x > 0$ (that is, when x is positive), graph the line $y = x$. This creates a V-shaped graph that is the parent function for absolute value functions.

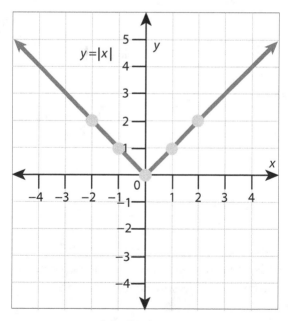

Figure 2.4. Absolute Value Parent Function

Examples

1. Solve for x: $|x - 3| = 27$

Answer:

Set the quantity inside the parentheses equal to 27 or –27, and solve:

$$x - 3 = 27$$
$$\mathbf{x = 30}$$

$$x - 3 = -27$$
$$\mathbf{x = -24}$$

2. Solve for r: $\frac{|r-7|}{5} = 27$

Answer:

The first step is to isolate the absolute value part of the equation. Multiplying both sides by 5 gives:

$|r - 7| = 135$

If the quantity in the absolute value bars is 135 or −135, then the absolute value would be 135:

$$r - 7 = 135$$
$$\mathbf{r = 142}$$

$$r - 7 = -135$$
$$\mathbf{r = -128}$$

3. Find the solution set for the following inequality: $\left|\frac{3x}{7}\right| \geq 4 - x$.

Answer:

$\left\|\frac{3x}{7}\right\| \geq 4 - x$	
$\frac{\|3x\|}{7} \geq 4 - x$ $\|3x\| \geq 28 - 7x$	Simplify the equation.
$3x \geq 28 - 7x$ $10x \geq 28$ $x \geq \frac{28}{10}$ $-(3x) \leq 28 - 7x$ $-3x \leq 28 - 7x$ $4x \leq 28$ $x \leq 7$	Create and solve two inequalities. When including the negative answer, flip the inequality.
$\frac{28}{10} \leq x \leq 7$	Combine the two answers to find the solution set.

DESCRIBING SETS OF DATA

Measures of central tendency help identify the center, or most typical, value within a data set. There are three such central tendencies that describe the "center" of the data in different ways. The **MEAN** is the arithmetic average and is found by dividing the sum of all measurements by the number of measurements. The mean of a population is written as μ and the mean of a sample is written as $\bar{x}$.

$$\text{population mean} = \mu = \frac{x_1 + x_2 + \dots x_N}{N} = \frac{\sum x}{N} \qquad \text{sample mean} = \bar{x} = \frac{x_1 + x_2 + \dots x_n}{n} = \frac{\sum x}{n}$$

The data points are represented by x's with subscripts; the sum is denoted using the Greek letter sigma (Σ); N is the number of data points in the entire population; and n is the number of data points in a sample set.

The **MEDIAN** divides the measurements into two equal halves. The median is the measurement right in the middle of an odd set of measurements or the average of the two middle numbers in an even data set. When calculating the median, it is important to order the data values from least to greatest before attempting to locate the middle value. The MODE is simply the measurement that occurs most often. There can be many modes in a data set, or no mode. Since measures of central tendency describe a *center* of the data, all three of these measures will be between the lowest and highest data values (inclusive).

Unusually large or small values, called OUTLIERS, will affect the mean of a sample more than the mode. If there is a high outlier, the mean will be greater than the median; if there is a low outlier, the mean will be lower than the median. When outliers are present, the median is a better measure of the data's center than the mean because the median will be closer to the terms in the data set.

When the same value is added to each term in a set, the mean increases by that value and the standard deviation is unchanged. When each term in a set is multiplied by the same value, both the mean and standard deviation will also be multiplied by that value.

The values in a data set can be very close together (close to the mean), or very spread out. This is called the SPREAD or DISPERSION of the data. There are a few MEASURES OF VARIATION (or MEASURES OF DISPERSION) that quantify the spread within a data set. RANGE is the difference between the largest and smallest data points in a set:

$$R = \text{largest data point} - \text{smallest data point}$$

Notice range depends on only two data points (the two extremes). Sometimes these data points are outliers; regardless, for a large data set, relying on only two data points is not an exact tool.

The understanding of the data set can be improved by calculating QUARTILES. To calculate quartiles, first arrange the data in ascending order and find the set's median (also called quartile 2 or Q2). Then find the median of the lower half of the data, called quartile 1 (Q1), and the median of the upper half of the data, called quartile 3 (Q3). These three points divide the data into four equal groups of data (thus the word *quartile*). Each quartile contains 25% of the data.

INTERQUARTILE RANGE (IQR) provides a more reliable range that is not as affected by extremes. IQR is the difference between the third quartile data point and the first quartile data point and gives the spread of the middle 50% of the data:

$$IQR = Q_3 - Q_1$$

A measure of variation that depends on the mean is STANDARD DEVIATION, which uses every data point in a set and calculates the average distance of each data point from the mean of the data. Standard deviation can be computed for an entire population (written σ) or for a sample of a population (written s):

$$\sigma = \sqrt{\frac{\sum(x_i - \mu)^2}{N}} \qquad s = \sqrt{\frac{\sum(x_i - \bar{x})^2}{n - 1}}$$

Thus, to calculate standard deviation, the difference between the mean and each data point is calculated. Each of these differences is squared (so that each is positive). The average of the squared values is computed by summing the squares and dividing by N or $(n - 1)$. Then the square root is taken, to "undo" the previous squaring.

The VARIANCE of a data set is simply the square of the standard variation:

Standard deviation and variance are also affected by extreme values. Though much simpler to calculate, interquartile range is the more accurate depiction of how the data is scattered when there are outlier values.

$$V = \sigma^2 = \frac{1}{N} \sum_{i=1}^{N} (x_i - \mu)^2$$

Variance measures how narrowly or widely the data points are distributed. A variance of zero means every data point is the same; a large variance means the data is widely spread out.

Examples

1. What is the mean of the following data set? {1000, 0.1, 10, 1}

   Answer:

   Use the equation to find the mean of a sample:

   $$\frac{1000 + 0.1 + 10 + 1}{4} = \textbf{252.78}$$

2. What is the median of the following data set? {1000, 10, 1, 0.1}

   Answer:

   Since there is an even number of data points in the set, the median will be the mean of the two middle numbers. Order the numbers from least to greatest: 0.1, 1, 10, and 1000. The two middle numbers are 1 and 10, and their mean is:

   $$\frac{1 + 10}{2} = \textbf{5.5}$$

3. Josey has an average of 81 on four equally weighted tests she has taken in her statistics class. She wants to determine what grade she must receive on her fifth test so that her mean is 83, which will give her a B in the course, but she does not remember her other scores. What grade must she receive on her fifth test?

   Answer:

   Even though Josey does not know her test scores, she knows her average. Therefore it can be assumed that each test score was 81, since four scores of 81 would average to 81. To find the score, x, that she needs use the equation for the mean of a sample:

   $$\frac{4(81) + x}{5} = 83$$
   $$324 + x = 415$$
   $$x = \textbf{91}$$

4. What are the range and interquartile range of the following set? {3, 9, 49, 64, 81, 100, 121, 144, 169}

   Answer:

R = largest point − smallest point = 169 − 3 = **166**	Use the equation for range.
3 9 → Q1 = $\frac{49 + 9}{2}$ = 29 49 64 81 → Q2 100 121 → Q3 = $\frac{121 + 144}{2}$ = 132.5 144 169	Place the terms in numerical order and identify Q1, Q2, and Q3.

$IQR = Q3 - Q1$ $= 132.5 - 29$ $= \mathbf{103.5}$	Find the IQR by subtracting Q1 from Q3.

5. In a group of 7 people, 1 person has no children, 2 people have 1 child, 2 people have 2 children, 1 person has 5 children, and 1 person has 17 children. To the nearest hundredth of a child, what is the standard deviation in this group?

Answer:

$\{0, 1, 1, 2, 2, 5, 17\}$	Create a data set out of this scenario.
$\mu = \dfrac{x_1 + x_2 + \ldots x_N}{N} = \dfrac{\Sigma x}{N}$ $\mu = \dfrac{0 + 1 + 1 + 2 + 2 + 5 + 17}{7} = 4$	Calculate the population mean.
$(0 - 4)^2 = (-4)^2 = 16$ $(1 - 4)^2 = (-3)^2 = 9$ $(1 - 4)^2 = (-3)^2 = 9$ $(2 - 4)^2 = (-2)^2 = 4$ $(2 - 4)^2 = (-2)^2 = 4$ $(5 - 4)^2 = (1)^2 = 1$ $(17 - 4)^2 = (13)^2 = 169$	Find the square of the difference of each term and the mean $(x_i - \mu)^2$.
$\sigma = \sqrt{\dfrac{\Sigma(x_i - \mu)^2}{N}}$ $\sigma = \sqrt{\dfrac{212}{7}} = \sqrt{30.28} = \mathbf{5.50}$	Plug the sum (Σ) of these squares, 212, into the standard deviation formula.

PROBABILITY

Probability describes how likely something is to happen. In probability, an **EVENT** is the single result of a trial, and an **OUTCOME** is a possible event that results from a trial. The collection of all possible outcomes for a particular trial is called the **SAMPLE SPACE**. For example, when rolling a die, the sample space is the numbers 1 – 6. Rolling a single number, such as 4, would be a single event.

Probability of a Single Event

The probability of a single event occurring is the number of outcomes in which that event occurs (called **FAVORABLE EVENTS**) divided by the number of items in the sample space (total possible outcomes):

$$P \text{ (an event)} = \frac{number\ of\ favorable\ outcomes}{total\ number\ of\ possible\ outcomes}$$

The probability of any event occurring will always be a fraction or decimal between 0 and 1. It may also be expressed as a percent. An event with 0 probability will never occur and an event with a probability of 1 is certain to occur. The probability of an event not occurring is referred to as that event's **COMPLEMENT**. The sum of an event's probability and the probability of that event's complement will always be 1.

Examples

1. What is the probability that an even number results when a six-sided die is rolled? What is the probability the die lands on 5?

   Answer:

   $P(rolling\ even) = \dfrac{number\ of\ favorable\ outcomes}{total\ number\ of\ possible\ outcomes} = \dfrac{3}{6} = \dfrac{1}{2}$

   $P(rolling\ 5) = \dfrac{number\ of\ favorable\ outcomes}{total\ number\ of\ possible\ outcomes} = \dfrac{1}{6}$

2. Only 20 tickets were issued in a raffle. If someone were to buy 6 tickets, what is the probability that person would not win the raffle?

   Answer:

   $P(not\ winning) = \dfrac{number\ of\ favorable\ outcomes}{total\ number\ of\ possible\ outcomes} = \dfrac{14}{20} = \dfrac{7}{10}$

   or

   $P(not\ winning) = 1 - P(winning) = 1 - \dfrac{6}{20} = \dfrac{14}{20} = \dfrac{7}{10}$

3. A bag contains 26 tiles representing the 26 letters of the English alphabet. If 3 tiles are drawn from the bag without replacement, what is the probability that all 3 will be consonants?

   Answer:

   $P = \dfrac{number\ of\ favorable\ outcomes}{total\ number\ of\ possible\ outcomes}$

   $= \dfrac{number\ of\ 3\text{-}consonant\ combinations}{number\ of\ 3\text{-}tile\ combinations}$

   $= \dfrac{_{21}C_3}{_{26}C_3}$

   $= \dfrac{54{,}264}{65{,}780}$

   $= 0.82 = \mathbf{82\%}$

Probability of Multiple Events

If events are **INDEPENDENT**, the probability of one occurring does not affect the probability of the other event occurring. Rolling a die and getting one number does not change the probability of getting any particular number on the next roll. The number of faces has not changed, so these are independent events.

If events are **DEPENDENT**, the probability of one occurring changes the probability of the other event occurring. Drawing a card from a deck without replacing it will affect the probability of the next card drawn because the number of available cards has changed.

> ⚠
> When drawing objects, the phrase *with replacement* describes independent events, and *without replacement* describes dependent events.

To find the probability that two or more independent events will occur (A and B), simply multiply the probabilities of each individual event together. To find the probability that one, the other, or both will occur (A or B), it's necessary to add their probabilities and then subtract their overlap (which prevents the same values from being counted twice).

CONDITIONAL PROBABILITY is the probability of an event occurring given that another event has occurred. The notation $P(B|A)$ represents the probability that event B occurs, given that event A has already occurred (it is read "probability of B, given A").

Table 2.8. Probability Formulas

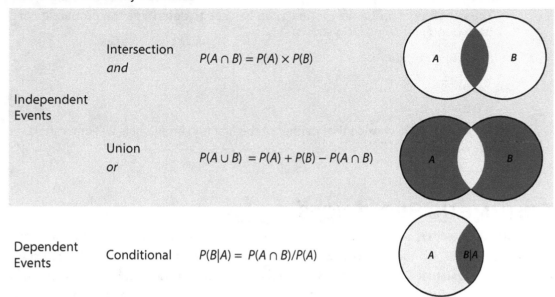

Independent Events	Intersection *and*	$P(A \cap B) = P(A) \times P(B)$	
	Union *or*	$P(A \cup B) = P(A) + P(B) - P(A \cap B)$	
Dependent Events	Conditional	$P(B|A) = P(A \cap B)/P(A)$	

Two events that are MUTUALLY EXCLUSIVE CANNOT happen at the same time. This is similar to disjoint sets in set theory. The probability that two mutually exclusive events will occur is zero. MUTUALLY INCLUSIVE events share common outcomes.

Examples

1. A card is drawn from a standard 52-card deck. What is the probability that it is either a queen or a heart?

   Answer:

   This is a union (*or*) problem.

   $P(A)$ = the probability of drawing a queen = $\frac{1}{13}$

   $P(B)$ = the probability of drawing a heart = $\frac{1}{4}$

   $P(A \cap B)$ = the probability of drawing a heart and a queen = $\frac{1}{52}$

   $P(A \cup B) = P(A) + P(B) - P(A \cap B)$

   $= \frac{1}{13} + \frac{1}{4} - \frac{1}{52}$

   $= \mathbf{0.31}$

2. A group of ten individuals is drawing straws from a group of 28 long straws and 2 short straws. If the straws are not replaced, what is the probability, as a percentage, that neither of the first two individuals will draw a short straw?

   Answer:

   This scenario includes two events, *A* and *B*.

   The probability of the first person drawing a long straw is an independent event: $P(A) = \frac{28}{30}$

   The probability the second person draws a long straw changes because one long straw has already been drawn. In other words, it is the probability of event *B* given that event *A* has already happened:

$$P(B|A) = \frac{27}{29}$$

The conditional probability formula can be used to determine the probability of both people drawing long straws:

$$P(A \cap B) = P(A)P(B|A)$$

$$= \left(\frac{28}{30}\right)\left(\frac{27}{29}\right)$$

$$= 0.87$$

There is an **87% chance** that neither of the first two individuals will draw short straws.

ARITHMETIC SEQUENCES

ARITHMETIC GROWTH is constant growth, meaning that the difference between any one term in the series and the next consecutive term will be the same constant. This constant is called the COMMON DIFFERENCE. Thus, to list the terms in the sequence, one can just add (or subtract) the same number repeatedly. For example, the series {20, 30, 40, 50} is arithmetic since 10 is added each time to get from one term to the next. One way to represent this sequence is using a RECURSIVE definition, which basically says: *next term = current term + common difference*. For this example, the recursive definition would be $a_{n+1} = a_n + 10$ because the *next* term a_{n+1} in the sequence is the current term a_n plus 10. In general, the recursive definition of a series is:

$$a_{n+1} = a_n + d, \text{ where } d \text{ is the common difference.}$$

Often, the objective of arithmetic sequence questions is to find a specific term in the sequence or the sum of a certain series of terms. The formulas to use are:

Table 2.9. Formulas for Arithmetic Sequences and Series

FINDING THE *N*TH TERM . . .

$a_n = a_1 + d(n-1)$ $a_n = a_m + d(n-m)$	d = the common difference of the sequence a_n = the nth term in the sequence n = the number of the term a_m = the mth term in the sequence m = the number of the term a_1 = the first term in the sequence

FINDING THE PARTIAL SUM . . .

$S_n = \frac{n(a_1 + a_n)}{2}$	S_n = sum of the terms through the nth term a_n = the nth term in the sequence n = the number of the term a_1 = the first term in the sequence

Examples

1. Find the ninth term of the sequence: $-57, -40, -23, -6 \ldots$

Answer:

$a_1 = -57$ $d = -57 - (-40) = 17$ $n = 9$	Identify the variables given.
$a_9 = -57 + 17(9 - 1)$	Plug these values into the formula for the specific term of an arithmetic sequence.
$a_9 = -57 + 17(8)$ $a_9 = -57 + 136$ $\boldsymbol{a_9 = 79}$	Solve for a_9.

2. If the 23rd term in an arithmetic sequence is 820, and the 5th term is 200, find the common difference between each term.

Answer:

$a_5 = 200$ $a_{23} = 820$ $n = 23$ $m = 5$ $d = ?$	Idenfity the variables given.
$a_n = a_m + d(n - m)$ $820 = 200 + d(23 - 5)$ $620 = d(18)$ $\boldsymbol{d = 34.\overline{44}}$	Plug these values into the equation for using one term to find another in an arithmetic sequence.

3

WORD KNOWLEDGE

The ASVAB Word Knowledge section tests vocabulary. Each question will provide either a word on its own or a word in the context of a sentence. The correct answer will be the choice whose meaning most closely matches the definition of the given word. It's a fast-moving section: questions need to be answered in less than 30 seconds. Having a large vocabulary will obviously help with this section, but there are also strategies that can be used to determine the meaning of unfamiliar words.

WORD STRUCTURE

In addition to the context of a sentence or passage, an unfamiliar word itself can provide clues about its meaning. Most words consist of discrete pieces that determine its meaning; these pieces include word roots, prefixes, and suffixes.

WORD ROOTS are the bases from which many words take their form and meaning. The most common word roots are Greek and Latin, and a broad knowledge of these roots can make it much easier to determine the meaning of words. The root of a word does not always point to the word's exact meaning, but combined with an understanding of the word's place in a sentence, it will often be enough to answer a question about meaning or relationships.

Table 3.1. Common Word Roots

ROOT	MEANING	EXAMPLES
alter	other	alternate, alter ego
ambi	both	ambidextrous
ami, amic	love	amiable
amphi	both ends, all sides	amphibian
anthrop	man, human, humanity	misanthrope, anthropologist
apert	open	aperture
aqua	water	aqueduct, aquarium

Table 3.1. Common Word Roots (continued)

ROOT	MEANING	EXAMPLES
aud	to hear	audience
auto	self	autobiography
bell	war	belligerent, bellicose
bene	good	benevolent
bio	life	biology
ced	yield, go	secede, intercede
cent	one hundred	century
chron	time	chronological
circum	around	circumference
contra, counter	against	contradict
crac, crat	rule, ruler	autocrat, bureaucrat
crypt	hidden	cryptogram, cryptic
curr, curs, cours	to run	precursory
dict	to say	dictator, dictation
dyna	power	dynamic
dys	bad, hard, unlucky	dysfunctional
equ	equal, even	equanimity
fac	to make, to do	factory
form	shape	reform, conform
fort	strength	fortitude
fract	to break	fracture
grad, gress	step	progression
gram	thing written	epigram
graph	writing	graphic
hetero	different	heterogeneous
homo	same	homogenous
hypo	below, beneath	hypothermia
iso	identical	isolate
ject	throw	projection
logy	study of	biology
luc	light	elucidate
mal	bad	malevolent
meta, met	behind, between	metacognition, behind the thinking
meter, metr	measure	thermometer
micro	small	microbe
mis, miso	hate	misanthrope
mit	to send	transmit

ROOT	MEANING	EXAMPLES
mono	one	monologue
morph	form, shape	morphology
mort	death	mortal
multi	many	multiple
phil	love	philanthropist
port	carry	transportation
pseudo	false	pseudonym
psycho	soul, spirit	psychic
rupt	to break	disruption
scope	viewing instrument	microscope
scrib, scribe	to write	inscription
sect, sec	to cut	section
sequ, secu	follow	consecutive
soph	wisdom, knowledge	philosophy
spect	to look	spectator
struct	to build	restructure
tele	far off	telephone
terr	earth	terrestrial
therm	heat	thermal
vent, vene	to come	convene
vert	turn	vertigo
voc	voice, call	vocalize, evocative

PREFIXES

In addition to understanding the base of a word, it's helpful to know common affixes that change the meaning of words and demonstrate their relationships to other words. PREFIXES are added to the beginning of words and frequently change their meaning (sometimes even to the opposite meaning).

Table 3.2. Common Prefixes

PREFIX	MEANING	EXAMPLES
a, an	without, not	anachronism, anhydrous
ab, abs, a	apart, away from	abscission, abnormal
ad	toward	adhere
agere	act	agent
amphi, ambi	round, both sides	ambivalent
ante	before	antedate, anterior
anti	against	antipathy

Table 3.2. Common Prefixes (continued)

PREFIX	MEANING	EXAMPLES
archos	leader, first, chief	oligarchy
bene	well, favorable	benevolent, beneficent
bi	two	binary, bivalve
caco	bad	cacophony
circum	around	circumnavigate
corpus	body	corporeal
credo	belief	credible
demos	people	demographic
di	two, double	dimorphism, diatomic
dia	across, through	dialectic
dis	not, apart	disenfranchise
dynasthai	be able	dynamo, dynasty
ego	I, self	egomaniac, egocentric
epi	upon, over	epigram, epiphyte
ex	out	extraneous, extemporaneous
geo	earth	geocentric, geomancy
ideo	idea	ideology, ideation
in	in	induction, indigenous
in, im	not	ignoble, immoral
inter	between	interstellar
lexis	word	lexicography
liber	free, book	liberal
locus	place	locality
macro	large	macrophage
micro	small	micron
mono	one, single	monocle, monovalent
mortis	death	moribund
olig	few	oligarchy
peri	around	peripatetic, perineum
poly	many	polygamy
pre	before	prescient
solus	alone	solitary
subter	under, secret	subterfuge
un	not	unsafe
utilis	useful	utilitarian

SUFFIXES

SUFFIXES are added to the end of words, and like preffixes they modify the meaning of the word root. Suffixes also serve an important grammatical function, and can change a part of speech or indicate if a word is plural or related to a plural.

Table 3.3. Common Suffixes

SUFFIX	MEANING	EXAMPLES
able, ible	able, capable	visible
age	act of, state of, result of	wreckage
al	relating to	gradual
algia	pain	myalgia
an, ian	native of, relating to	riparian
ance, ancy	action, process, state	defiance
ary, ery, ory	relating to, quality, place	aviary
cian	processing a specific skill or art	physician
cule, ling	very small	sapling, animalcule
cy	action, function	normalcy
dom	quality, realm	wisdom
ee	one who receives the action	nominee
en	made of, to make	silken
ence, ency	action, state of, quality	urgency
er, or	one who, that which	professor
escent	in the process of	adolescent, senescence
esis, osis	action, process, condition	genesis, neurosis
et, ette	small one, group	baronet, lorgnette
fic	making, causing	specific
ful	full of	frightful
hood	order, condition, quality	adulthood
ice	condition, state, quality	malice
id, ide	connected with, belonging to	bromide
ile	relating to, suited for, capable of	puerile, juvenile
ine	nature of	feminine
ion, sion, tion	act, result, state of	contagion
ish	origin, nature, resembling	impish
ism	system, manner, condition, characteristic	capitalism
ist	one who, that which	artist, flautist
ite	nature of, quality of, mineral product	graphite
ity, ty	state of, quality	captivity

Table 3.3. Common Suffixes (continued)

SUFFIX	MEANING	EXAMPLES
ive	causing, making	exhaustive
ize, ise	make	idolize, bowdlerize
ment	act of, state or, result	containment
nomy	law	autonomy, taxonomy
oid	resembling	asteroid, anthropoid
some	like, apt, tending to	gruesome
strat	cover	strata
tude	state of, condition of	aptitude
um	forms single nouns	spectrum
ure	state of, act, process, rank	rupture, rapture
ward	in the direction of	backward
y	inclined to, tend to	faulty

Examples

1. <u>Monograph</u> most nearly means

   (A) a mathematical concept

   (B) a written study of a single subject

   (C) an illness caused by a virus

   (D) a boring piece of art

   (B) is correct. The prefix *mono-* means one, and the word root *graph* means written, so a monograph is a written document about one subject.

2. My sister is a <u>polyglot</u>, and comfortably travels all over the world.

   (A) a person who speaks many language

   (B) a person who loves to travel

   (C) a person who is extremely intelligent

   (D) a person who is unafraid of new places

   (A) is correct. The prefix *poly-* means many, and the suffix *-glot* means in a language or tongue. Therefore, the sister speaks many languages.

4

PARAGRAPH COMPREHENSION

The ASVAB Paragraph Comprehension section includes short reading passages followed by questions about those passages. The passages will cover simple, easy-to-understand topics, and no outside knowledge will be needed to answer the questions. The CAT-ASVAB includes 11 questions to be answered in 22 minutes, and the pen-and-paper ASVAB has 15 questions to be answered in 13 minutes.

THE MAIN IDEA

The **MAIN IDEA** of a text describes the author's main topic and general concept; it also generalizes the author's point of view about a subject. It is contained within and throughout the text. The reader can easily find the main idea by considering how the main topic is addressed throughout a passage. In the reading test, the expectation is not only to identify the main idea but also to differentiate it from a text's theme and to summarize the main idea clearly and concisely.

The main idea is closely connected to topic sentences and how they are supported in a text. Questions may deal with finding topic sentences, summarizing a text's ideas, or locating supporting details. The sections and practice examples that follow detail the distinctions between these aspects of text.

Identifying the Main Idea

To identify the main idea, first identify the topic. The difference between these two things is simple: the **TOPIC** is the overall subject matter of a passage; the main idea is what the author wants to say about that topic. The main idea covers the author's direct perspective about a topic, as distinct from the **THEME**, which is a generally true idea that the reader might derive from a text. Most of the time, fiction has a theme, whereas nonfiction has a main idea. This is the case because in a nonfiction text, the author speaks more directly to the audience about a topic—his or her perspective is more visible.

The author's perspective on the subject of the text and how he or she has framed the argument or story hints at the main idea. For example, if the author framed the story with a description, image, or short anecdote, this suggests a particular idea or point of view.

For example, the following passage conveys the topic as well as what the author wants to communicate about that topic.

> The "shark mania" of recent years can be largely pinned on the sensationalistic media surrounding the animals: from the release of *Jaws* in 1975 to the week of ultra-hyped shark feeding frenzies and "worst shark attacks" countdowns known as Shark Week, popular culture both demonizes and fetishizes sharks until the public cannot get enough. Swimmers and beachgoers may look nervously for the telltale fin skimming the surface, but the reality is that shark bites are extremely rare and they are almost never unprovoked. Sharks attack people at very predictable times and for very predictable reasons. Rough surf, poor visibility, or a swimmer sending visual and physical signals that mimic a shark's normal prey are just a few examples.
>
> Of course, some places are just more dangerous to swim. Shark attack "hot spots," such as the coasts of Florida, South Africa, and New Zealand try a variety of solutions to protect tourists and surfers. Some beaches employ "shark nets," meant to keep sharks away from the beach, though these are controversial because they frequently trap other forms of marine life as well. Other beaches use spotters in helicopters and boats to alert beach officials when there are sharks in the area. In addition, there is an array of products that claim to offer personal protection from sharks, ranging from wetsuits in different colors to devices that broadcast electrical signals in an attempt to confuse the sharks' sensory organs. At the end of the day, though, beaches like these remain dangerous, and swimmers must assume the risk every time they paddle out from shore.

The author of this passage has a clear topic: sharks and the relationship between humans and sharks. In order to identify the main idea of the passage, the reader must ask what the author wants to say about this topic, what the reader is meant to think or understand. The author makes sure to provide information about several different aspects of the relationship between sharks and humans, and points out that humans must respect sharks as dangerous marine animals, without sensationalizing the risk of attack. This conclusion results from looking at the various pieces of information the author includes as well as the similarities between them. The passage describes sensationalistic media, then talks about how officials and governments try to protect beaches, and ends with the observation that people must take personal responsibility. These details clarify what the author's main idea is. Summarizing that main idea by focusing on the connection between the different details helps the reader draw a conclusion.

Readers should identify the topic of a text and pay attention to how the details about it relate to one another. A passage may discuss, for example, topic similarities, characteristics, causes, and/or effects.

Examples

The art of the twentieth and twenty-first centuries demonstrates several aspects of modern societal advancement. A primary example is the advent and ascendancy of technology: New technologies have developed new avenues for art making, and the globalization brought about by the Internet has both diversified the art world and brought it together simultaneously. Even as artists are able to engage in a global conversation about the categories and characteristics of art, creating a more uniform understanding, they can now express themselves in a diversity of ways for a diversity of audiences. The result has been a rapid change in how art is made and consumed.

1. This passage is primarily concerned with

    (A) the importance of art in the twenty-first century.

    (B) the use of art to communicate overarching ideals to diverse communities.

    (C) the importance of technology to art criticism.

    (D) the change in understanding and creation of art in the modern period.

    Answers:

    (A) is incorrect. The focus of the passage is what the art of the twentieth and twenty-first centuries demonstrates.

    (B) is incorrect. Although the passage mentions a diversity of audiences, it discusses the artists expressing themselves, not attempting to communicate overarching ideals.

    (C) is incorrect. The passage discusses how new technologies have "developed new avenues for art making," but nothing about criticism.

    (D) is correct. The art of the modern period reflects the new technologies and globalization possible through the Internet.

2. Which of the following best describes the main idea of the passage?

    (A) Modern advances in technology have diversified art making and connected artists to distant places and ideas.

    (B) Diversity in modern art is making it harder for art viewers to understand and talk about that art.

    (C) The use of technology to discuss art allows us to create standards for what art should be.

    (D) Art making before the invention of technology such as the Internet was disorganized and poorly understood.

    Answers:

    (A) is correct. According to the text, technology and the Internet have "diversified the art world and brought it together simultaneously."

    (B) is incorrect. The passage explains that the global conversation about art has created a more uniform understanding.

    (C) is incorrect. The passage indicates that artists now engage in a global conversation about art, but this is one detail in the passage. The main idea of the passage concerns the advances in art in the twentieth and twenty-first centuries.

    (D) is incorrect. The invention of technology and the Internet have diversified art; however, that does not mean it was disorganized previously.

Topic and Summary Sentences

Identifying the main idea requires understanding the structure of a piece of writing. In a short passage of one or two paragraphs, the topic and summary sentences quickly relate what the paragraphs are about and what conclusions the author wants the reader to draw. These sentences function as bookends to a paragraph or passage, telling readers what to think and keeping the passage tied tightly together.

Generally, the TOPIC SENTENCE is the first, or very near the first, sentence in a paragraph. It is a general statement that introduces the topic, clearly and specifically directing the reader to access any previous experience with that topic.

A **summary** is a very brief restatement of the most important parts of an argument or text. Building a summary begins with the most important idea in a text. A longer summary also includes supporting details. The text of a summary should be much shorter than the original.

The SUMMARY SENTENCE, on the other hand, frequently—but not always!—comes at the end of a paragraph or passage, because it wraps up all the ideas presented. This sentence provides an understanding of what the author wants to say about the topic and what conclusions to draw about it. While a topic sentence acts as an introduction to a topic, allowing the reader to activate his or her own ideas and experiences, the summary statement asks the reader to accept the author's ideas about that topic. Because of this, a summary sentence helps the reader quickly identify a piece's main idea.

Examples

Altogether, Egypt is a land of tranquil monotony. The eye commonly travels either over a waste of waters, or over a green plain unbroken by elevations. The hills which inclose (*sic*) the Nile valley have level tops, and sides that are bare of trees, or shrubs, or flowers, or even mosses. The sky is generally cloudless. No fog or mist enwraps the distance in mystery; no rainstorm sweeps across the scene; no rainbow spans the empyrean; no shadows chase each other over the landscape. There is an entire absence of picturesque scenery. A single broad river, unbroken within the limits of Egypt even by a rapid, two flat strips of green plain at its side, two low lines of straight-topped hills beyond them, and a boundless open space where the river divides itself into half a dozen sluggish branches before reaching the sea, constitute Egypt, which is by nature a southern Holland—"weary, stale, flat and unprofitable."

—from *Ancient Egypt* by George Rawlinson

1. Which of the following best explains the general idea and focus indicated by the topic sentence?

   (A) Egypt is a boring place without much to do.

   (B) The land of Egypt is undisturbed; the reader will read on to find out what makes it so dull.

   (C) Egypt is a peaceful place; its people live with a sense of predictability.

   (D) The land of Egypt is quiet; the reader wants to know what is missing.

Answers:

(A) is incorrect. The word *monotony* does suggest the idea of being bored; however, the focus is the land of Egypt, not what people have to do. In addition, tranquility is part of the general idea.

(B) is correct. This option indicates both the main idea and what the reader will focus on while reading.

(C) is incorrect. This option leaves out what the focus will be.

(D) is incorrect. This option leaves out the general idea of monotony.

2. Which of the following best states what the author wants the reader to understand after reading the summary sentence?

   (A) There is not much to get excited about while visiting Egypt.

   (B) Egypt is a poverty-stricken wasteland.

   (C) The land of Egypt is worn out from overuse.

   (D) The land of Egypt lacks anything fresh or inspiring.

Answers:

(A) is incorrect. The summary describes the place, not a visit to the place.

(B) is incorrect. The word *unprofitable* suggests that the land of Egypt is unrewarding, not poverty stricken.

(C) is incorrect. The reason the land is stale and weary may not be due to overuse. This summary describes; it does not explain the reasons the land is worn.

(D) is correct. The words *weary*, *stale*, and *unprofitable* suggest a lack of freshness or anything that stimulates enthusiasm.

SUPPORTING DETAILS

Between a topic sentence and a summary sentence, the rest of a paragraph is built with SUPPORTING DETAILS. Supporting details come in many forms; the purpose of the passage dictates the type of details that will support the main idea. A persuasive passage may use facts and data or detail specific reasons for the author's opinion. An informative passage will primarily use facts about the topic to support the main idea. Even a narrative passage will have supporting details—specific things the author says to develop the story and characters.

The most important aspect of supporting details is exactly what the term states: They support the main idea. Examining the various supporting details and how they work with one another will solidify how the author views a topic and what the main idea of the passage is. Supporting details are key to understanding a passage.

Identifying Supporting Details

How can the reader identify the most important pieces of information in a passage? Supporting details build an argument and contain the concepts upon which the main idea rests. While supporting details will help the reader determine the main idea, it is actually easier to find the most important supporting details by first understanding the main idea; the pieces that make up the main argument then become clear.

SIGNAL WORDS—transitions and conjunctions—explain to the reader how one sentence or idea is connected to another. These words and phrases can be anywhere in a sentence, and it is important to understand what each signal word means. Signal words can add information, provide counterarguments, create organization in a passage, or draw conclusions. Some common signal words include *in particular*, *in addition*, *besides*, *contrastingly*, *therefore*, and *because*.

Examples

The war is inevitable—and let it come! I repeat it, sir, let it come! It is in vain, sir, to extenuate the matter. Gentlemen may cry, "Peace! Peace!"—but there is no peace. The war is actually begun! The next gale that sweeps from the north will bring to our ears the clash of resounding arms! Our brethren are already in the field! Why stand we here idle? What is it that gentlemen wish? What would they have? Is life so dear, or peace so sweet, as to be purchased at the price of chains and slavery? Forbid it, Almighty God! I know not what course others may take; but as for me, give me liberty or give me death!

—from "Give Me Liberty or Give Me Death" speech by Patrick Henry

1. In the fourth sentence of the text, the word *but* signals

   (A) an example.

   (B) a consequence.

   (C) an exception.

   (D) a counterargument.

   Answers:

   (A) is incorrect. The author includes an example that the war has begun when he says "Our brethren are already in the field!" The word *but* does not signal this example.

   (B) is incorrect. The phrase "but there is no peace" is a fact, not a consequence.

   (C) is incorrect. In order to be an exception, the word *but* would have to be preceded by a general point or observation. In this case, *but* is preceded by a demand for peace.

   (D) is correct. The argument or claim that the country should be at peace precedes the word *but*. *But* counters the demand for peace with the argument that there is no peace; the war has begun.

2. What argument does the author use to support his main point?

   (A) Life in slavery is not the goal of the country.

   (B) To die bravely is worthwhile.

   (C) Life without freedom is intolerable.

   (D) The cost of going to war is too great.

   Answers:

   (A) is incorrect. The main point is that the country has to go to war with England to be free. The author does not support his point with a discussion of the goals of the country.

   (B) is incorrect. This does not relate to the main point of going to war.

   (C) is correct. The author indicates that life is not so dear, nor peace so sweet, "as to be purchased at the price of chains and slavery."

   (D) is incorrect. This is inaccurate. The author insists that the cost of not fighting for freedom is too great.

Evaluating Supporting Details

Besides using supporting details to help understand a main idea, the reader must evaluate them for relevance and inconsistency. An author selects details to help organize a passage and support its main idea. Sometimes, the author's bias results in details left out that don't directly support the main idea or that support an opposite idea. The reader has to be able to notice not only what the author says but also what the author leaves out.

To understand how a supporting detail relates to the main idea, the purpose of the passage should be discerned: what the author is trying to communicate and what the author wants from the reader. Every passage has a specific goal, and each paragraph in a passage is meant to support that goal. For each supporting detail, the position in the text, the signal words, and the specific content work together to alert the reader to the relationship between the supporting ideas and the main idea.

Close reading involves noticing the striking features of a text. For example, does a point made in the text appeal to the reader's sense of justice? Does a description seem rather exaggerated or overstated? Do certain words—such as *agonizing*—seem emotive? Are rhetorical questions being used to lead the reader to a certain conclusion?

Though the author generally includes details that support the text's main idea, the reader must decide how those details relate to one another as well as find any gaps in the support of the author's argument. This is particularly important in a persuasive piece of writing, when an author may allow bias to show through. Discovering the author's bias and how the supporting details reveal that bias is also key to understanding a text.

Examples

In England in the 'fifties came the Crimean War, with the deep stirring of national feeling which accompanied it, and the passion of gratitude and admiration which was poured forth on Miss Florence Nightingale for her work on behalf of our wounded soldiers. It was universally felt that there was work for women, even in war—the work of cleansing, setting in order, breaking down red tape, and soothing the vast sum of human suffering which every war is bound to cause. Miss Nightingale's work in war was work that never had been done until women came forward to do it, and her message to her countrywomen was educate yourselves, prepare, make ready; never imagine that your task can be done by instinct, without training and preparation. Painstaking study, she insisted, was just as necessary as a preparation for women's work as for men's work; and she bestowed the whole of the monetary gift offered her by the gratitude of the nation to form training-schools for nurses at St. Thomas's and King's College Hospitals.

—from *Women's Suffrage: A Short History of a Great Movement* by Millicent Garrett Fawcett

1. Which of the following best states the bias of the passage?
   (A) Society underestimates the capacity of women.
   (B) Generally, women are not prepared to make substantial contributions to society.
   (C) If women want power, they need to prove themselves.
   (D) One strong woman cannot represent all women.

Answers:

(A) is correct. The author is suggesting that the work Florence Nightingale did had not been done before women came forward. Up till that point, what a woman could do had not been recognized.

(B) is incorrect. This fact may have been true at the time this text was written, but only because educational opportunities were not available to women, and women were not encouraged to develop their abilities. Including this fact reveals the bias that women should be granted opportunities to train and to contribute.

(C) is incorrect. This option does not apply; Florence Nightingale did more than prove herself.

(D) is incorrect. The fact that Florence Nightingale donated the money awarded her to the training of women indicates that other women were preparing themselves to contribute.

2. Which of the following best summarizes what the author left out of the passage?

   (A) Women can fight in wars.

   (B) Other women should be recognized.

   (C) Women need to stop wasting time giving speeches at conventions and start proving themselves.

   (D) Without the contributions of women, society suffers.

Answers:

(A) is incorrect. "It was universally felt that there was work for women, even in war" suggests that women had much to offer and didn't need to be sheltered; however, "there was work" does not mean the author thought women should engage in combat.

(B) is incorrect. Since the passage is specifically about Florence Nightingale, nothing in it suggests the author included information about what other women did.

(C) is incorrect. Information about women's suffrage conventions is unrelated to the topic of the paragraph.

(D) is correct. The author emphasizes that "Miss Nightingale's work in war was work that never had been done until women came forward to do it."

DRAWING CONCLUSIONS

Reading text begins with making sense of the explicit meanings of information or a narrative. Understanding occurs as the reader draws conclusions and makes logical inferences. To draw a conclusion, the reader considers the details or facts. He or she then comes to a conclusion—the next logical point in the thought sequence. For example, in a Hemingway story, an old man sits alone in a café. A young waiter says that the café is closing, but the old man continues to drink. The waiter starts closing up, and the old man signals for a refill. Based on these details, the reader might conclude that the old man has not understood the young waiter's desire for him to leave.

When considering a character's motivations, the reader should ask what the character wants to achieve, what the character will get by accomplishing this, and what the character seems to value the most.

An inference is distinguished from a conclusion drawn. An INFERENCE is an assumption the reader makes based on details in the text as well as his or her own knowledge. It is more of an educated guess that extends the literal meaning. Inferences begin with the given details; however, the reader uses the facts to determine additional facts. What the reader already knows informs what is being suggested by the details of decisions or situations in the text. Returning to the example of the Hemingway story, the reader might infer that the old man is lonely, enjoys being in the café, and is reluctant to leave.

When reading fictional text, inferring character motivations is essential. The actions of the characters move the plot forward; a series of events is understood by making sense of why the characters did what they did. Hemingway includes contrasting details as the young waiter and an older waiter discuss the old man. The older waiter sympathizes with the old man; both men have no one at home and experience a sense of emptiness in life, which motivates them to seek the café.

Another aspect of understanding text is connecting it to other texts. Readers may connect the Hemingway story about the old man in the café to other Hemingway stories about individuals struggling to deal with loss and loneliness in a dignified way. They can extend their initial connections to people they know or their personal experiences. When readers read a persuasive text, they often connect the arguments made to counterarguments and opposing evidence of which they are aware. They use these connections to infer meaning.

Conclusions are drawn by thinking about how the author wants the reader to feel. A group of carefully selected facts can cause the reader to feel a certain way.

Examples

I believe it is difficult for those who publish their own memoirs to escape the imputation of vanity; nor is this the only disadvantage under which they labor: it is also their misfortune, that what is uncommon is rarely, if ever, believed, and what is obvious we are apt to turn from with disgust, and to charge the writer with impertinence. People generally think those memoirs only worthy to be read or remembered which abound in great or striking events, those, in short, which in a high degree excite either admiration or pity: all others they consign to contempt and oblivion. It is therefore, I confess, not a little hazardous in a private and obscure individual, and a stranger too, thus to solicit the indulgent attention of the public; especially when I own I offer here the history of neither a saint, a hero, nor a tyrant. I believe there are few events in my life, which have not happened to many: it is true the incidents of it are numerous; and, did I consider myself an European, I might say my sufferings were great: but when I compare my lot with that of most of my countrymen, I regard myself as a *particular favorite of Heaven*, and acknowledge the mercies of Providence in every occurrence of my life. If then the following narrative does not appear sufficiently interesting to engage general attention, let my motive be some excuse for its publication. I am not so foolishly vain as to expect from it either immortality or literary reputation. If it affords any satisfaction to my numerous friends, at whose request it has been written, or in the smallest degree promotes the interests of humanity, the ends for which it was undertaken will be fully attained, and every wish of my heart gratified. Let it therefore be remembered, that, in wishing to avoid censure, I do not aspire to praise.

—from *The Interesting Narrative of the Life of Olaudah Equiano, or Gustavus Vassa, The African* by Olaudah Equiano

CONTINUE

1. Which of the following best explains the primary motivation of the narrator?

   (A) He wants his audience to know that he is not telling his story out of vanity.

   (B) He is hoping people will praise his courage.

   (C) He wants to give credit to God for protecting him.

   (D) He is not seeking personal notoriety; he is hoping people will be influenced by his story and the human condition will improve.

   Answers:

   (A) is incorrect. That motive is how the passage begins, but it is not his primary motive.

   (B) is incorrect. He says he does not aspire to praise, and he does not suggest that he was courageous.

   (C) is incorrect. He does state that the "mercies of Providence" were always with him; however, that acknowledgement is not his primary motive.

   (D) is correct. In the passage "If it…in the smallest degree promotes the interests of humanity, the ends for which it was undertaken will be fully attained, and every wish of my heart gratified," the narrator's use of the word *humanity* could mean he wants to improve the human condition or he wants to increase human benevolence, or brotherly love.

2. Given the details of what the narrator says he is *not*, as well as what he claims his story is *not*, it can be inferred that his experience was

   (A) a story that could lead to his success.

   (B) an amazing story of survival and struggle that will be unfamiliar to many readers.

   (C) an adventure that will thrill the audience.

   (D) a narrow escape from suffering.

   Answers:

   (A) is incorrect. The narrator says that what is obvious in his story is what people "are apt to turn from with disgust, and to charge the writer with impertinence." The narrator is telling a story that his audience couldn't disagree with and might consider rude.

   (B) is correct. By saying "what is uncommon is rarely, if ever, believed, and what is obvious we are apt to turn from with disgust," the narrator suggests that his experience wasn't common or ordinary and could cause disgust.

   (C) is incorrect. The reader can infer that the experience was horrific; it will inspire disgust, not excitement.

   (D) is incorrect. The narrator admits he suffered; he indicates that he narrowly escaped death. This is not an inference.

UNDERSTANDING THE AUTHOR

Many questions on the Paragraph Comprehension section will ask for an interpretation of an author's intentions and ideas. This requires an examination of the author's perspective and purpose as well as the way the author uses language to communicate these things.

In every passage, an author chooses words, structures, and content with specific purpose and intent. With this in mind, the reader can begin to comprehend why an author opts for particular words and structures and how these ultimately relate to the content.

The Author's Purpose

The author of a passage sets out with a specific goal in mind: to communicate a particular idea to an audience. The AUTHOR'S PURPOSE is determined by asking why the author wants the reader to understand the passage's main idea. There are four basic purposes to which an author can write: narrative, expository, technical, and persuasive. Within each of these general purposes, the author may direct the audience to take a clear action or respond in a certain way.

The purpose for which an author writes a passage is also connected to the structure of that text. In a NARRATIVE, the author seeks to tell a story, often to illustrate a theme or idea the reader needs to consider. In a narrative, the author uses characteristics of storytelling, such as chronological order, characters, and a defined setting, and these characteristics communicate the author's theme or main idea.

In an EXPOSITORY passage, on the other hand, the author simply seeks to explain an idea or topic to the reader. The main idea will probably be a factual statement or a direct assertion of a broadly held opinion. Expository writing can come in many forms, but one essential feature is a fair and balanced representation of a topic. The author may explore one detailed aspect or a broad range of characteristics, but he or she mainly seeks to prompt a decision from the reader.

Similarly, in TECHNICAL writing, the author's purpose is to explain specific processes, techniques, or equipment in order for the reader to use that process or equipment to obtain a desired result. Writing like this employs chronological or spatial structures, specialized vocabulary, and imperative or directive language.

In PERSUASIVE writing, though the reader is free to make decisions about the message and content, the author actively seeks to convince him or her to accept an opinion or belief. Much like expository writing, persuasive writing is presented in many organizational forms, but the author will use specific techniques, or RHETORICAL STRATEGIES, to build an argument. Readers can identify these strategies in order to clearly understand what an author wants them to believe, how the author's perspective and purpose may lead to bias, and whether the passage includes any logical fallacies.

Reading persuasive text requires an awareness of what the author believes about the topic.

Common rhetorical strategies include the appeals to ethos, logos, and pathos. An author uses these to build trust with the reader, explain the logical points of his or her argument, and convince the reader that his or her opinion is the best option.

An ETHOS—ETHICAL—APPEAL uses balanced, fair language and seeks to build a trusting relationship between the author and the reader. An author might explain his or her credentials, include the reader in an argument, or offer concessions to an opposing argument.

Readers should consider how different audiences will react to a text. For example, how a slave owner's reactions to the narrative of Olaudah Equiano (on page 89) will differ from a slave trader's.

A LOGOS—LOGICAL—APPEAL builds on that trust by providing facts and support for the author's opinion, explaining the argument with clear connections and reasoning. At this point, the reader should beware of logical fallacies that connect unconnected ideas and build arguments on incorrect premises. With a logical appeal, an author strives to convince the reader to accept an opinion or belief by demonstrating that not only is it the most logical option but it also satisfies his or her emotional reaction to a topic.

A PATHOS—EMOTIONAL—APPEAL does not depend on reasonable connections between ideas; rather, it seeks to remind the reader, through imagery, strong language, and personal connections, that the author's argument aligns with his or her best interests.

Many persuasive passages seek to use all three rhetorical strategies to best appeal to the reader.

Clues will help the reader determine many things about a passage, from the author's purpose to the passage's main idea, but understanding an author's purpose is essential to fully understanding the text.

Examples

Evident truth. Made so plain by our good Father in Heaven, that all *feel* and *understand* it, even down to brutes and creeping insects. The ant, who has toiled and dragged a crumb to his nest, will furiously defend the fruit of his labor, against whatever robber assails him. So plain, that the most dumb and stupid slave that ever toiled for a master, does constantly *know* that he is wronged. So plain that no one, high or low, ever does mistake it, except in a plainly *selfish* way; for although volume upon volume is written to prove slavery a very good thing, we never hear of the man who wishes to take the good of it, *by being a slave himself.*

Most governments have been based, practically, on the denial of the equal rights of men, as I have, in part, stated them; *ours* began, by *affirming* those rights. *They* said, some men are too *ignorant*, and *vicious*, to share in government. Possibly so, said we; and, by your system, you would always keep them ignorant and vicious. We proposed to give *all* a chance; and we expected the weak to grow stronger, the ignorant, wiser; and all better, and happier together.

We made the experiment; and the fruit is before us. Look at it. Think of it. Look at it, in its aggregate grandeur, of extent of country, and numbers of population, of ship, and steamboat.

—fragment from Abraham Lincoln's speech on slavery

1. The author's purpose is to
   (A) explain ideas.
   (B) narrate a story.
   (C) describe a situation.
   (D) persuade to accept an idea.

Answers:

(A) is incorrect. The injustice of slavery in America is made clear, but only to convince the audience that slavery cannot exist in America.

(B) is incorrect. The author briefly mentions the narrative of America in terms of affirming the equal rights of all people, but he does not tell a story or relate the events that led to slavery.

(C) is incorrect. The author does not describe the conditions of slaves or the many ways their human rights are denied.

(D) is correct. The author provides logical reasons and evidence that slavery is wrong, that it violates the American belief in equal rights.

2. To achieve his purpose, the author primarily uses

   (A) concrete analogies.

   (B) logical reasoning.

   (C) emotional appeals.

   (D) images.

Answers:

(A) is incorrect. The author mentions the ant's willingness to defend what is his but does not make an explicit and corresponding conclusion about the slave; instead, he says, "So plain, that the most dumb and stupid slave that ever toiled for a master, does constantly *know* that he is wronged." The implied parallel is between the ant's conviction about being wronged and the slave knowing he is wronged.

(B) is correct. The author uses logic when he points out that people who claim slavery is good never wish "to take the good of it, *by being a slave*." The author also points out that the principle of our country is to give everyone, including the "ignorant," opportunity; then he challenges his listeners to look at the fruit of this principle, saying, "Look at it, in its aggregate grandeur, of extent of country, and numbers of population, of ship, and steamboat."

(C) is incorrect. The author relies on logic and evidence, and makes no emotional appeals about the suffering of slaves.

(D) is incorrect. The author does offer evidence of his point with an image of the grandeur of America, but his primary appeal is logic.

The Audience

The structure, purpose, main idea, and language of a text all converge on one target: the intended audience. An author makes decisions about every aspect of a piece of writing based on that audience, and readers can evaluate the writing through the lens of that audience. By considering the probable reactions of an intended audience, readers can determine many things: whether or not they are part of that intended audience; the author's purpose for using specific techniques or devices; the biases of the author and how they appear in the writing; and how the author uses rhetorical strategies. While readers evaluate each of these things separately, identifying and considering the intended audience adds depth to the understanding of a text and helps highlight details with more clarity.

⚠️ When reading a persuasive text, students should maintain awareness of what the author believes about the topic.

Several aspects identify the text's intended audience. First, when the main idea of the passage is known, the reader considers who most likely cares about that idea, benefits from it, or needs to know about it. Many authors begin with the main idea and then determine the audience in part based on these concerns.

Then the reader considers language. The author tailors language to appeal to the intended audience, so the reader can narrow down a broad understanding of that audience. The figurative language John Steinbeck uses in his novel *The Grapes of Wrath* reveals the suffering of the migrant Americans who traveled to California to find work during the Great Depression of the 1930s. Steinbeck spoke concretely to the Americans who were discriminating against the migrants. Instead of finding work in the "land of milk and honey," migrants faced unbearable poverty and injustice. The metaphor that gives the novel its title is "and in the eyes of the people there is the failure; and in the eyes of the hungry there is a growing wrath. In the souls of the people the grapes of wrath are filling and growing heavy, growing heavy for the vintage." Steinbeck, used the image of ripening grapes, familiar to those surrounded by vineyards, to condemn this harsh treatment, provide an education of the human heart, and inspire compassion in his audience. Readers who weren't directly involved in the exodus of people from Oklahoma to the West, could have little difficulty grasping the meaning of Steinbeck's language in the description: "66 is the path of a people in flight, refugees from dust and shrinking land, from the thunder of tractors and invasion, from the twisting winds that howl up out of Texas, from floods that bring no richness to the land and steal what little richness is there."

> A logical argument includes a claim, a reason that supports the claim, and an assumption that the reader makes based on accepted beliefs. All parts of the argument need to make sense to the reader, so authors often consider the beliefs of their audience as they construct their arguments.

Examples

In the following text, consideration should be made for how an English political leader of 1729 might have reacted.

It is a melancholy object to those, who walk through this great town, or travel in the country, when they see the streets, the roads and cabin-doors crowded with beggars of the female sex, followed by three, four, or six children, all in rags, and importuning every passenger for an alms. These mothers instead of being able to work for their honest livelihood, are forced to employ all their time in strolling to beg sustenance for their helpless infants who, as they grow up, either turn thieves for want of work, or leave their dear native country, to fight for the Pretender in Spain, or sell themselves to the Barbados.

I shall now therefore humbly propose my own thoughts, which I hope will not be liable to the least objection.

I have been assured by a very knowing American of my acquaintance in London, that a young healthy child well nursed, is, at a year old, a most delicious nourishing and wholesome food, whether stewed, roasted, baked, or boiled; and I make no doubt that it will equally serve in a fricassee.

I do therefore humbly offer it to public consideration, that of the hundred and twenty thousand children, already computed, twenty thousand may be reserved for breed, whereof only one fourth part to be males; which is more than we allow to sheep, black cattle, or swine, and my reason is, that these children are seldom the fruits of marriage, a circumstance not much regarded by our savages, therefore, one male will be sufficient to serve four females. That the remaining hundred thousand may, at a year old, be offered in sale to the persons of quality and fortune, through the kingdom, always advising the mother to let them suck plentifully in the last month, so as to render them plump, and fat for a good table. A child will make two dishes at an entertainment for friends, and when the family dines alone, the fore or hind quarter will make a reasonable dish, and seasoned with a little pepper or salt, will be very good boiled on the fourth day, especially in winter.

—from *A Modest Proposal for Preventing the Children of Poor People in Ireland From Being a Burden on Their Parents or Country, and for Making Them Beneficial to the Public* by Jonathan Swift

1. Which of the following best states the central idea of the passage?

   (A) Irish mothers are not able to support their children.

   (B) The Irish people lived like savages.

   (C) The people of England are quality people of fortune.

   (D) The kingdom of England has exploited the weaker country of Ireland to the point that the Irish people cannot support their families.

   Answers:

   (A) is incorrect. This is a fact alluded to in the passage, not a central idea.

   (B) is incorrect. Although the author does refer to the Irish as savages, the reader recognizes that the author is being outrageously satirical.

   (C) is incorrect. The author does say "That the remaining hundred thousand may, at a year old, be offered in sale to the persons of quality and fortune, through the kingdom," referring to the English. However, this is not the central idea; the opposite is, given that this is satire.

   (D) is correct. The author is hoping to use satire to shame England.

2. The author's use of phrases like "humbly propose," "liable to the least objection," "wholesome food" suggests which of the following purposes?

   (A) to inform people about the attitudes of the English

   (B) to use satire to reveal the inhumane treatment of the Irish by the English

   (C) to persuade people to survive by any means

   (D) to express his admiration of the Irish people

   Answers:

   (A) is incorrect. The author's subject is the poverty of the Irish, and his audience is the English who are responsible for the suffering of the Irish.

   (B) is correct. The intended meaning of a satire sharply contradicts the literal meaning. Swift's proposal is not humble; it is meant to humble the arrogant. He expects the audience to be horrified. The children would make the worst imaginable food.

   (C) is incorrect. The author is not serious. His intent is to shock his English audience.

   (D) is incorrect. The author is expressing sympathy for the Irish.

Tone and Mood

Two important aspects of the communication between author and audience occur subtly. The **TONE** of a passage describes the author's attitude toward the topic, distinct from the **MOOD**, which is the pervasive feeling or atmosphere in a passage that provokes specific emotions in the reader. The distinction between these two aspects lies once again in the audience: the mood influences the reader's emotional state in response to the piece, while the tone establishes a relationship between the audience and the author. Does the author intend to instruct the audience? Is the author more experienced than the audience, or does he or she wish to convey a friendly or equal relationship? In each of these cases, the author uses a different tone to reflect the desired level of communication.

To determine the author's tone, students should examine what overall feeling they are experiencing.

Primarily **DICTION**, or word choice, determines mood and tone in a passage. Many readers make the mistake of thinking about the ideas an author puts forth and using those alone to determine particularly tone; a much better practice is to separate specific words from the text and look for patterns in connotation and emotion. By considering categories of words used by the author, the reader can discover both the overall emotional atmosphere of a text and the attitude of the author toward the subject.

> ⚠️ To decide the connotation of a word, the reader examines whether the word conveys a positive or negative association in the mind. Adjectives are often used to influence the feelings of the reader, such as in the phrase "an ambitious attempt to achieve."

Every word has not only a literal meaning but also a **CONNOTATIVE MEANING**, relying on the common emotions, associations, and experiences an audience might associate with that word. The following words are all synonyms: *dog, puppy, cur, mutt, canine, pet*. Two of these words—*dog* and *canine*—are neutral words, without strong associations or emotions. Two others—*pet* and *puppy*—have positive associations. The last two—*cur* and *mutt*—have negative associations. A passage that uses one pair of these words versus another pair activates the positive or negative reactions of the audience.

Examples

Day had broken cold and grey, exceedingly cold and grey, when the man turned aside from the main Yukon trail and climbed the high earth-bank, where a dim and little-travelled trail led eastward through the fat spruce timberland. It was a steep bank, and he paused for breath at the top, excusing the act to himself by looking at his watch. It was nine o'clock. There was no sun nor hint of sun, though there was not a cloud in the sky. It was a clear day, and yet there seemed an intangible *pall* over the face of things, a subtle gloom that made the day dark, and that was due to the absence of sun. This fact did not worry the man. He was used to the lack of sun. It had been days since he had seen the sun, and he knew that a few more days must pass before that cheerful orb, due south, would just peep above the sky-line and dip immediately from view.

—from "To Build a Fire" by Jack London

1. Which of the following best describes the mood of the passage?

   (A) exciting and adventurous

   (B) fierce and determined

   (C) bleak and forbidding

   (D) grim yet hopeful

Answers:

(A) is incorrect. The man is on some adventure as he turns off the main trail, but the context is one of gloom and darkness, not excitement.

(B) is incorrect. The cold, dark day is fierce, and the man may be determined; however, the overall mood of the entire passage is one of grim danger.

(C) is correct. The man is oblivious to the gloom and darkness of the day, which was "exceedingly cold and grey."

(D) is incorrect. The atmosphere is grim, and there is no indication the man is hopeful about anything. He is aware only of his breath and steps forward.

2. The connotation of the words intangible *pall* is

(A) a death-like covering.

(B) a vague sense of familiarity.

(C) an intimation of communal strength.

(D) an understanding of the struggle ahead.

Answers:

(A) is correct. Within the context of the sentence "It was a clear day, and yet there seemed an intangible *pall* over the face of things, a subtle gloom that made the day dark," the words *gloom* and *dark* are suggestive of death; the words *over the face* suggest a covering.

(B) is incorrect. The word *intangible* can mean a vague sense, but there is nothing especially familiar about a clear day that is dark, with no sunlight.

(C) is incorrect. The word *intangible* suggests intimation; however, from the beginning, the author shows the man alone, and reports, "the man turned aside from the main Yukon trail."

(D) is incorrect. A struggle may be indicated by the darkness and gloom, but the man has no understanding of this possibility. The text refers to the darkness, saying, "This fact did not worry the man. He was used to the lack of sun."

MEANING OF WORDS AND PHRASES

Vocabulary in context questions ask about the meaning of specific words in the passage. The questions will ask which answer choice is most similar in meaning to the specified word, or which answer choice could be substituted for that word in the passage.

When confronted with unfamiliar words, the passage itself can help clarify their meaning. Often, identifying the tone or main idea of the passage can help eliminate answer choices. For example, if the tone of the passage is generally positive, try eliminating the answer choices with a negative connotation. Or, if the passage is about a particular occupation, rule out words unrelated to that topic.

 Look in the Word Knowledge section to learn more strategies for determining the meaning of unfamiliar words.

Passages may also provide specific context clues that can help determine the meaning of a word.

One type of context clue is a **DEFINITION**, or **DESCRIPTION**, **CLUE**. Sometimes, authors use a difficult word, then include *that is* or *which is* to signal that they are providing a definition. An author also may provide a synonym or restate the idea in more familiar words:

> *Teachers often prefer teaching students with intrinsic motivation; these students have an internal desire to learn.*

The meaning of *intrinsic* is restated as an *internal desire*.

Similarly, authors may include an **EXAMPLE CLUE**, providing an example phrase that clarifies the meaning of the word:

> *Teachers may view extrinsic rewards as efficacious; however, an individual student may not be interested in what the teacher offers. For example, a student who is diabetic may not feel any incentive to work when offered a sweet treat.*

Efficacious is explained with an example that demonstrates how an extrinsic reward may not be effective.

Another commonly used context clue is the CONTRAST, or ANTONYM, CLUE. In this case, authors indicate that the unfamiliar word is the opposite of a familiar word:

> *In contrast to intrinsic motivation, extrinsic motivation is contingent on teachers offering rewards that are appealing.*

The phrase "in contrast" tells the reader that *extrinsic* is the opposite of *intrinsic*.

Examples

1. One challenge of teaching is finding ways to incentivize, or to motivate, learning.

   Which of the following is the meaning of *incentivize* as used in the sentence?

   (A) encourage

   (B) determine

   (C) challenge

   (D) improve

   Answers:

   (A) is correct. The word *incentivize* is defined immediately with the synonym *motivate*, or *encourage*.

   (B) is incorrect. *Determine* is not a synonym for *motivate*. In addition, the phrase "to determine learning" does not make sense in the sentence.

   (C) is incorrect. *Challenge* is not a synonym for *motivate*.

   (D) is incorrect. *Improve* is closely related to motivation, but it is not the best synonym provided.

2. If an extrinsic reward is extremely desirable, a student may become so apprehensive he or she cannot focus. The student may experience such intense pressure to perform that the reward undermines its intent.

   Which of the following is the meaning of *apprehensive* as used in the sentence?

   (A) uncertain

   (B) distracted

   (C) anxious

   (D) forgetful

   Answers:

   (A) is incorrect. Nothing in the sentence suggests the student is uncertain.

   (B) is incorrect. *Distracted* is related to the clue "focus" but does not address the clue "pressure to perform."

   (C) is correct. The reader can infer that the pressure to perform is making the student anxious.

   (D) is incorrect. Nothing in the sentence suggests the student is forgetful.

5

MATH KNOWLEDGE

The Math Knowledge section on the CAT-ASVAB includes 16 questions to be answered in 20 minutes. The pen-and-paper ASVAB has 25 questions to be answered in 24 minutes. The questions cover a broad range of topics, including operations with exponents and radicals, equations and inequalities, and properties of geometric figures. In addition, many of the basic operations tested in the Arithmetic Reasoning section may be needed to answer Math Knowledge questions.

ALGEBRAIC EXPRESSIONS

The foundation of algebra is the **VARIABLE**, an unknown number represented by a symbol (usually a letter such as x or a). Variables can be preceded by a **COEFFICIENT**, which is a constant (i.e., a real number) in front of the variable, such as $4x$ or $-2a$. An **ALGEBRAIC EXPRESSION** is any sum, difference, product, or quotient of variables and numbers (for example $3x^2$, $2x + 7y - 1$, and $\frac{5}{x}$ are algebraic expressions). **TERMS** are any quantities that are added or subtracted (for example, the terms of the expression $x^2 - 3x + 5$ are x^2, $3x$, and 5). A **POLYNOMIAL EXPRESSION** is an algebraic expression where all the exponents on the variables are whole numbers. A polynomial with only two terms is known as a **BINOMIAL**, and one with three terms is a **TRINOMIAL**. A **MONOMIAL** has only one term.

EVALUATING EXPRESSIONS is another way of saying "find the numeric value of an expression if the variable is equal to a certain number." To evaluate the expression, simply plug the given value(s) for the variable(s) into the equation and simplify. Remember to use the order of operations when simplifying:

1.	Parentheses		4.	Division
2.	Exponents		5.	Addition
3.	Multiplication		6.	Subtraction

Example

If $m = 4$, find the value of the following expression:

$5(m - 2)^3 + 3m^2 - \frac{m}{4} - 1$

Answer:

$5(m-2)^3 + 3m^2 - \frac{m}{4} - 1$	
$= 5(4-2)^3 + 3(4)^2 - \frac{4}{4} - 1$	Plug the value 4 in for m in the expression.
$= 5(2)^3 + 3(4)^2 - \frac{4}{4} - 1$	Calculate all the expressions inside the parentheses.
$= 5(8) + 3(16) - \frac{4}{4} - 1$	Simplify all exponents.
$= 40 + 48 - 1 - 1$	Perform multiplication and division from left to right.
$= \mathbf{86}$	Perform addition and subtraction from left to right.

Operations with Expressions

Adding and Subtracting

Expressions can be added or subtracted by simply adding and subtracting LIKE TERMS, which are terms with the same variable part (the variables must be the same, with the same exponents on each variable). For example, in the expressions $2x + 3xy - 2z$ and $6y + 2xy$, the like terms are $3xy$ and $2xy$. Adding the two expressions yields the new expression $2x + 5xy - 2z + 6y$. Note that the other terms did not change; they cannot be combined because they have different variables.

Example

If $a = 12x + 7xy - 9y$ and $b = 8x - 9xz + 7z$, what is $a + b$?

Answer:

$a + b = (12x + 8x) + 7xy - 9y - 9xz + 7z =$ $\mathbf{20x + 7xy - 9y - 9xz + 7z}$	The only like terms in both expressions are $12x$ and $8x$, so these two terms will be added, and all other terms will remain the same.

Distributing and Factoring

Distributing and factoring can be seen as two sides of the same coin. DISTRIBUTION multiplies each term in the first factor by each term in the second factor to get rid of parentheses. FACTORING reverses this process, taking a polynomial in standard form and writing it as a product of two or more factors.

> ⚠️ Operations with polynomials can always be checked by evaluating equivalent expressions for the same value.

When distributing a monomial through a polynomial, the expression outside the parentheses is multiplied by each term inside the parentheses. Using the rules of exponents, coefficients are multiplied and exponents are added.

When simplifying two polynomials, each term in the first polynomial must multiply each term in the second polynomial. A binomial (two terms) multiplied by a binomial, will require 2 × 2 or 4 multiplications. For the binomial × binomial case, this process is sometimes called **FOIL**, which stands for first, outside, inside, and last. These terms refer to the placement of each term of the expression:

multiply the first term in each expression, then the outside terms, then the inside terms, and finally the last terms. A binomial (two terms) multiplied by a trinomial (three terms), will require 2 × 3 or 6 products to simplify. The first term in the first polynomial multiplies each of the three terms in the second polynomial, then the second term in the first polynomial multiplies each of the three terms in the second polynomial. A trinomial (three terms) by a trinomial will require 3 × 3 or 9 products, and so on.

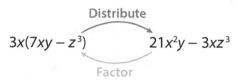

Figure 4.1. Distribution and Factoring

Factoring is the reverse of distributing: the first step is always to remove ("undistribute") the GCF of all the terms, if there is a GCF (besides 1). The GCF is the product of any constants and/or variables that <u>every</u> term shares. (For example, the GCF of $12x^3$, $15x^2$ and $6xy^2$ is $3x$ because $3x$ evenly divides all three terms.) This shared factor can be taken out of each term and moved to the outside of the parentheses, leaving behind a polynomial where each term is the original term divided by the GCF. (The remaining terms for the terms in the example would be $4x^2$, $5x$, and $2y^2$.) It may be possible to factor the polynomial in the parentheses further, depending on the problem.

Example

1. Expand the following expression: $5x(x^2 - 2c + 10)$

   Answer:

$5x(x^2 - 2c + 10)$	
$(5x)(x^2) = 5x^3$	Distribute and multiply the term outside the parentheses to all three terms inside the parentheses.
$(5x)(-2c) = -10xc$	
$(5x)(10) = 50x$	
$= 5x^3 - 10xc + 50x$	

2. Expand the following expression: $(x^2 - 5)(2x - x^3)$

   Answer:

$(x^2 - 5)(2x - x^3)$	
$(x^2)(2x) = 2x^3$	Apply FOIL: first, outside, inside, and last.
$(x^2)(-x^3) = -x^5$	
$(-5)(2x) = -10x$	
$(-5)(-x^3) = 5x^3$	
$= 2x^3 - x^5 - 10x + 5x^3$	Combine like terms and put them in order.
$= -x^5 + 7x^3 - 10x$	

3. Factor the expression $16z^2 + 48z$

   Answer:

$16z^2 + 48z$	Both terms have a z, and 16 is a common factor of both 16 and 48. So the greatest common factor is $16z$. Factor out the GCF.
$= 16z(z + 3)$	

4. Factor the expression $6m^3 + 12m^3n - 9m^2$

Answer:

$6m^3 + 12m^3n - 9m^2$ $= 3m^2(2m + 4mn - 3)$	All the terms share the factor m^2, and 3 is the greatest common factor of 6, 12, and 9. So, the GCF is $3m^2$.

LINEAR EQUATIONS

An EQUATION states that two expressions are equal to each other. Polynomial equations are categorized by the highest power of the variables they contain: the highest power of any exponent of a linear equation is 1, a quadratic equation has a variable raised to the second power, a cubic equation has a variable raised to the third power, and so on.

Solving Linear Equations

Solving an equation means finding the value or values of the variable that make the equation true. To solve a linear equation, it is necessary to manipulate the terms so that the variable being solved for appears alone on one side of the equal sign while everything else in the equation is on the other side.

The way to solve linear equations is to "undo" all the operations that connect numbers to the variable of interest. Follow these steps:

On multiple choice tests, it is often easier to plug the possible values into the equation and determine which solution makes the equation true than to solve the equation.

1. Eliminate fractions by multiplying each side by the least common multiple of any denominators.

2. Distribute to eliminate parentheses, braces, and brackets.

3. Combine like terms.

4. Use addition or subtraction to collect all terms containing the variable of interest to one side, and all terms not containing the variable to the other side.

5. Use multiplication or division to remove coefficients from the variable of interest.

Sometimes there are no numeric values in the equation or there are a mix of numerous variables and constants. The goal is to solve the equation for one of the variables in terms of the other variables. In this case, the answer will be an expression involving numbers and letters instead of a numeric value.

Examples

1. Solve for x: $\dfrac{100(x + 5)}{20} = 1$

Answer:

$\dfrac{100(x + 5)}{20} = 1$	
$(20)(\dfrac{100(x + 5)}{20}) = (1)(20)$ $100(x + 5) = 20$	Multiply both sides by 20 to cancel out the denominator.
$100x + 500 = 20$	Distribute 100 through the parentheses.

$100x = -480$	"Undo" the $+500$ by subtracting 500 on both sides of the equation to isolate the variable term.
$x = \dfrac{-480}{100}$	"Undo" the multiplication by 100 by dividing by 100 on both sides to solve for x.
$x = -4.8$	

2. Solve for x: $2(x + 2)^2 - 2x^2 + 10 = 42$

Answer:

$2(x + 2)^2 - 2x^2 + 10 = 42$	
$2(x + 2)(x + 2) - 2x^2 + 10 = 42$	Eliminate the exponents on the left side.
$2(x^2 + 4x + 4) - 2x^2 + 10 = 42$	Apply FOIL.
$2x^2 + 8x + 8 - 2x^2 + 10 = 42$	Distribute the 2.
$8x + 18 = 42$	Combine like terms on the left-hand side.
$8x = 24$	Isolate the variable. "Undo" $+18$ by subtracting 18 on both sides.
$x = 3$	"Undo" multiplication by 8 by dividing both sides by 8.

3. Solve the equation for D: $\dfrac{A(3B + 2D)}{2N} = 5M - 6$

Answer:

$\dfrac{A(3B + 2D)}{2N} = 5M - 6$	
$3AB + 2AD = 10MN - 12N$	Multiply both sides by $2N$ to clear the fraction, and distribute the A through the parentheses.
$2AD = 10MN - 12N - 3AB$	Isolate the term with the D in it by moving $3AB$ to the other side of the equation.
$D = \dfrac{(10MN - 12N - 3AB)}{2A}$	Divide both sides by $2A$ to get D alone on the right-hand side.

Graphs of Linear Equations

The most common way to write a linear equation is **SLOPE-INTERCEPT FORM**, $y = mx + b$. In this equation, m is the slope, which describes how steep the line is, and b is the y-intercept. Slope is often described as "rise over run" because it is calculated as the difference in y-values (rise) over the difference in x-values (run). The slope of the line is also the rate of change of the dependent variable y with respect to the independent variable x. The y-intercept is the point where the line crosses the y-axis, or where x equals zero.

To graph a linear equation, identify the y-intercept and place that point on the y-axis. If the slope is not written as a fraction,

Use the phrase "Begin, Move" to remember that b is the y-intercept (where to begin) and m is the slope (how the line moves).

make it a fraction by writing it over 1 $\left(\frac{m}{1}\right)$. Then use the slope to count up (or down, if negative) the "rise" part of the slope and over the "run" part of the slope to find a second point. These points can then be connected to draw the line.

To find the equation of a line, identify the y-intercept, if possible, on the graph and use two easily identifiable points to find the slope. If the y-intercept is not easily identified, identify the slope by choosing easily identifiable points; then choose one point on the graph, plug the point and the slope values into the equation, and solve for the missing value b.

⚠

slope-intercept form:
$y = mx + b$

slope: $m = \dfrac{y_2 - y_1}{x_2 - x_1}$

- standard form: $Ax + By = C$
- $m = -\dfrac{A}{B}$

- x-intercept = $\dfrac{C}{A}$
- y-intercept = $\dfrac{C}{B}$

Another way to express a linear equation is standard form: $Ax + By = C$. In order to graph equations in this form, it is often easiest to convert them to point-slope form. Alternately, it is easy to find the x- or y-intercept from this form, and once these two points are known, a line can be drawn through them. To find the x-intercept, simply make $y = 0$ and solve for x. Similarly, to find the y-intercept, make $x = 0$ and solve for y.

Examples

1. What is the slope of the line whose equation is $6x - 2y - 8 = 0$?

   Answer:

$6x - 2y - 8 = 0$	
$-2y = -6x + 8$ $y = \dfrac{-6x + 8}{-2}$ $y = 3x - 4$	Rearrange the equation into slope-intercept form by solving the equation for y.
$m = 3$	The slope is 3, the value attached to x.

2. What is the equation of the following line?

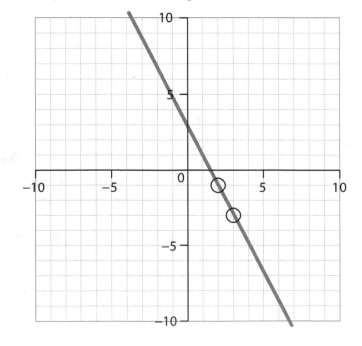

Answer:

$b = 3$	The y-intercept can be identified on the graph as $(0, 3)$.
$m = \dfrac{(-3) - (-1)}{3 - 2} = \dfrac{-2}{1} = -2$	To find the slope, choose any two points and plug the values into the slope equation. The two points chosen here are $(2, -1)$ and $(3, -3)$.
$y = -2x + 3$	Replace m with -2 and b with 3 in $y = mx + b$.

3. Write the equation of the line which passes through the points $(-2, 5)$ and $(-5, 3)$.

Answer:

$(-2, 5)$ and $(-5, 3)$	
$m = \dfrac{3 - 5}{(-5) - (-2)}$ $= \dfrac{-2}{-3}$ $= \dfrac{2}{3}$	Calculate the slope.
$5 = \dfrac{2}{3}(-2) + b$ $5 = \dfrac{-4}{3} + b$ $b = \dfrac{19}{3}$	To find b, plug into the equation $y = mx + b$ the slope for m and a set of points for x and y.
$y = \dfrac{2}{3}x + \dfrac{19}{3}$	Replace m and b to find the equation of the line.

4. What is the equation of the following graph?

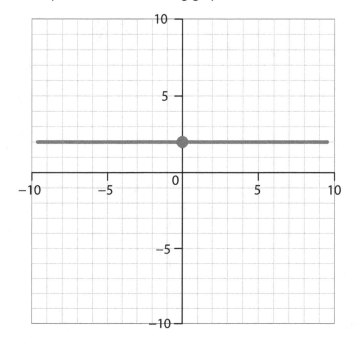

$y = 0x + 2$, or $y = 2$

The line has a rise of 0 and a run of 1, so the slope is $\frac{0}{1} = 0$. There is no *x*-intercept. The *y*-intercept is (0, 2), meaning that the *b*-value in the slope-intercept form is 2.

The Distance and Midpoint Formulas

The distance formula finds the distance of a line drawn between two points that terminates at those two points:

$$d = \sqrt{(x_2 - x_1)^2 + (y_2 - y_1)^2}$$

The distance formula resembles the Pythagorean theorem because it is essentially finding the hypotenuse of the right triangle with legs of length $\Delta x = x_2 - x_1$ and $\Delta y = y_2 - y_1$.

The midpoint formula finds the coordinates of a point exactly in the middle of two other points. To find the midpoint, average the *x* values and then average the *y* values. These are the coordinates of the midpoint:

$$\text{Midpoint } M = (\frac{x_1 + x_2}{2}, \frac{y_1 + y_2}{2})$$

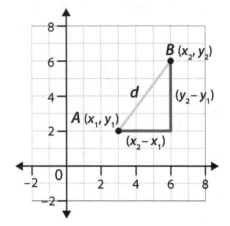

Figure 4.2. The Distance Formula

Examples

1. If $(-3, 8)$ is the midpoint of segment $\overline{AB}$ and point *A* is at $(-10, -17)$, what are the coordinates of point *B*?

Answer:

$A = (x_1, y_1) = (-10, -17)$ $B = (x_2, y_2)$ $M = (-3, 8)$	Identify the given variables.
$M_x = \frac{x_2 + x_1}{2}$ $-3 = \frac{x_2 + (-10)}{2}$ $x_2 = 4$ $M_y = \frac{y_2 + y_1}{2}$ $8 = \frac{y_2 + (-17)}{2}$ $y_2 = 33$ $B = (4, 33)$	Use the midpoint formula to find point *B*.

2. Find the distance between the points $(-10, 50)$ and $(50, 10)$.

Answer:

$(x_1, y_1) = (-10, 50)$ $(x_2, y_2) = (50, 10)$	Identify the given variables.
$d = \sqrt{(x_2 - x_1)^2 + (y_2 - y_1)^2}$ $d = \sqrt{(50 - (-10))^2 + (10 - 50)^2}$ $d = \sqrt{(60)^2 + (-40)^2}$ $d = \sqrt{3600 + 1600}$ $d = \sqrt{5200}$ $d \approx 72.11$	Plug these values into the distance formula and solve.

Building Equations

In word problems, it is often necessary to translate a verbal description of a relationship into a mathematical equation. No matter the problem, this process can be done using the same steps:

1. Read the problem carefully and identify what value needs to be solved for.
2. Identify the known and unknown quantities in the problem, and assign the unknown quantities a variable.
3. Create equations using the variables and known quantities.
4. Solve the equations.
5. Check the solution: Does it answer the question asked in the problem? Does it make sense?

> ⚠️ Use the acronym STAR to remember word-problem strategies: Search the problem, Translate into an expression or equation, Answer, and Review.

Examples

1. A school is holding a raffle to raise money. There is a $3 entry fee, and each ticket costs $5. If a student paid $28, how many tickets did he buy?

Answer:

Number of tickets $= x$ Cost per ticket $= 5$ Cost for x tickets $= 5x$ Total cost $= 28$ Entry fee $= 3$	Identify the quantities.
$5x + 3 = 28$	Set up equations. The total cost for x tickets will be equal to the cost for x tickets plus the $3 flat fee.
$5x + 3 = 28$ $5x = 25$ $x = 5$ The student bought **5 tickets**.	Solve the equation for x.

2. Kelly is selling shirts for her school swim team. There are two prices: a student price and a nonstudent price. During the first week of the sale, Kelly raised $84 by selling 10 shirts to students and 4 shirts to nonstudents. She earned $185 in the second week by selling 20 shirts to students and 10 shirts to nonstudents. What is the student price for a shirt?

Answer:

Student price = s Nonstudent price = n	Assign variables.
$10s + 4n = 84$ $20s + 10n = 185$	Create two equations using the number of shirts Kelly sold and the money she earned.
$10s + 4n = 84$ $10n = -20s + 185$ $n = -2s + 18.5$ $10s + 4(-2s + 18.5) = 84$ $10s - 8s + 74 = 84$ $2s + 74 = 84$ $2s = 10$ $s = 5$	Solve the system of equations using substitution.
The student cost for shirts is **$5**.	

LINEAR INEQUALITIES

Solving Linear Inequalities

An inequality shows the relationship between two expressions, much like an equation. However, the equal sign is replaced with an inequality symbol that expresses the following relationships:

- < less than
- ≤ less than or equal to
- > greater than
- ≥ greater than or equal to

Inequalities are read from left to right. For example, the inequality $x \leq 8$ would be read as "x is less than or equal to 8," meaning x has a value smaller than or equal to 8. The set of solutions of an inequality can be expressed using a number line. The shaded region on

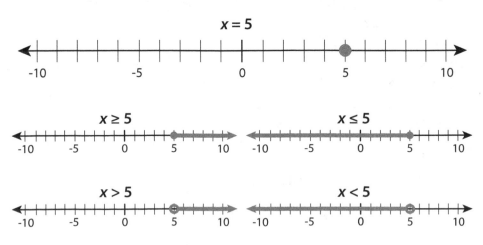

Figure 4.3. Inequalities on a Number Line

the number line represents the set of all the numbers that make an inequality true. One major difference between equations and inequalities is that equations generally have a finite number of solutions, while inequalities generally have infinitely many solutions (an entire interval on the number line containing infinitely many values).

Linear inequalities can be solved in the same way as linear equations, with one exception. When multiplying or dividing both sides of an inequality by a negative number, the direction of the inequality sign must reverse—"greater than" becomes "less than" and "less than" becomes "greater than."

Examples

1. Solve for z: $3z + 10 < -z$

Answer:

$3z + 10 < -z$	
$3z < -z - 10$	Collect nonvariable terms to one side.
$4z < -10$	Collect variable terms to the other side.
$\mathbf{z < -2.5}$	Isolate the variable.

2. Solve for x: $2x - 3 > 5(x - 4) - (x - 4)$

Answer:

$2x - 3 > 5(x - 4) - (x - 4)$	
$2x - 3 > 5x - 20 - x + 4$	Distribute 5 through the parentheses and −1 through the parentheses.
$2x - 3 > 4x - 16$	Combine like terms.
$-2x > -13$	Collect x-terms to one side, and constant terms to the other side.
$x < 6.5$	Divide both sides by −2; since dividing by a negative, reverse the direction of the inequality.

6.5

Compound Inequalities

Compound inequalities have more than one inequality expression. Solutions of compound inequalities are the sets of all numbers that make *all* the inequalities true. Some compound inequalities may not have any solutions, some will have solutions that contain some part of the number line, and some will have solutions that include the entire number line.

CONTINUE

Table 4.1. Unions and Intersections

INEQUALITY	MEANING IN WORDS	NUMBER LINE
$a < x < b$	All values x that are greater than a and less than b	
$a \leq x \leq b$	All values x that are greater than or equal to a and less than or equal to b	
$x < a \, or \, x > b$	All values of x that are less than a or greater than b	
$x \leq a \, or \, x \geq b$	All values of x that are less than or equal to a or greater than or equal to b	

Compound inequalities can be written, solved, and graphed as two separate inequalities. For compound inequalities in which the word *and* is used, the solution to the compound inequality will be the set of numbers on the number line where both inequalities have solutions (where both are shaded). For compound inequalities where *or* is used, the solution to the compound inequality will be *all* the shaded regions for *either* inequality.

Examples

1. Solve the compound inequalities: $2x + 4 < -10 \, or \, 4(x + 2) > 18$

Answer:

$2x + 4 < -10 \, or \, 4(x + 2) > 18$	
$2x < -14 \quad\quad 4x + 8 > 18$ $x < -7 \quad\quad\quad 4x > 10$ $\quad\quad\quad\quad\quad\quad x > 2.5$ The solution to the original compound inequality is **the set of all x for which** $x < -7$ **or** $x > 2.5$**.**	Solve each inequality independently.

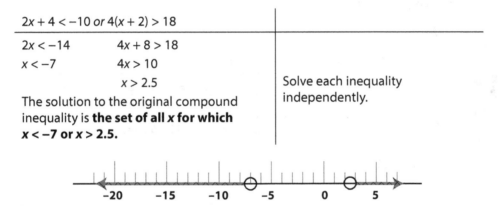

2. Solve the inequality: $-1 \leq 3(x + 2) - 1 \leq x + 3$

Answer:

$-1 \leq 3(x + 2) - 1 \leq x + 3$	
$-1 \leq 3(x + 2) - 1 \, and$ $3(x + 2) - 1 \leq x + 3$	Break up the compound inequality into two inequalities.
$-1 \leq 3x + 6 - 1 \quad\quad 3x + 6 - 1 \leq x + 3$ $-6 \leq 3x \quad\quad\quad\quad\quad 2x \leq -2$ $-2 \leq x \quad\quad and \quad\quad x \leq -1$	Solve separately.
$-2 \leq x \leq -1$	The only values of x that satisfy *both* inequalities are the values between −2 and −1 (inclusive).

QUADRATIC EQUATIONS

Quadratic equations are degree 2 polynomials; the highest power on the dependent variable is two. While linear functions are represented graphically as lines, the graph of a quadratic function is a **PARABOLA**. The graph of a parabola has three important components. The **VERTEX** is where the graph changes direction. In the parent graph $y = x^2$, the origin $(0, 0)$ is the vertex. The **AXIS OF SYMMETRY** is the vertical line that cuts the graph into two equal halves. The line of symmetry always passes through the vertex. On the parent graph, the y-axis is the axis of symmetry. The **ZEROS** or **ROOTS** of the quadratic are the x-intercepts of the graph.

Forms of Quadratic Equations

Quadratic equations can be expressed in two forms:

- **STANDARD FORM: $y = ax^2 + bx + c$**

  Axis of symmetry: $x = -\dfrac{b}{2a}$ Vertex: $(-\dfrac{b}{2a}, f(-\dfrac{b}{2a}))$

- **VERTEX FORM: $y = a(x - h)^2 + k$**

  Vertex: (h, k) Axis of symmetry: $x = h$

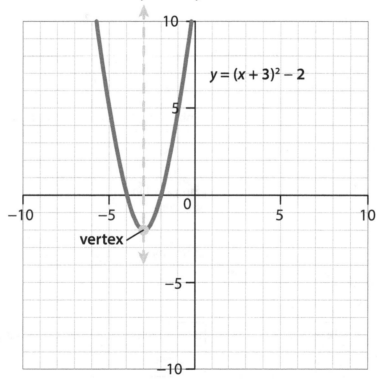

Figure 4.4. Parabola

In both equations, the sign of a determines which direction the parabola opens: if a is positive, then it opens upward; if a is negative, then it opens downward. The wideness or narrowness is also determined by a. If the absolute value of a is less than one (a proper fraction), then the parabola will get wider the closer $|a|$ is to zero. If the absolute value of a is greater than one, then the larger $|a|$ becomes, the narrower the parabola will be.

Equations in vertex form can be converted to standard form by squaring out the $(x - h)^2$ part (using FOIL), distributing the a, adding k, and simplifying the result.

Equations can be converted from standard form to vertex form by COMPLETING THE SQUARE. Take an equation in standard form, $y = ax^2 + bc + c$.

1. Move c to the left side of the equation.
2. Divide the entire equation through by a (to make the coefficient of x^2 be 1).
3. Take half of the coefficient of x, square that number, and then add the result to both sides of the equation.
4. Convert the right side of the equation to a perfect binomial squared, $(x + m)^2$.
5. Isolate y to put the equation in proper vertex form.

Examples

1. What is the line of symmetry for $y = -2(x + 3)^2 + 2$?

Answer:

This quadratic is given in vertex form, with $h = -3$ and $k = 2$. The vertex of this equation is $(-3, 2)$. The line of symmetry is the vertical line that passes through this point. Since the x-value of the point is -3, the line of symmetry is **$x = -3$**.

2. What is the vertex of the parabola $y = -3x^2 + 24x - 27$?

Answer:

$y = -3x^2 + 24x - 27$	
$x = -\dfrac{b}{2a}$ where $a = -3$, $b = 24$ $x = -\dfrac{24}{2(-3)} = 4$	This quadratic equation is in standard form. Use the formula for finding the x-value of the vertex.
$y = -3(4)^2 + 24(4) - 27 = 21$ The vertex is at **$(4, 21)$**.	Plug $x = 4$ into the original equation to find the corresponding y-value.

3. Write $y = -3x^2 + 24x - 27$ in vertex form by completing the square.

Answer:

$y = -3x^2 + 24x - 27$	
$y + 27 = -3x^2 + 24x$	Move c to the other side of the equation.
$\dfrac{y}{-3} - 9 = x^2 - 8x$	Divide through by a (-3 in this example).
$\dfrac{y}{-3} - 9 + 16 = x^2 - 8x + 16$	Take half of the new b, square it, and add that quantity to both sides: $\frac{1}{2}(-8) = -4$. Squaring it gives $(-4)^2 = 16$.
$\dfrac{y}{-3} + 7 = (x - 4)^2$	Simplify the left side, and write the right side as a binomial squared.
$y = -3(x - 4)^2 + 21$	Subtract 7, and then multiply through by -3 to isolate y.

Solving Quadratic Equations

Solving the quadratic equation $ax^2 + bx + c = 0$ finds x-intercepts of the parabola (by making $y = 0$). These are also called the **ROOTS** or **ZEROS** of the quadratic function. A quadratic equation may have zero, one, or two real solutions. There are several ways of finding the zeros. One way is to factor the quadratic into a product of two binomials, and then use the zero product property. (If $m \times n = 0$, then either $m = 0$ or $n = 0$.) Another way is to complete the square and square root both sides. One way that works every time is to memorize and use the **QUADRATIC FORMULA**:

$$x = \frac{-b \pm \sqrt{b^2 - 4ac}}{2a}$$

The a, b, and c come from the standard form of quadratic equations above. (Note that to use the quadratic equation, the right-hand side of the equation must be equal to zero.)

The part of the formula under the square root radical ($b^2 - 4ac$) is known as the **DISCRIMINANT**. The discriminant tells how many and what type of roots will result without actually calculating the roots.

> ⚠ With all graphing problems, putting the function into the $y =$ window of a graphing calculator will aid the process of elimination when graphs are examined and compared to answer choices with a focus on properties like axis of symmetry, vertices, and roots of formulas.

Table 4.2. Discriminants

IF $B^2 - 4AC$ IS	THERE WILL BE	AND THE PARABOLA
zero	only 1 real root	has its vertex on the x-axis
positive	2 real roots	has **two** x-intercepts
negative	0 real roots 2 complex roots	has **no** x-intercepts

Examples

1. Find the zeros of the quadratic equation: $y = -(x + 3)^2 + 1$.

   Answer:

   Method 1: Make $y = 0$; isolate x by square rooting both sides:

$0 = -(x + 3)^2 + 1$	Make $y = 0$.
$-1 = -(x + 3)^2$	Subtract 1 from both sides.
$1 = (x + 3)^2$	Divide by -1 on both sides.
$(x + 3) = \pm 1$	Square root both sides. Don't forget to write plus OR minus 1.
$(x + 3) = 1$ or $(x + 3) = -1$	Write two equations using $+1$ and -1.
$x = -2$ or $x = -4$	Solve both equations. These are the zeros.

   Method 2: Convert vertex form to standard form, and then use the quadratic formula.

$y = -(x + 3)^2 + 1$ $y = -(x^2 + 6x + 9) + 1$ $y = -x^2 - 6x - 8$	Put the equation in standard form by distributing and combining like terms.

$$x = \frac{-b \pm \sqrt{(b^2 - 4ac)}}{2a}$$

$$x = \frac{-(-6) \pm \sqrt{(-6)^2 - 4(-1)(-8)}}{2(-1)}$$

$$x = \frac{6 \pm \sqrt{36 - 32}}{-2}$$

$$x = \frac{6 \pm \sqrt{4}}{-2}$$

$x = -4, -2$

Find the zeros using the quadratic formula.

2. Find the root(s) for: $z^2 - 4z + 4 = 0$

Answer:

This polynomial can be factored in the form $(z - 2)(z - 2) = 0$, so the only root is $z = 2$. There is only one x-intercept, and the vertex of the graph is *on* the x-axis.

3. Write a quadratic function that has zeros at $x = -3$ and $x = 2$ that passes through the point $(-2, 8)$.

Answer:

If the quadratic has zeros at $x = -3$ and $x = 2$, then it has factors of $(x + 3)$ and $(x - 2)$. The quadratic function can be written in the factored form $y = a(x + 3)(x - 2)$. To find the a-value, plug in the point $(-2, 8)$ for x and y:

$8 = a(-2 + 3)(-2 - 2)$

$8 = a(-4)$

$a = -2$

The quadratic function is **$y = -2(x + 3)(x - 2)$**.

PROPERTIES OF SHAPES

Basic Definitions

The basic figures from which many other geometric shapes are built are points, lines, and planes. A **POINT** is a location in a plane. It has no size or shape, but is represented by a dot. It is labeled using a capital letter.

A **LINE** is a one-dimensional collection of points that extends infinitely in both directions. At least two points are needed to define a line, and any points that lie on the same line are **COLINEAR**. Lines are represented by two points, such as A and B, and the line symbol: ($\overleftrightarrow{AB}$). Two lines on the same plane will intersect unless they are **PARALLEL**, meaning they have the same slope. Lines that intersect at a 90 degree angle are **PERPENDICULAR**.

A **LINE SEGMENT** has two endpoints and a finite length. The length of a segment, called the measure of the segment, is the distance from A to B. A line segment is a subset of a line, and is also denoted with two points, but with a segment symbol: ($\overline{AB}$). The **MIDPOINT** of a line segment is the point at which the segment is divided into two equal parts. A line, segment, or plane that passes through the midpoint of a segment is called a **BISECTOR** of the segment, since it cuts the segment into two equal segments.

A **RAY** has one endpoint and extends indefinitely in one direction. It is defined by its endpoint, followed by any other point on the ray: $\overrightarrow{AB}$. It is important that the first letter represents the endpoint. A ray is sometimes called a half line.

Table 4.3. Basic Geometric Figures

TERM	DIMENSIONS	GRAPHIC	SYMBOL
point	zero	●	$\cdot A$
line segment	one	*A* ——— *B*	$\overline{AB}$
ray	one	*A* —→ *B*	$\overrightarrow{AB}$
line	one	←——→	$\overleftrightarrow{AB}$
plane	two	▱	Plane *M*

A **PLANE** is a flat sheet that extends indefinitely in two directions (like an infinite sheet of paper). A plane is a two-dimensional (2D) figure. A plane can always be defined through any three noncollinear points in three-dimensional (3D) space. A plane is named using any three points that are in the plane (for example, plane ***ABC***). Any points lying in the same plane are said to be **COPLANAR**. When two planes intersect, the intersection is a line.

Example

1) Which points and lines are not contained in plane *M* in the diagram below?

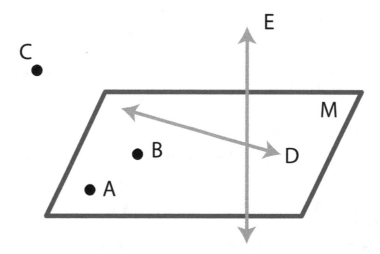

Answer:

Points *A* and *B* and line *D* are all on plane *M*. Point *C* is above the plane, and line *E* cuts through the plane and thus does not lie on plane *M*. The point at which line *E* intersects plane *M* is on plane *M* but the line as a whole is not.

Angles

ANGLES are formed when two rays share a common endpoint. They are named using three letters, with the vertex point in the middle (for example $\angle ABC$, where *B* is the vertex).

They can also be labeled with a number or named by their vertex alone (if it is clear to do so). Angles are also classified based on their angle measure. A RIGHT ANGLE has a measure of exactly 90°. ACUTE ANGLES have measures that are less than 90°, and OBTUSE ANGLES have measures that are greater than 90°.

⚠ Angles can be measured in degrees or radians. Use the conversion factor 1 rad = 57.3 degrees to convert between them.

Any two angles that add to make 90° are called COMPLEMENTARY ANGLES. A 30° angle would be complementary to a 60° angle. SUPPLEMENTARY ANGLES add up to 180°. A supplementary angle to a 60° angle would be a 120° angle; likewise, 60° is the SUPPLEMENT of 120°. The complement and supplement of any angle must always be positive. For example, a 140 degree has no complement. Angles that are next to each other and share a common ray are called ADJACENT ANGLES.

Angles that are adjacent and supplementary are called a LINEAR PAIR of angles. Their nonshared rays form a line (thus the *linear* pair). Note that angles that are supplementary do not need to be adjacent; their measures simply need to add to 180°.

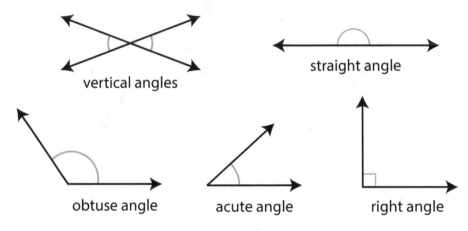

Figure 4.5. Types of Angles

VERTICAL ANGLES are formed when two lines intersect. Four angles will be formed; the vertex of each angle is at the intersection point of the lines. The vertical angles across from each other will be equal in measure. The angles adjacent to each other will be linear pairs and therefore supplementary.

A ray, line, or segment that divides an angle into two equal angles is called an ANGLE BISECTOR.

Examples

1. If angles *M* and *N* are supplementary and ∠**M** is 30° less than twice ∠*N*, what is the degree measurement of each angle?

Answer:

∠*M* + ∠*N* = 180° ∠*M* = 2∠*N* – 30°	Set up a system of equations.
∠*M* + ∠*N* = 180° (2∠*N* – 30°) + ∠*N* = 180° 3∠*N* – 30° = 180° 3∠*N* = 210° ∠**N = 70°**	Use substitution to solve for ∠*N*.

$$\angle M + \angle N = 180°$$
$$\angle M + 70° = 180°$$
$$\angle M = \textbf{110°}$$

Solve for $\angle M$ using the original equation.

2. How many linear pairs of angles are there in the following figure?

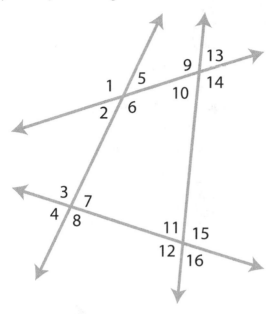

Answers:

Any two adjacent angles that are supplementary are linear pairs, so there are 16 linear pairs in the figure ($\angle 1$ and $\angle 5$, $\angle 2$ and $\angle 6$, $\angle 5$ and $\angle 6$, $\angle 2$ and $\angle 1$, and so on).

Circles

A **CIRCLE** is the set of all the points in a plane that are the same distance from a fixed point called the **CENTER**. The distance from the center to any point on the circle is the **RADIUS** of the circle. The distance around the circle (the perimeter) is called the **CIRCUMFERENCE**.

The ratio of a circle's circumference to its diameter is a constant value called pi (π), an irrational number which is commonly rounded to 3.14. The formula to find a circle's circumference is $C = 2\pi r$. The formula to find the enclosed area of a circle is $A = \pi r^2$.

Circles have a number of unique parts and properties:

- The **DIAMETER** is the largest measurement across a circle. It passes through the circle's center, extending from one side of the circle to the other. The measure of the diameter is twice the measure of the radius.

- A line that cuts across a circle and touches it twice is called a **SECANT** line. The part of a secant line that lies within a circle is called a **CHORD**. Two chords within a circle are of equal length if they are are the same distance from the center.

Trying to square a circle means attempting to create a square that has the same area as a circle. Because the area of a circle depends on π, which is an irrational number, this task is impossible. The phrase is often used to describe trying to do something that can't be done.

- A line that touches a circle or any curve at one point is TANGENT to the circle or the curve. These lines are always exterior to the circle. A line tangent to a circle and a radius drawn to the point of tangency meet at a right angle (90°).

- An ARC is any portion of a circle between two points on the circle. The MEASURE of an arc is in degrees, whereas the LENGTH OF THE ARC will be in linear measurement (such as centimeters or inches). A MINOR ARC is the small arc between the two points (it measures less than 180°), whereas a MAJOR ARC is the large arc between the two points (it measures greater than 180°).

- An angle with its vertex at the center of a circle is called a CENTRAL ANGLE. For a central angle, the measure of the arc intercepted by the sides of the angle (in degrees) is the same as the measure of the angle.

- A SECTOR is the part of a circle *and* its interior that is inside the rays of a central angle (its shape is like a slice of pie).

	Area of Sector	Length of an Arc
Degrees	$A = \dfrac{\theta}{360°} \times \pi r^2$	$s = \dfrac{\theta}{360°} \times 2\pi r$
Radians	$A = \dfrac{1}{2}\, \pi^2 \theta$	$s = r\theta$

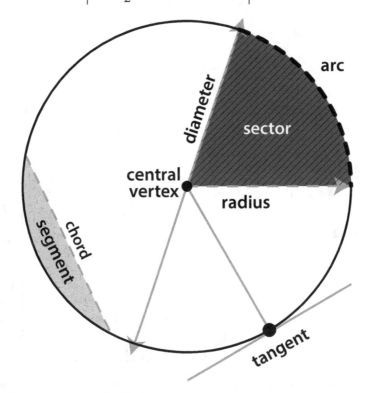

Figure 4.6. Parts of a Circle

- An INSCRIBED ANGLE has a vertex on the circle and is formed by two chords that share that vertex point. The angle measure of an inscribed angle is one-half the angle measure of the central angle with the same endpoints on the circle.

- A CIRCUMSCRIBED ANGLE has rays tangent to the circle. The angle lies outside of the circle.

- Any angle outside the circle, whether formed by two tangent lines, two secant lines, or a tangent line and a secant line, is equal to half the difference of the intercepted arcs.

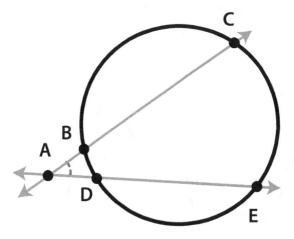

$m\angle A = \frac{1}{2}(\overarc{CE} - \overarc{BD})$

Figure 4.7. Angles Outside a Circle

- Angles are formed within a circle when two chords intersect in the circle. The measure of the smaller angle formed is half the sum of the two smaller arc measures (in degrees). Likewise, the larger angle is half the sum of the two larger arc measures.

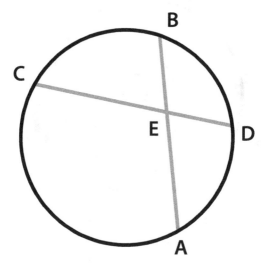

$m\angle E = \frac{1}{2}(\overarc{AC} + \overarc{BD})$

Figure 4.8. Intersecting Chords

- If a chord intersects a line tangent to the circle, the angle formed by this intersection measures one half the measurement of the intercepted arc (in degrees).

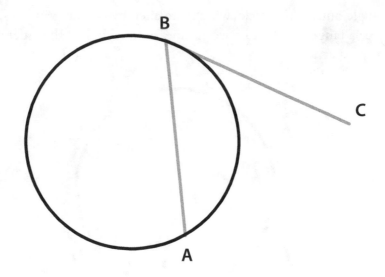

$m\angle ABC = \frac{1}{2}m\widehat{AB}$

Figure 2.11. Intersecting Chord and Tangent

Examples

1. Find the area of the sector *NHS* of the circle below with center at *H*:

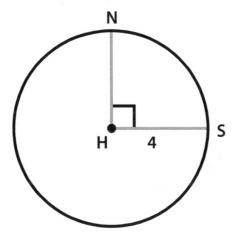

Answer:

$r = 4$ $\angle NHS = 90°$	Identify the important parts of the circle.
$A = \frac{\theta}{360°} \times \pi r^2$ $= \frac{90}{360} \times \pi (4)^2$	Plug these values into the formula for the area of a sector.
$= \frac{1}{4} \times 16\pi$ $\mathbf{= 4\pi}$	Plug these values into the formula for the area of a sector (continued).

2. In the circle below with center *O*, the minor arc *ACB* measures 5 feet. What is the measurement of *m∠AOB*?

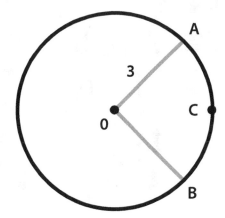

Answer:

$r = 3$
length of $\overset{\frown}{ACB} = 5$

Identify the important parts of the circle.

$s = \frac{\theta}{360°} \times 2\pi r$

$5 = \frac{\theta}{360} \times 2\pi(3)$

$\frac{5}{6\pi} = \frac{\theta}{360}$

Plug these values into the formula for the length of an arc and solve for *θ*.

$\theta = 95.5°$

$\mathbf{\mathit{m∠AOB} = 95.5°}$

Triangles

Much of geometry is concerned with triangles as they are commonly used shapes. A good understanding of triangles allows decomposition of other shapes (specifically polygons) into triangles for study.

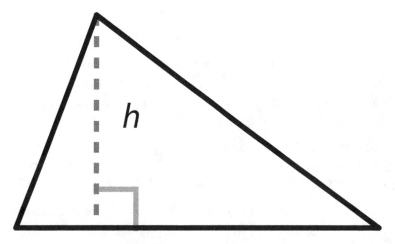

Figure 4.9. Finding the Base and Height of Triangles

Triangles have three sides, and the three interior angles always sum to 180°. The formula for the area of a triangle is $A = \frac{1}{2} bh$ or one-half the product of the base and height (or altitude) of the triangle.

Some important segments in a triangle include the angle bisector, the altitude, and the median. The **ANGLE BISECTOR** extends from the side opposite an angle to bisect that angle. The **ALTITUDE** is the shortest distance from a vertex of the triangle to the line containing the base side opposite that vertex. It is perpendicular to that line and can occur on the outside of the triangle. The **MEDIAN** extends from an angle to bisect the opposite side.

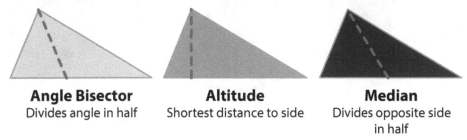

Angle Bisector
Divides angle in half

Altitude
Shortest distance to side

Median
Divides opposite side in half

Figure 4.10. Important Segments in a Triangle

Triangles have two "centers." The **CENTROID** is where a triangle's three medians meet. The **ORTHOCENTER** is formed by the intersection of a triangle's three altitudes.

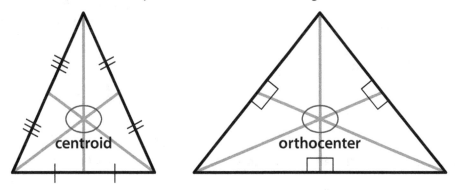

Figure 4.11. Centroid and Orthocenter of a Triangle

Triangles can be classified in two ways: by sides and by angles.

A **SCALENE TRIANGLE** has no equal sides or angles. An **ISOSCELES TRIANGLE** has two equal sides and two equal angles, often called **BASE ANGLES**. In an **EQUILATERAL TRIANGLE**, all three sides are equal as are all three angles. Moreover, because the sum of the angles of a triangle is always 180°, each angle of an equilateral triangle must be 60°.

A **RIGHT TRIANGLE** has one right angle (90°) and two acute angles. An **ACUTE TRIANGLE** has three acute angles (all angles are less than 90°). An **OBTUSE TRIANGLE** has one obtuse angle (more than 90°) and two acute angles.

Trigonometric functions can be employed to find missing sides and angles of a triangle.

For any triangle, the side opposite the largest angle will have the longest length, while the side opposite the smallest angle will have the shortest length. The **TRIANGLE INEQUALITY THEOREM** states that the sum of any two sides of a triangle must be greater than the third side. If this inequality does not hold, then a triangle cannot be formed. A consequence of this theorem is the **THIRD-SIDE RULE**: if *b* and *c* are two sides of a triangle, then the measure of the third side *a* must be between the sum of the other two sides and the difference of the other two sides: $c - b < a < c + b$.

Triangles Based on Sides

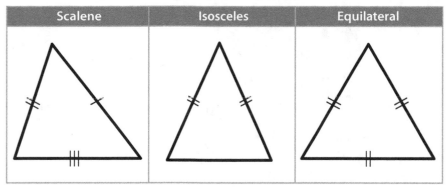

Triangles Based on Angles

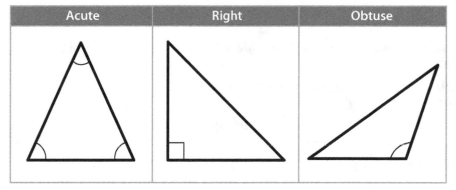

Figure 4.12. Types of Triangles

Solving for missing angles or sides of a triangle is a common type of triangle problem. Often a right triangle will come up on its own or within another triangle. The relationship among a right triangle's sides is known as the **PYTHAGOREAN THEOREM**: $a^2 + b^2 = c^2$, where *c* is the hypotenuse and is across from the 90° angle. Right triangles with angle measurements of 90° – 45° – 45° and 90° – 60° – 30° are known as "special" right triangles and have specific relationships between their sides and angles.

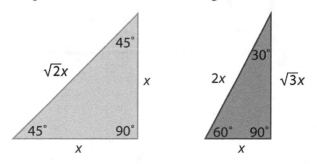

Figure 4.13. Special Right Triangles

CONTINUE

Examples

1. Examine and classify each of the following triangles:

[1]

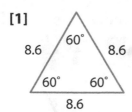

[2]

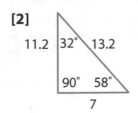

[3]

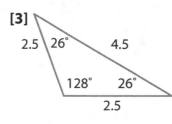

[4]

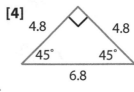

Answers:

Triangle 1 is an equilateral triangle (all 3 sides are equal, and all 3 angles are equal)

Triangle 2 is a scalene, right triangle (all 3 sides are different, and there is a 90° angle)

Triangle 3 is an obtuse, isosceles triangle (there are 2 equal sides and, consequently, 2 equal angles)

Triangle 4 is a right, isosceles triangle (there are 2 equal sides and a 90° angle)

2. Given the diagram, if $XZ = 100$, $WZ = 80$, and $XU = 70$, then $WY = ?$

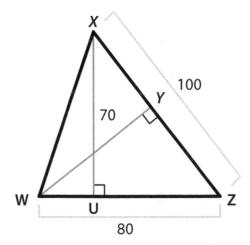

Answer:

$WZ = b_1 = 80$
$XU = h_1 = 7.0$
$XZ = b_2 = 100$
$WY = h_2 = ?$

$A = \frac{1}{2}bh$

$A_1 = \frac{1}{2}(80)(70) = 2800$

$A_2 = \frac{1}{2}(100)(h_2)$

The given values can be used to write two equation for the area of $\triangle WXZ$ with two sets of bases and heights.

$2800 = \frac{1}{2}(100)(h_2)$

$h_2 = 56$

WY = 56

Set the two equations equal to each other and solve for WY.

3. What are the minimum and maximum values of x to the nearest hundredth?

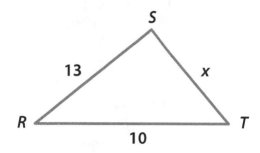

Answers:

The sum of two sides is 23 and their difference is 3. To connect the two other sides and enclose a space, x must be less than the sum and greater than the difference (that is, $3 < x < 23$). Therefore, **x's minimum value to the nearest hundredth is 3.01 and its maximum value is 22.99.**

Quadrilaterals

All closed, four-sided shapes are QUADRILATERALS. The sum of all internal angles in a quadrilateral is always 360°. (Think of drawing a diagonal to create two triangles. Since each triangle contains 180°, two triangles, and therefore the quadrilateral, must contain 360°.) The AREA OF ANY QUADRILATERAL is $A = bh$, where b is the base and h is the height (or altitude).

A **PARALLELOGRAM** is a quadrilateral with two pairs of parallel sides. A rectangle is a parallelogram with two pairs of equal sides and four right angles. A **KITE** also has two pairs of equal sides, but its equal sides are consecutive. Both a **SQUARE** and a **RHOMBUS** have four equal sides. A square has four right angles, while a rhombus has a pair of acute opposite angles and a pair of obtuse opposite angles. A **TRAPEZOID** has exactly one pair of parallel sides.

⚠️ All squares are rectangles and all rectangles are parallelograms; however, not all parallelograms are rectangles and not all rectangles are squares.

Table 4.4 Properties of Parallelograms

TERM	SHAPE	PROPERTIES
Parallelogram		Opposite sides are parallel. Consecutive angles are supplementary. Opposite angles are equal. Opposite sides are equal. Diagonals bisect each other.

Table 4.4 Properties of Parallelograms (continued)

TERM	SHAPE	PROPERTIES
Rectangle		All parallelogram properties hold. Diagonals are congruent *and* bisect each other. All angles are right angles.
Square		All rectangle properties hold. All four sides are equal. Diagonals bisect angles. Diagonals intersect at right angles and bisect each other.
Kite		One pair of opposite angles is equal. Two pairs of consecutive sides are equal. Diagonals meet at right angles.
Rhombus		All four sides are equal. Diagonals bisect angles. Diagonals intersect at right angles and bisect each other.
Trapezoid		One pair of sides is parallel. Bases have different lengths. Isosceles trapezoids have a pair of equal sides (and base angles).

Examples

1. In parallelogram *ABCD*, the measure of angle *m* is is $m° = 260°$. What is the measure of $n°$?

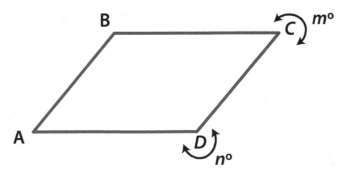

Answers:

$260° + m\angle C = 360°$ $m\angle C = 100°$	Find $\angle C$ using the fact that the sum of $\angle C$ and *m* is 360°.
$m\angle C + m\angle D = 180°$ $100° + m\angle D = 180°$ $m\angle D = 80°$	Solve for $\angle D$ using the fact that consecutive interior angles in a quadrilateral are supplementary.
$m\angle D + n = 360°$ $\mathbf{n = 280°}$	Solve for *n* by subtracting $m\angle D$ from 360°.

2. A rectangular section of a football field has dimensions of x and y and an area of 1000 square feet. Three additional lines drawn vertically divide the section into four smaller rectangular areas as seen in the diagram below. If all the lines shown need to be painted, calculate the total number of linear feet, in terms of x, to be painted.

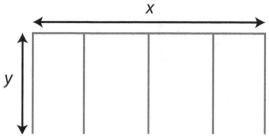

Answer:

$A = 1000 = xy$ $L = 2x + 5y$	Find equations for the area of the field and length of the lines to be painted (L) in terms of x and y.
$y = \frac{1000}{x}$ $L = 2x + 5y$ $L = 2x + 5(\frac{1000}{x})$ $\mathbf{L = 2x + \frac{5000}{x}}$	Substitute to find L in terms of x.

Polygons

Any closed shape made up of three or more line segments is a polygon. In addition to triangles and quadrilaterals, OCTAGONS and HEXAGONS are two common polygons.

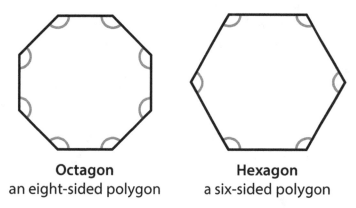

Octagon
an eight-sided polygon

Hexagon
a six-sided polygon

Figure 4.14. Common Polygons

The two polygons depicted above are REGULAR POLYGONS, meaning that they are equilateral (all sides having equal lengths) and equiangular (all angles having equal measurements). Angles inside a polygon are INTERIOR ANGLES, whereas those formed by one side of the polygon and a line extending outside the polygon are EXTERIOR ANGLES.

The sum of all the exterior angles of a polygon is always 360°. Dividing 360° by the number of a polygon's sides finds the measure of the polygon's exterior angles.

⚠ Breaking an irregular polygon down into triangles and quadrilaterals helps in finding its area.

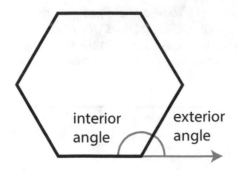

Figure 4.15. Interior and Exterior Angles

To determine the sum of a polygon's interior angles, choose one vertex and draw diagonals from that vertex to each of the other vertices, decomposing the polygon into multiple triangles. For example, an octagon has six triangles within it, and therefore the sum of the interior angles is $6 \times 180° = 1080°$. In general, the formula for finding the sum of the angles in a polygon is *sum of angles* $= (n - 2) \times 180°$, where n is the number of sides of the polygon.

To find the measure of a single interior angle in a regular polygon, simply divide the sum of the interior angles by the number of angles (which is the same as the number of sides). So, in the octagon example, each angle is $\frac{1080}{8} = 135°$.

In general, the formula to find the measure of a regular polygon's interior angles is: *interior angle* $= \frac{(n - 2)}{n} \times 180°$ where n is the number of sides of the polygon.

To find the area of a polygon, it is helpful to know the perimeter of the polygon (p), and the **APOTHEM** (a). The apothem is the shortest (perpendicular) distance from the polygon's center to one of the sides of the polygon. The formula for the area is: *area* $= \frac{ap}{2}$.

Finally, there is no universal way to find the perimeter of a polygon (when the side length is not given). Often, breaking the polygon down into triangles and adding the base of each triangle all the way around the polygon is the easiest way to calculate the perimeter.

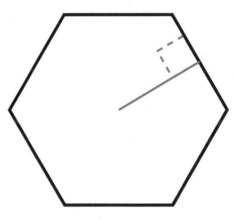

Figure 4.16. Apothem in a Hexagon

Examples

1. What is the measure of an exterior angle and an interior angle of a regular 400-gon?

   Answer:

   The sum of the exterior angles is 360°. Dividing this sum by 400 gives $\frac{360°}{400} =$ **0.9°**. Since an interior angle is supplementary to an exterior angle, all the interior angles have measure $180 - 0.9 =$ **179.1°**. Alternately, using the formula for calculating the interior angle gives the same result:

   interior angle $= \frac{400 - 2}{400} \times 180° = 179.1°$

2. The circle and hexagon below both share center point T. The hexagon is entirely inscribed in the circle. The circle's radius is 5. What is the area of the shaded area?

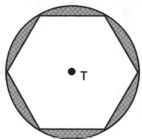

Answer:

$A_C = \pi r^2$ $= \pi(5)^2$ $= 25\pi$	The area of the shaded region will be the area of the circle minus the area of the hexagon. Use the radius to find the area of the circle.
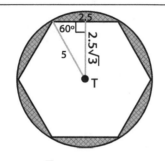 $a = 2.5\sqrt{3}$ $A_H = \dfrac{ap}{2}$ $\quad = \dfrac{(2.5\sqrt{3})(30)}{2}$ $\quad = 64.95$	To find the area of the hexagon, draw a right triangle from the vertex, and use special right triangles to find the hexagon's apothem. Then, use the apothem to calculate the area.
$= A_C - A_H$ $= 25\pi - 64.95$ $\approx \mathbf{13.59}$	Subtract the area of the hexagon from the circle to find the area of the shaded region.

THREE-DIMENSIONAL SHAPES

THREE-DIMENSIONAL SHAPES have depth in addition to width and length. VOLUME is expressed as the number of cubic units any shape can hold—that is, what it takes to fill it up. SURFACE AREA is the sum of the areas of the two-dimensional figures that are found on its surface. Some three-dimensional shapes also have a unique property called a slant height (ℓ), which is the distance from the base to the apex along a lateral face.

→

CONTINUE

Table 4.5 Three-Dimensional Shapes and Formulas

TERM	SHAPE	FORMULA	

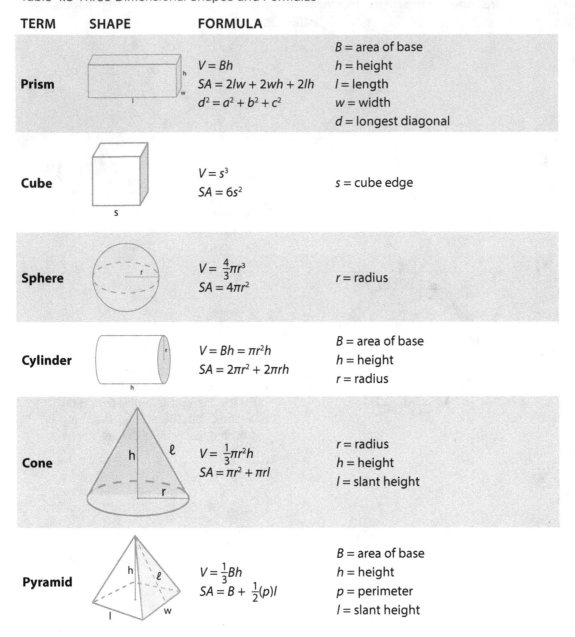

Prism
$V = Bh$
$SA = 2lw + 2wh + 2lh$
$d^2 = a^2 + b^2 + c^2$

B = area of base
h = height
l = length
w = width
d = longest diagonal

Cube
$V = s^3$
$SA = 6s^2$

s = cube edge

Sphere
$V = \frac{4}{3}\pi r^3$
$SA = 4\pi r^2$

r = radius

Cylinder
$V = Bh = \pi r^2 h$
$SA = 2\pi r^2 + 2\pi rh$

B = area of base
h = height
r = radius

Cone
$V = \frac{1}{3}\pi r^2 h$
$SA = \pi r^2 + \pi rl$

r = radius
h = height
l = slant height

Pyramid
$V = \frac{1}{3}Bh$
$SA = B + \frac{1}{2}(p)l$

B = area of base
h = height
p = perimeter
l = slant height

Finding the surface area of a three-dimensional solid can be made easier by using a **net**. This two-dimensional "flattened" version of a three-dimensional shape shows the component parts that comprise the surface of the solid.

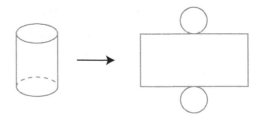

Figure 4.17. Net of a Cylinder

Examples

1. A sphere has a radius z. If that radius is increased by t, by how much is the surface area increased? Write the answer in terms of z and t.

   Answer:

$SA_1 = 4\pi z^2$	Write the equation for the area of the original sphere.
$SA_2 = 4\pi(z + t)^2$ $= 4\pi(z^2 + 2zt + t^2)$ $= 4\pi z^2 + 8\pi zt + 4\pi t^2$	Write the equation for the area of the new sphere.
$A_2 - A_1 = 4\pi z^2 + 8\pi zt + 4\pi t^2 - 4\pi z^2$ $= \mathbf{4\pi t^2 + 8\pi zt}$	To find the difference between the two, subtract the original from the increased surface area.

2. A cube with volume 27 cubic meters is inscribed within a sphere such that all of the cube's vertices touch the sphere. What is the length of the sphere's radius?

   Answer:

   Since the cube's volume is 27, each side length is equal to $\sqrt[3]{27} = 3$. The long diagonal distance from one of the cube's vertices to its opposite vertex will provide the sphere's diameter:

   $$d = \sqrt{3^2 + 3^2 + 3^2} = \sqrt{27} = 5.2$$

   Half of this length is the radius, which is **2.6 meters**.

6

ELECTRONICS

THE BASICS OF ELECTRICITY

Electric Charge

Electric **CHARGE** is a fundamental property of matter, like mass. When something is without charge, it is called **NEUTRAL**. Experimentally it was determined that there are two types of charges, named positive (+) and negative (–). As more was discovered about electric charge, it was shown that negative charge came from **ELECTRONS**, and positive charge came from **PROTONS.**

The unit of charge, e, is a fundamental constant (meaning it never changes) and has a value of e = 1.602 x 10^{-19} C, where C is coulombs. The charge of an electron is –e, and the charge of a proton is +e. Therefore, the total charge is always a multiple of e, and fractional values of e do not exist. For example, a charge of 14 e means there are 14 protons providing that charge.

As discussed in previous chapters, mass attracts other mass via the gravitational force. Similarly, an electric charge interacts with other electric charges through an electric force. Through experiments scientists determined that like charges repel (positive charges will repel positive charges and negative charges will repel negative charges), and unlike charges attract (positive charges will attract negative charges).

The magnitude of the electrical force, F, between charges is given in newtons, N, and is given by the equation:

$$F = \frac{kq_a q_b}{r^2}$$

where q_a and q_b are the charges, and r is the separation between them. k is a proportionality constant; $k = 9 \times 10^9$ Nm²/C². It is important to consider direction when applying the force equation. For example, two electrons will each experience a force due to the other that pushes them apart. An electron and a proton will each experience a force due to the other that pulls them together.

Charges interact through this force through an **ELECTRIC FIELD** that is created by each individual charge. The electric field has

The words *force* and *field* are commonly used in our language. Think of your understanding of the words compared to how they are described here. It will help you remember!

direction and always moves away from positive charges and toward negative charges. The magnitude of the electric field (units N/C) at distance r from a charge q is given by:

$$E = \frac{kq}{r^2}$$

If another charge, q', is placed at r, the previous equation for the electric force is recovered:

$$F = q'E$$

Charges behave differently when placed in an electric field. A positive charge will be pushed along the direction of the electric field, while a negative charge will be pushed in the opposite direction of the electric field.

Examples

1. Consider two scenarios: A) a proton and electron separated by 1 meter and B) two protons separated by 1 meter. What can be said about the electric force for each case?

    (A) The electric force will be the same strength, but for A) it will pull them together and for B) it will push them apart.

    (B) The electric force will be the same strength, but for A) it will push them apart and for B) it will pull them together.

    (C) The electric force will be stronger for case A) than case B).

    (D) The electric force will be stronger for case B) than case A).

    Answers:

    (A) is correct. The electric force equation will give the same value for both cases. Opposite charges attract and like charges repel.

    (B) is incorrect. The electric force equation will give the same value for both cases. Opposite charges attract and like charges repel.

    (C) is incorrect. The electric force equation will give the same value for both cases.

    (D) is incorrect. The electric force equation will give the same value for both cases.

2. What comment about the electric field is true?

    (A) The electric field can turn a proton turn into an electron.

    (B) The electric field gets stronger the farther it is from a charge.

    (C) The electric field always points from positive to negative charges.

    (D) The electric field always points from negative to positive charges.

    Answers:

    (A) is incorrect. An electric field cannot turn a proton into an electron.

    (B) is incorrect. The electric field gets weaker the farther it is from a charge.

    (C) is correct. The electric field does point from positive to negative charges.

    (D) is incorrect. The electric field always points from positive to negative charges.

Atomic Structure

Opposite charges attract, where the electric force will pull them together. However, this does not mean they will collide and stick together. Although the reasons are beyond the scope of this text, opposite charges will form systems called ATOMS when they are brought close together. In atoms, negatively charged electrons will orbit around a positively charged nucleus that contains protons and neutral particles called NEUTRONS.

Although it is possible for the number of protons in an atom to change (through nuclear reactions, like in the sun or a nuclear weapon), it is uncommon in daily experience. Outside of nuclear reactions, it is important to remember that electrons and protons are not created or destroyed.

 The neutron will radioactively decay into a positively charged proton and negatively charged electron (among other things).

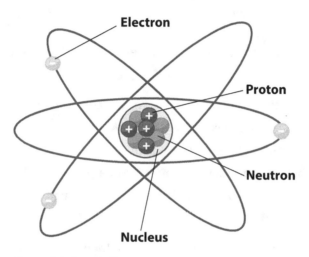

Figure 6.1. Atomic Structure

The mass of a proton is 1.673×10^{-27} kg (kilograms), and the mass of an electron is almost 2,000 times lighter, at 9.109×10^{-31} kg. Although their charges are equal and opposite, it is much harder to move the proton than the electron. Therefore, the much heavier nucleus may be considered rigid while the electrons move freely.

Electrons move around the nucleus in levels called shells. An atom's outermost shell is occupied by VALENCE ELECTRONS, which are farthest from the nucleus and therefore the most reactive of the atom's electrons. Atoms with a full valence shell are unreactive. Valence shells that are close to full will more easily accept electrons, and nearly empty valence shells will more easily lose electrons.

Valence shells determine a material's conductivity. The atoms in an INSULATOR have nearly full valence shells, meaning the electrons do not easily move. In a CONDUCTOR, the atoms have nearly empty valence shells, and electrons move freely. A SEMICONDUC-TOR'S atoms are neither full nor empty, making them poor conductors and insulators. A semiconductor on its own will not conduct charge. However, other elements, or *dopants*, are added to change the material's electrical properties.

⟶
CONTINUE

Examples

1. What configuration of particles can make an atom?

    (A) two neutrons

    (B) one proton and one electron

    (C) one neutron and one electron

    (D) two electrons

    Answers:

    (A) is incorrect. Neutrons are neutral and will not attract and create an atom.

    (B) is correct. The proton and electron will attract and create an atomic system (in this case, a hydrogen atom).

    (C) is incorrect. The neutron has no charge, so it will not attract the electron to form an atom.

    (D) is incorrect. The two electrons will repel and separate and will not create an atom.

2. What best describes the properties of a semiconductor?

    (A) It is an insulator unless dopants are added.

    (B) It is a conductor unless dopants are added.

    (C) It has half the conducting properties of a conductor.

    (D) It is a conductor surrounded by an insulating material.

    Answers:

    (A) is correct. A semiconductor is an insulator whose conducting properties can be altered with dopants.

    (B) is incorrect. A semiconductor without dopants is an insulator.

    (C) is incorrect. Despite the name, a semiconductor does not have half the conducting properties of a conductor.

    (D) is incorrect. A semiconductor is a type of material, not an electrical structure or device.

Current

CURRENT (I) is the amount of charge flow per time and is given by the equation:

$$I = \frac{\Delta q}{\Delta t}$$

where Δq is the amount of charge that moved past a location in Δt, the amount of time passed. Current is measured in amperes (amps), A.

Although current, by definition, does not need to be inside a material, for electronics, current flow is considered within a conductor (or semiconductor). As discussed previously, electrons are much lighter and therefore move much more easily than the heavy nuclei (nuclei are seen as basically rigid). Thus current flow is actually the flow of electrons. However, historically in electronics and circuits, current flow is positive in the direction of positive charge flow. This is called CONVENTIONAL CURRENT.

If a straight segment of conducting wire has an electric field applied along the wire, the electrons will move in the opposite direction of the field. If the nuclei are rigid and do not move, how is there positive charge flow? A simple analogy is bubbles in a liquid. The bubbles (air) are moving up through the liquid. The liquid moves down to fill the space left by the air. In electronics, the electrons act as the liquid, and the air (lack of electrons, also called HOLES) moves in the opposite direction. Therefore, conventional current flow is the direction of the flow of holes through a circuit.

Conceptually, a single electron or hole does not travel through the entire wire to create current. For example, a hole does not start at the battery and then move through the circuit back to the battery. Instead, the holes are colliding and moving at high speed in generally random directions in the wire. The electric field introduces a trend, or drift, in the hole movement that will make the holes move in the direction of the field, but rather slowly. Therefore, the electric field that is introducing the slow drift direction to the charge movement throughout the entire wire or circuit is what is measured as current flow.

There are two types of current sources, DIRECT CURRENT (DC) and ALTERNATING CURRENT (AC). Direct current is a constant current value, like that from a battery. For example, a battery will supply a constant 10mA to a circuit as long as the battery is good. In alternating current sources, the current value changes sign at a certain frequency.

As shown later in this chapter, alternating current is created by alternators, like those in a car and in power plants. Power outlets in our homes and businesses are AC sources (with typical frequencies of f = 60 Hz, ω = 377 Hz). It is common to have electronic devices that convert AC sources to DC sources to power electronics, like laptops and smartphones.

Voltage from a battery, power supply, or across a circuit element is usually notated with + and − signs. Current always flows from + to − in the circuit.

Resistance

RESISTIVITY is a measure of how easily an electron can move through a material. An insulator, where electrons are held close to the nuclei, will have a high resistivity. A conductor, where electrons can freely move throughout the entire material, has a low resistivity. The reciprocal of resistivity is called the conductivity; insulators have low conductivity and conductors have high conductivity. Resistivity is a material property and can vary by a huge amount.

Table 6.1. Resistivity of Common Materials

CONDUCTORS		SEMICONDUCTORS		INSULATORS	
Copper	1.72×10^{-8}	Silicon	2300	Glass	$10^{10} - 10^{14}$
Gold	2.44×10^{-8}			Teflon	$>10^{13}$

RESISTANCE has units of ohms, Ω, and includes the material resistivity as well as the actual size of the device. For the case of a wire of length, L, cross-sectional area, A, and resistivity, ρ, the resistance is given by:

$$R = \frac{\rho L}{A}$$

Therefore, the resistance of a wire increases if the wire is made longer or if the wire is made thinner. Relatively, short and fat wires will have less resistance that long and thin wires.

Example

What is the best type of wire to use to get the highest resistance? Assume the material resistivity in the wire is identical.

(A) long, thin wire

(B) long, thick wire

(C) short, thin wire

(D) short, thick wire

Answers:

(A) is correct. From the equation $R = \rho L / A$, a larger length, L, means a higher resistance, R. A thinner wire (smaller A) will also have a higher resistance, R.

(B) is incorrect. The long wire will increase resistance, but a thick wire will have less resistance than a thin wire.

(C) is incorrect. The thin wire will increase resistance, but a short wire will decrease it.

(D) is incorrect. The short and thick wire will have the least resistance.

Voltage

To understand voltage, it is helpful to revisit the concept of gravitational potential energy. Consider an individual standing on a box. She is not moving and therefore has zero kinetic energy. However, she has potential energy because if the box moves, she would fall to the floor. When the box moves, the person falls, and her potential energy becomes kinetic energy. As she falls, her kinetic energy increases and her potential energy decreases until she reaches the floor. There, her potential energy is zero because she cannot fall any further. (Her kinetic energy changes to other types of energy when she strikes the floor.)

Kinetic energy is the energy associated with moving objects. Potential energy is the energy stored in an object.

Potential energy is defined by the relative position of the object. The woman on the box would have more potential energy if the box was tall because she would be farther from the floor; she'd have less potential energy if she was standing on a shorter box. In this analogy, potential (not potential energy) is defined only by the height of the box, not by the size of the person standing on the box.

In electronics, the electrical potential energy is conceptually the same. If two charges are separated by a distance, there is the potential for their energy to be turned into kinetic energy. For example, two opposite charges at a distance r that start at rest will be pulled together and have kinetic energy. Also, two similar charges (both positive or both negative) that start at rest at a distance r will move away and gain kinetic energy.

The ELECTRICAL POTENTIAL is defined as the electrical potential energy per unit charge. A higher electrical potential at a location means that a charge placed at that location has a higher potential energy. The potential difference is defined as the difference between the potentials at two separate locations. In electronics, the ELECTRIC POTENTIAL DIFFERENCE is called VOLTAGE and is given in volts, V.

It is important to remember that voltage is a relative measurement. If a measurement of voltage is relative to zero potential, for example, the reading may be 1,000 V at point A. If the same measurement is made at point B, the reading may be 1,001 V. The potential difference, or voltage, between points A and B is only 1 V. Therefore, a charged particle moving from A to B would have much less kinetic energy than a charged particle moving from A to zero potential (a difference of 1,000 V).

An important concept to consider is called the ELECTROMOTIVE FORCE, or EMF. EMF is also measured in volts. If the terminals of a AAA battery (1.5 V) are connected with a conducting copper wire, the electrons in the wire will move from the negative terminal to the positive terminal through the wire. (The electric field goes from the positive to the negative terminal through the wire, and the negatively charged electrons move opposite to the electric field.)

But why do the electrons flow through the wire and not directly through the battery itself? The field inside the battery will oppose the flow of electrons in the wire, so how does this work? The battery has a chemical process that moves the electrons in the opposite direction of the field (they move from the positive to negative terminals, not vice versa). This chemical process provides the EMF that drives the electrons through the wire (a simple circuit). EMF can be provided by photovoltaic cells (solar power), batteries (chemical processes), and generators (mechanical processes). As shown later in this chapter, the EMF in generators is created by a changing magnetic field.

Example

What is the source of the electromotive force in a battery?

(A) changing magnetic field

(B) mechanical movement

(C) chemical processes

(D) A battery does not supply an electromotive force.

Answers:

(A) is incorrect. Generators (not batteries) supply an electromotive force through a changing magnetic field.

(B) is incorrect. Generators (not batteries) supply an electromotive force by converting mechanical movement into electricity.

(C) is correct. A battery contains chemicals that produce an electromotive force through chemical reactions.

(D) is incorrect. All power supplies supply an electromotive force.

CIRCUITS

Circuit Basics

An electronic CIRCUIT is made up of conducting wires that connect circuit elements, such as resistors, capacitors, and inductors. To operate, an electric circuit requires a source of power. Some common circuit symbols are shown in Figure 6.2.

An important concept for circuits is GROUND. This is when the circuit is connected to the ground, or earth, which is ideally where charge of any amount can flow. Many buildings literally have a wire that goes into the earth outside as their ground. Ground is at zero potential.

There are many types of VOLTAGE SOURCES. The most common is the power outlet in our homes and businesses, and it provides V_{rms} = 120 V at 60Hz AC (the voltage goes from positive to negative to positive again at 60 times per second). Common DC sources include 9 V AA, AAA, C, and D batteries as well as batteries for our automobiles, smartphones, tablets, and laptops. These sources maintain a constant voltage. All voltage sources have an internal resistance, which is often assumed to be zero. However, this internal resistance can lead to actual voltage values that are less than expected. For example, a 1.5 V AAA battery may have a voltage measured at 1.3 V while connected to a device.

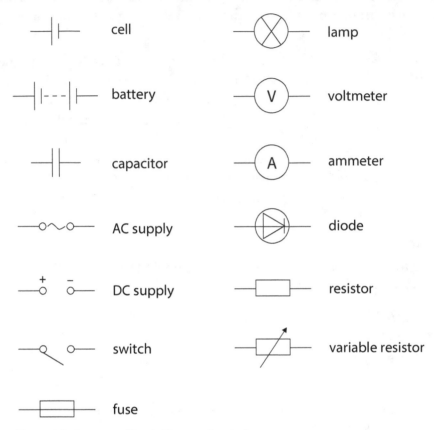

Figure 6.2. Common Circuit Element Symbols

The electrical **LOAD** in a circuit consists of everything except for the power supply. The load is effectively the part of the circuit that uses power and performs a function. As shown later in this chapter, a complicated load circuit can often be reduced to a simpler, but equivalent, circuit. An example circuit with a power supply, an internal resistance, and a load resistance is shown in Figure 6.3.

A common circuit element is a **SWITCH**. It can either be an actual lever moved to connect or disconnect two wires, or it can be automated electronically. When the switch is open, the circuit is an open circuit, and current will not flow through it. When the switch is closed, the circuit is a closed circuit, allowing current to flow.

A **FUSE** is a device that breaks the circuit (creates an open circuit) when too much current is flowing through it. At high currents, the heat caused by the power dissipated in the material will vaporize the material. Fuses can only be used once, and it is often easy to see when fuses have blown (the thin wire disappears).

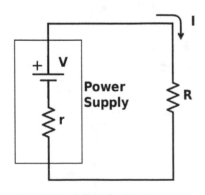

Figure 6.3. A Simple Circuit

In homes, 10A and 20A to 40A fuses are common. A CIRCUIT BREAKER serves the same function as a fuse; however, it is a switch that is opened at high current and can be reused. It is common to have to manually reset the circuit breaker switch in homes.

Examples

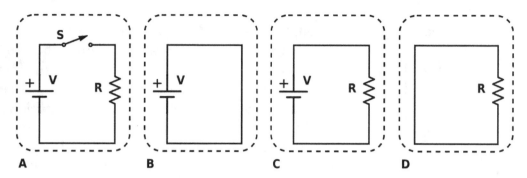

1. Which circuit in the figure above shows a closed circuit with a power source and a load?

   (A) A

   (B) B

   (C) C

   (D) D

   Answers:

   (A) is incorrect. The circuit is not closed.

   (B) is incorrect. There is no load on the power supply in this circuit.

   (C) is correct. This circuit contains a power supply and a load.

   (D) is incorrect. This circuit has no power source.

2. Which electrical component would best turn a computer on and off?

   (A) switch

   (B) fuse

   (C) circuit breaker

   (D) resistor

   Answers:

   (A) is correct. A switch would allow power to flow through the circuit when the computer is on, and it would not allow power to flow when it is off.

   (B) is incorrect. A fuse is used to protect a circuit, and it breaks when too much current is applied.

   (C) is incorrect. A circuit breaker is used to protect a circuit, and it flips a switch when too much current is applied.

   (D) is incorrect. A resistor does not typically change its properties and therefore cannot be used to turn a computer on and off.

Ohm's Law

OHM'S LAW is perhaps the most commonly used equation in electronics. When a voltage is applied across a resistive circuit element, the electrons in that material begin to move in the opposite direction of the electric field created. This creates a flow of charge and therefore a current flow. Remember that current is positive in the opposite direction of the flow of electrons.

The voltage from the power supply provides the energy to move the charges to create current, but the material limits the amount of current that can flow. This limitation is represented as the material's resistance. Through experimentation, current flow was found to be directly proportional to the voltage applied. This is understandable, as a stronger field should lead to more charge movement. Current flow was also found to be inversely proportional to the resistance of the material. Again, this is understandable, as less resistance from the material should allow more charge flow. Writing this mathematically gives Ohm's law:

> ⚠️ When two values are directly proportional, they increase or decrease at the same time. When two values are indirectly proportional, one goes up when the other goes down (and vice versa).

Where V is the voltage across the resistive element, I is the current through the element, and R is the element's resistance.

Example

What is the current flowing through a 100 kΩ resistor when a voltage of 2 V is applied across it?

(A) 20 μA

(B) 200 mA

(C) 20 A

(D) 200 kA

Answers:

(A) is correct.

$V - IR$	Identify the appropriate equation.
$I = \frac{V}{R}$ $I + \frac{2V}{100k\Omega} = 0.00002A = \textbf{20 μA}$	Rewrite equation in terms of I, plug in values, and solve for the current.

Power

POWER is defined as the energy per unit of time (joules per second) and is measured in watts, W. Power is described by the equation:

$$P = \frac{\text{energy}}{\text{time}} = VI$$

Where V is the voltage and I is the current through a circuit.

> Power companies sell electric energy in units of kilowatt hours (kWh). 1 kWh = 3.6 × 10⁶ J.

Using Ohm's law to replace V and I in the above equation, the equation for power can be written as:

$$P = VI = I^2R = \frac{V^2}{R}$$

Where R is the resistance.

As charges move through a material, they collide with other charges and nuclei, which leads to heat. Therefore, the majority of electrical power used is converted into heat (except for an electrical motor, where electrical power is turned into mechanical power). This is why electronics get hot during use.

Example

What is the power dissipated in a 1 kΩ resistor when a voltage of 350 V is applied across it?

(A) 350 μW

(B) 0.35 W

(C) 122.5 W

(D) 350 kW

Answers:

(C) is correct.

$P = \dfrac{V^2}{R}$	Identify the appropriate equation.
$P = \dfrac{(350V)^2}{1k\,\Omega} = 122.5W$	Plug in values and solve for power.

Series Circuits

When elements are in a **SERIES CIRCUIT**, the current flows through the elements along a single path. The current through elements in series will always be constant, and the total voltage for the resistors can be found by adding the voltage at each individual resistor.

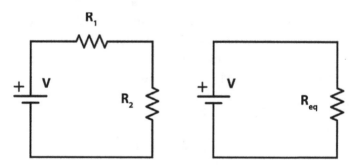

Figure 6.4. A Simple Series Circuit and its Equivalent

The **EQUIVALENT RESISTANCE** of the circuit, which models a complicated circuit with many resistors as a single resistor, is found by adding the resistance of each resistor. This equivalent resistance can then be used to find the power for the circuit.

Table 6.2. Series Circuits

Current	$I_1 = I_2 = I_3 = \ldots = I_n$
Voltage	$V_t = V_1 + V_2 + V_3 + \ldots + V_n$
Resistance	$R_{eq} = R_1 + R_2 + R_3 + \ldots + R_n$

Example

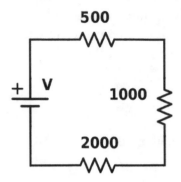

Find the equivalent resistance for the circuit in the figure above.

(A) 500 Ω

(B) 1.5 kΩ

(C) 2.5 kΩ

(D) 3.5 kΩ

Answer:

(D) is correct.

$R_{eq} = R_1 + R_2 + R_3$	Identify the appropriate equation.
$R_{eq} = 500 \, \Omega + 1 \, k\Omega + 2 \, k\Omega = 3{,}500 \, \Omega = \textbf{3.5 k}\boldsymbol{\Omega}$	Plug in values and solve for equivalent resistance.

Parallel Circuits

When elements are in a **PARALLEL CIRCUIT**, current may flow through multiple paths. For this type of circuit, the voltage across each element is constant, and the current for the circuit is found by adding the current passing through each resistor. Because electricity can flow through multiple paths (meaning it passes through each resistor) the equivalent resistance of the circuit will decrease as resistors are added.

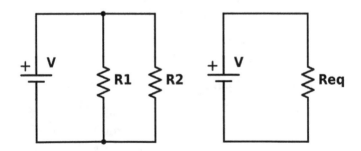

Figure 6.5. A Simple Parallel Circuit and its Equivalent

Table 6.3. Parallel Circuits

Current	$I_t = I_1 + I_2 + I_3 + \ldots + I_n$
Voltage	$V_1 = V_2 = V_3 = \ldots = V_n$
Resistance	$\dfrac{1}{R_{eq}} = \dfrac{1}{R_1} + \dfrac{1}{R_2} + \ldots + \dfrac{1}{R_N}$

Example

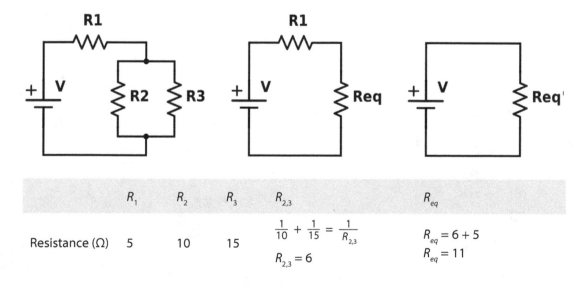

Find the equivalent resistance for the circuit in the figure above.

(A) 285.7 Ω

(B) 571.4 Ω

(C) 1.45 kΩ

(D) 3.5 kΩ

Answer:

(A) is correct.

$\dfrac{1}{R_{eq}} = \dfrac{1}{R_1} + \dfrac{1}{R_2} + \dfrac{1}{R_3}$	Identify the appropriate equation.
$\dfrac{1}{R_{eq}} = \dfrac{1}{500\,\Omega} + \dfrac{1}{1\,k\Omega} + \dfrac{1}{2\,k\Omega} = 0.0035\dfrac{1}{\Omega}$ $R_{eq} = \mathbf{285.7\ \Omega}$	Plug in values to solve for equivalent resistance.

Complex Circuits

Series and parallel circuits can be combined to make more complex circuits. To determine the properties of these circuits, they must be broken down into individual series and parallel circuits that can be used to find the properties of each resistor or the overall circuit.

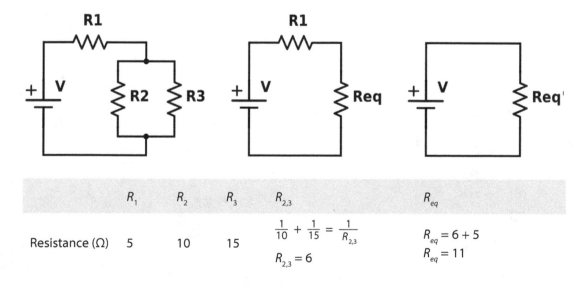

	R_1	R_2	R_3	$R_{2,3}$		R_{eq}
Resistance (Ω)	5	10	15	$\dfrac{1}{10} + \dfrac{1}{15} = \dfrac{1}{R_{2,3}}$ $R_{2,3} = 6$		$R_{eq} = 6 + 5$ $R_{eq} = 11$

Figure 6.6A. A Complex Circuit and its Equivalent

In Figure 6.6, resistors R_2 and R_3 are in parallel, and both are wired in series with resistor R_1. To find the equivalent resistance of the circuit, find $R_{2,3}$ for R_2 and R_3 using the rules for parallel circuits. $R_{2,3}$ and R_1 are now in series, so the equivalent resistance of the entire circuit can be found using the rules for series circuits, as shown below.

In the next example, resistor R_1 is in parallel with two resistors in series, R_2 and R_3. Again, the trick to finding the R_{eq} for this circuit is to work in steps. Using the equation for R_{eq} for series resistors, first reduce R_2 and R_3 to an equivalent resistance $R_{2,3}$. Now, R_1 and $R_{2,3}$ are in parallel, so use the rules for parallel circuits to find the equivalent resistance for the circuit.

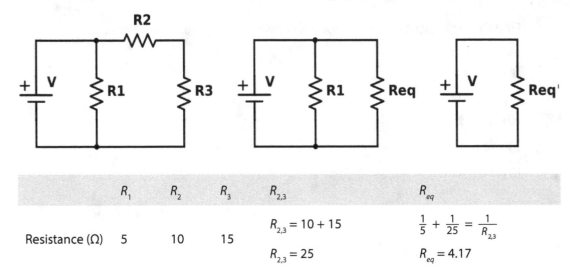

	R_1	R_2	R_3	$R_{2,3}$	R_{eq}
Resistance (Ω)	5	10	15	$R_{2,3} = 10 + 15$ $R_{2,3} = 25$	$\frac{1}{5} + \frac{1}{25} = \frac{1}{R_{2,3}}$ $R_{eq} = 4.17$

Figure 6.6B. A Complex Circuit and its Equivalent

Example

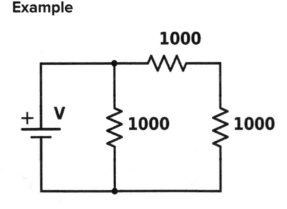

Find the equivalent resistance for the circuit in the figure above.

(A) 0.7 kΩ

(B) 1.5 kΩ

(C) 3.1 kΩ

(D) 4.1 kΩ

Answer:

(B) is correct.

$\dfrac{1}{R_{eq}} = \dfrac{1}{R_1} + \dfrac{1}{R_2} + \dfrac{1}{R_3}$ $R_{eq} = R_1 + R_2$	Identify the appropriate equations.
$\dfrac{1}{R_{eq}} = \dfrac{1}{1\ k\Omega} + \dfrac{1}{1\ k\Omega} = 0.0021\,\dfrac{1}{\Omega}$ $R_{eq} = 500\ \Omega$	First, find the equivalent resistance of the parallel resistors.
$R'_{eq} = R + R_{eq} = 1\ k\Omega + 500\ \Omega = \textbf{1.5 k}\boldsymbol{\Omega}$	Next, use that equivalent resistance in series with the last resistor to find the overall equivalent resistance.

Electrical Measurements

The previous sections discussed resistance, voltage, and current, all of which can all be measured with a device called a **MULTIMETER**.

Electrical current is measured using a device called an **AMMETER**. An ammeter must be placed in series with the circuit element to accurately measure the current. An ammeter should have approximately zero internal resistance. Conceptually, the current going through the element also must be going through the ammeter.

Electric voltage is measured using a device called a **VOLTMETER**. A voltmeter must be placed in parallel to the circuit element to correctly measure the element's voltage. A voltmeter should have infinite resistance (an open circuit) so no current will flow through it. Because no current moves through the detector, a voltmeter can measure the voltage across the element without changing the circuit.

Resistance is measured using a device called an **OHMMETER**. An ohmmeter will either provide a voltage across an element and read the current that flows through it, or it will provide a current through an element and read the voltage across it. In either case, the resistance is calculated using Ohm's law.

Example

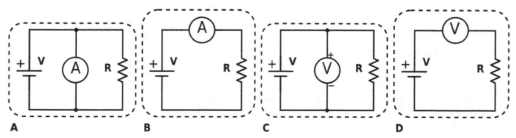

A   B   C   D

Which two diagrams in the figure above show the correct usage of an ammeter and a voltmeter to read the current through and voltage across the resistor shown?

(A) A, C

(B) B, C

(C) A, D

(D) B, D

ELECTRICAL SYSTEM COMPONENTS

Wire

A wire is a length of conducting material that carries current in a circuit. As expected, the choice of conductor (metal) for wire depends a great deal on the application. Oxidation (rust), weight, flexibility, conductivity, and cost concerns help determine the wire material. Copper is the most common material used for wires, and aluminum is also commonly used.

A **SOLID-CORE** wire is a solid strip of metal and therefore more rigid. It also has a lower risk of oxidation. A **STRANDED WIRE** is made from a bunch of small strands of wire (similar to a rope) and is more flexible. In addition, stranded wire can carry more current at higher frequencies.

Because of cost concerns all the copper wires need to be replaced with aluminum wire in a commercial product. Aluminum has a lower conductivity than copper, but the wires have to carry the same maximum current. Would the aluminum wire have a larger or smaller gauge number than the copper wires?

WIRE GAUGE is the size of the wire in terms of diameter or cross-section. There is no simple rule to remember the values, and a tool is usually used to determine the gauge. For example, a 10 gauge wire has a diameter of 0.102 inches, and a 20 gauge wire has a diameter of 0.032 inches.

The wire gauge is directly related to the relative amount of current a wire can carry. For smaller wires, a current that is too high can cause enough heat to melt or vaporize the wire. Larger gauge wires have a larger current range but may be too large, heavy, or expensive to use. It is important to choose the correct gauge, material, and type of wire for the application.

Example

How is wire gauge measured?

(A) with a specifically designed tool that measures the diameter of the wire

(B) The resistance of the wire is measured to give the gauge.

(C) with an ohmmeter

(D) The wire is bent to determine its flexibility.

Answers:

(A) is correct. The tool will give the correct gauge value for the wire.

(B) is incorrect. The resistance of the wire is not the gauge.

(C) is incorrect. An ohmmeter measures the resistance.

(D) Incorrect. The flexibility of the wire is not the wire gauge.

Resistors

Material resistivity, discussed previously, determines the ability to move charge through a wire as well as the amount of power dissipated (as heat). A RESISTOR is a circuit element that is constructed to have a known resistance and a maximum current level. A simple way to make a resistor is to construct a very long wire with reasonably high resistivity metal. It can be wrapped around a ceramic rod to minimize space and then covered with plastic as packaging. (The wire is wrapped in a manner that minimizes inductance, which is explained later in this text.)

A FIXED RESISTOR has a set resistance value, labeled with standard color codes. These codes are shown in Figure 6.8. Because resistors dissipate power as heat, too much current moving through them can lead to permanent damage. Therefore, the resistor must be able to handle the current that will flow through it.

A VARIABLE RESISTOR has a resistance value that can change and is usually constructed with a manual adjustment knob (many electronic knobs, like stereo volume, are variable resistors). Conceptually, imagine a wire sliding along a resistor of a certain length. As the wire moves, the current flowing through the circuit sees less or more of the resistor, therefore the resistance changes.

Resistors are often used to alter the voltage values seen by other circuit elements (review the section on series circuits to see how to do this). In addition, resistors can be used with capacitors and inductors (both discussed later) and alter the time-dependent behavior of a circuit. Perhaps the most obvious application is as a heating element: an electric stove top, space heater, and oven heating element are all basically resistors.

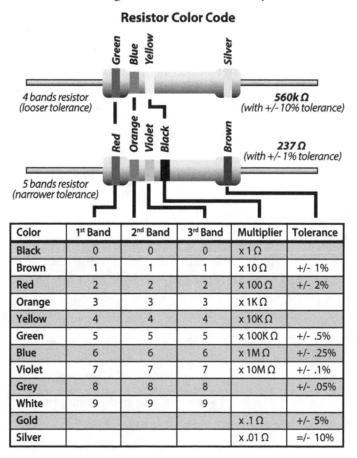

Resistor Color Code

Color	1st Band	2nd Band	3rd Band	Multiplier	Tolerance
Black	0	0	0	x 1 Ω	
Brown	1	1	1	x 10 Ω	+/- 1%
Red	2	2	2	x 100 Ω	+/- 2%
Orange	3	3	3	x 1K Ω	
Yellow	4	4	4	x 10K Ω	
Green	5	5	5	x 100K Ω	+/- .5%
Blue	6	6	6	x 1M Ω	+/- .25%
Violet	7	7	7	x 10M Ω	+/- .1%
Grey	8	8	8		+/- .05%
White	9	9	9		
Gold				x .1 Ω	+/- 5%
Silver				x .01 Ω	=/- 10%

Figure 6.7. Resistor Color Codes

Example

Example

Why would a variable resistor be used instead of a fixed resistor?

(A) The fixed resistor cannot have a voltage across it.

(B) A variable resistor stops current flow.

(C) The voltage across or the current through the variable resistor needs to change.

(D) A fixed resistor can only be used once.

Answers:

(A) is incorrect. A resistors will have a voltage if a current is passing through it.

(B) is incorrect. A resistor does not stop current flow.

(C) is correct. A variable resistor is used to change the voltage across or current through the resistor.

(D) is incorrect. Resistors can be used repeatedly.

Fuses and Circuit Breakers

Both FUSES and CIRCUIT BREAKERS are used to protect an electrical circuit from too much current.

A fuse, in its simplest form, is a device made from a thin wire (or a thin section of metal). If there is a power surge, or too much current flows through, the heat created in the material will literally melt or vaporize it and therefore break the circuit. When comparing a burnt fuse to a new fuse, it is readily apparent that the wire or thin film has broken or even disappeared.

The key difference between a CIRCUIT BREAKER and a fuse is that a circuit breaker can be reused. The operation of a breaker is beyond the scope of this text, but it also responds when there is too much current flowing through it. Conceptually, a large current will release a switch that breaks the circuit. The circuit will remain open until the switch is flipped back and allows current to flow.

A SHORT CIRCUIT (or SHORT) is when current flows from one point of the circuit to another, or to ground, when it is not supposed to. For example, if dust, water, or another material makes a connection between the power supply cables, a huge amount of current will start to flow and will most likely cause damage to the device or the wires. Fuses and circuit breakers protect the equipment from this kind of event.

Many circuits are connected to a battery, where the battery terminals set the voltage difference that drives the circuit. It is also common to construct circuits in which the power supply voltage is determined relative to ground. For example, a power outlet in a building will have a RMW voltage of 120 V, relative to ground. To use the full voltage, the device must be connected to earth. If not, the outlet could be a source of electrical noise and cause poor operation of the device.

Example

What is the primary difference between a fuse and a circuit breaker?

(A) A fuse will amplify a voltage; a circuit breaker amplifies current.

(B) They both protect circuits from too much power, so there is no difference.

(C) A circuit breaker can be used repeatedly. A fuse is used only once.

(D) A circuit breaker is another name for a fuse made of copper.

Capacitors

A CAPACITOR is an energy storage element, where the energy is stored in the capacitor's electric field. The simplest capacitor design is made from two relatively large parallel conducting plates separated by a thin insulator, usually plastic. Each plate will be connected to a circuit with a wire.

If a voltage is applied across a capacitor, charges will build up on each plate until the voltage across the capacitor matches the applied voltage. If the voltage supply is removed (and the capacitor is not connected to anything else), the capacitor will hold the charge, and therefore the voltage. This is how it stores energy. Once it is connected to a circuit manually or with a switch, the charge stored on the capacitor will drain and power the circuit.

CAPACITANCE is a measure of the ability of a capacitor to hold charge, has units of farads, F, and is given by:

$$C = \frac{Q}{V}$$

Where C is the capacitance, Q is the charge on the plates (+Q is on one, –Q is on the other), and V is the voltage across the capacitor.

An important concept to consider is the RC circuit, as shown in Figure 6.9. When a resistor is in a circuit with a capacitor (remember all wires and devices have some resistance), a charging time and a decay time are given by the RC time constant, τ = RC. This is a measure of the length of time it takes for a capacitor to charge or discharge and can be seen as the limit to a circuit turning on or off. It is especially important in digital circuits, like computers, where switching between on or off determines the speed of the computer.

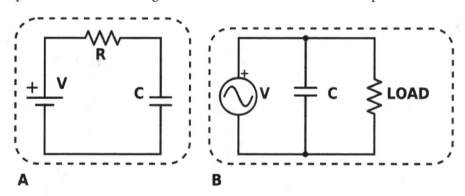

Figure 6.8. An RC Circuit; A High Frequency Filter

A capacitor that is fully charged or discharged is basically an open circuit (the insulator between the plates means that charge does not flow through it). Only immediately after a source is connected, or if the voltage across it is changed, does charge flow. For this reason, at low frequencies in AC circuits, a capacitor can be approximated as an open circuit, where current does not flow. At high frequencies (where the voltage is changing rapidly), the capacitor acts as if it were replaced by a wire.

A capacitor connected from the AC power supply to ground, like that shown in Figure 6.12, will work as a low-frequency filter (only a low-frequency AC signal will reach the circuit). Low frequencies will see a circuit as if the capacitor were not there are at all, and high frequencies will see a wire that directs the current to ground.

Capacitors are also used in series and parallel circuits and can be reduced to an equivalent capacitance using the equations below.

$$\text{Series:} \quad \frac{1}{C_{eq}} = \frac{1}{C_1} + \frac{1}{C_2} + \ldots + \frac{1}{C_N}$$

$$\text{Parallel:} \quad C_{eq} = C_1 + C_2 + \ldots + C_N$$

Example

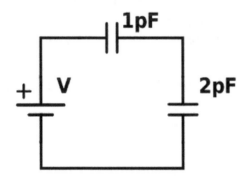

What is the equivalent capacitance for the circuit shown in the figure above?

(A) 0.33 pF

(B) 0.67 pF

(C) 1 pF

(D) 1.33 pF

Answer:

(B) is correct.

$\frac{1}{C_{eq}} = \frac{1}{C_1} + \frac{1}{C_2}$	Identify the appropriate equation.
$\frac{1}{C_{eq}} = \frac{1}{1\,pF} + \frac{1}{1\,pF} = 1.5 \times 10^{12}\frac{1}{F}$ $\frac{1}{C_{eq}} = 0.67 \times 10^{-12}F = 0.67\ pF$	Plug in the values to solve for equivalent capacitance.

Diodes

DIODES are made from semiconductors. As mentioned previously, a semiconductor is an insulator whose conduction properties can be altered by DOPING the material with other elements. Common semiconductors are made of silicon and gallium arsenide.

There are two outcomes from doping a semiconductor. The material can be made **N-TYPE**, where the dopants donate electrons to the conduction band. Common dopant materials are phosphorous and arsenic. In N-type semiconductors, electrons are the dominant charge carrier. The material can also be made **P-TYPE**, where electrons are taken away (accepted) from the valence band. Common dopant materials are selenium and tellurium. In P-type semiconductors, holes are the dominant charge carrier.

A **DIODE** is a semiconductor device made from connected N- and P-type regions. The excess electrons and holes in the two regions drift toward each other and create a depletion region at

> Most electronic symbols include information about the element's operation. The diode symbol has an arrow that shows the direction that current will flow. Current will not flow in the opposite direction.

the P- and N-interface. The depletion region is effectively a built-in voltage that is commonly around 0.5 V. This region has no excess charge carriers; therefore, current cannot flow through it.

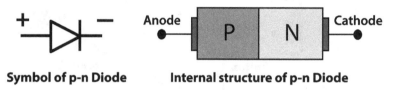

Symbol of p-n Diode   **Internal structure of p-n Diode**

Figure 6.9. The Structure of a Diode

However, a diode in **FORWARD-BIAS** configuration has a voltage applied that will counteract the built-in voltage and will allow current to flow. **REVERSE-BIAS** configuration has an applied voltage that adds to the built-in voltage and keeps the diode from conducting current. In this way, a diode will restrict current flow to only one direction. The **ANODE** is the contact where current enters the diode, and the **CATHODE** is the contact where current leaves the diode.

Example

How does current flow through a diode?

(A) The diode never allows current to flow.

(B) The diode always allows current to flow, but if too much is applied, it will shut off.

(C) The diode always allows current to flow, unless the correct voltage is applied.

(D) The diode only allows current to flow in one direction, and only if the correct voltage is applied.

Answers:

(A) is incorrect. A diode allows current to flow when the correct voltage is applied.

(B) is incorrect. A diode only allows current to flow in one direction and only when the correct voltage is applied.

(C) is incorrect. A diode only allows current to flow in one direction and only when the correct voltage is applied.

(D) is correct. A diode allows current to flow in one direction when the correct voltage is applied.

Transistors

TRANSISTORS have many configurations and designs and are the fundamental technology behind computer chips. In the most basic configuration discussed here, a transistor can be constructed with three doped regions in contact, as shown in Figure 6.11. These two configuration are known as a **NPN** or **PNP** TRANSISTORS.

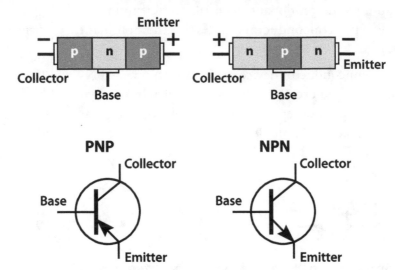

Figure 6.10. The Structure of PNP and NPN Transistors

A transistor has three connectors: the **COLLECTOR**, the **EMITTER**, and the **BASE**. Other types of transistors (field-effect transistors are the most common) may have the connections labeled as source (collector), drain (emitter), and gate (base).

At each N- and P-junction, there is a depletion region exactly as in a diode. Although the exact details are beyond the scope of this text, a transistor of this type operates as a switch. By changing the voltage drop between the emitter or collector and the base (depending on the type of transistor), the amount of current that flows between the collector and emitter can be controlled. To put it more simply, the voltage applied to the base can turn the current flow on or off, exactly like a switch.

Diodes and transistors, and other electrical devices that are made from semiconductor materials, are called **SOLID-STATE DEVICES**.

Example

What is a common application of transistor technology?

(A) light switch

(B) electrical generator

(C) computer chip

(D) oven heating element

Answers:

(A) is incorrect. A light switch is manually flipped and does not need a transistor.

(B) is incorrect. An electrical generator does not need transistor technology.

(C) is correct. A computer chip uses transistor technology.

(D) is incorrect. An oven heating element is essentially a resistor.

Rectifiers and Inverters

A **RECTIFIER** converts an AC input into a DC output. This circuit is commonly seen in the power bricks for laptops and other digital devices, usually after the voltage has been lowered with a transformer (discussed later in this text). The circuit includes diodes, capacitors, and resistors and is shown in Figure 6.12. The input voltage is sinusoidal, and the diodes work to keep the sign of the signal positive. Therefore, either a positive or negative input voltage will be positive on the output. The capacitors are charged slowly and release their charge slowly (via the RC time constant), which maintains a relatively stable output signal.

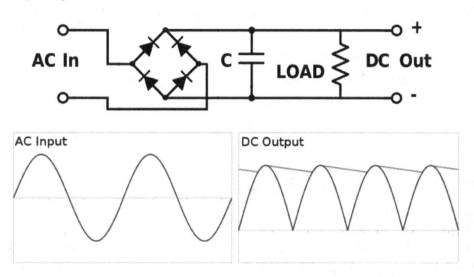

Figure 6.11. A Basic Rectifier Circuit

An **INVERTER** converts a DC input into an AC output. A common application is in battery backups for computer systems. Batteries supply DC power, while standard computers require an AC supply. An inverter circuit is usually used before a transformer to increase the voltage output. An example inverter circuit is shown in Figure 6.13. The two transformers act as a switch that flips the signal back and forth. The output will be a square wave, as shown, and other circuit elements can be added to approximate a sinusoidal wave output.

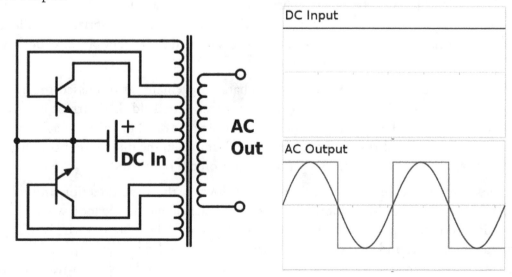

Figure 6.12. A Basic Inverter Circuit

Example

A car needs a DC power supply to recharge the car battery, and the alternator connected to the engine supplies AC power. What electric circuit is used to convert the AC power to DC to recharge the battery?

(A) inverter

(B) alternator

(C) rectifier

(D) transformer

Answers:

(A) is incorrect. An inverter converts DC to AC.

(B) is incorrect. An alternator converts mechanical movement into AC power.

(C) is correct. A rectifier converts AC power into DC power.

(D) is incorrect. A transformer converts an input voltage into a different output voltage.

MAGNETISM AND ELECTRICITY

Basics of Magnetism

MAGNETS are familiar items and perhaps need no introduction. Magnets have north and south poles, and a simple test with a refrigerator magnet will show that like poles repel each other and opposite poles attract. The magnetic field always points from the north pole to the south pole.

The magnetic field does not end or begin; it is always a complete loop. Stated in another way, there is no magnetic "charge" (called a magnetic monopole), so a north or south pole by itself does not exist.

Magnetic materials (magnets) and magnetic fields are created by moving charges. All materials have moving charges, either from electron orbits in an atom or a molecule or from an intrinsic spin of an electron (imagine the electron as a tiny ball spinning on an axis). In a magnet, the magnetic fields from all of these moving charges are aligned and combine to create a large magnetic field. A nonmagnetic material will still have moving charges, but the fields created are in random directions and will cancel each other out.

The north pole of a compass will point north. Therefore, the earth's geographic North Pole is actually the magnetic south pole.

Current is a measure of charge flow, or charge movement, as discussed previously. Therefore, it can be said that current will create a magnetic field. If a current is moving along a straight wire, the right-hand-rule will determine the direction of the magnetic field created. The right-hand-rule is as follows: if the thumb is in the direction of the current, the magnetic field is in the direction of the fingers on the right hand.

One example is a current loop. The current flows in the same direction around the loop, and the right-hand-rule shows that the magnetic field within the loop will be in the same direction and have a contribution from each point in the loop. If a wire is wrapped with many loops around an object (a coil), the contribution from each loop will combine to create a strong magnetic field. Wire is often wrapped around a piece of iron or other magnetic material to further amplify the created magnetic field. This device is a called a **SOLENOID** and is shown in Figure 6.14. Solenoids are commonly used in electronics.

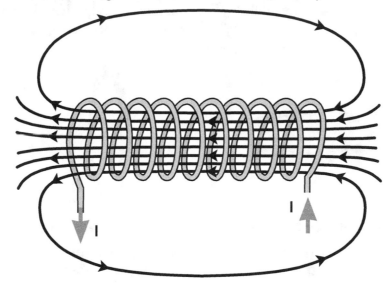

Figure 6.13. A Solenoid

Interestingly, it was discovered that not only does current flowing through a loop create a magnetic field, but a changing magnetic field within a wire loop can create a current. For instance, when current flows through wire, there must be an electric field that will supply a force to move the charges. (As a reminder, current is in the direction of positive charge flow, so the electric field and the current are in the same direction). In circuits previously discussed, the electric field in the wire is created by applying a power source that creates a voltage across the circuit.

A simple electromagnet can be made by wrapping a wire around a nail and connecting the wire to a battery.

However, a simple loop of wire with no power source will in fact have a current flow if the magnetic field within the loop changes. What is driving the flow of charge? If current is flowing, then there must be an electric field along the loop! From experiments like this, it was determined that the changing magnetic field within the loop creates an electric field along the loop that drives the current. Therefore, the changing magnetic field creates an EMF that moves the charges in the loop.

The direction of induced current flow in a loop can be remembered with a simple rule: the current in a loop will flow in the direction that will maintain the strength of the magnetic field within the loop. If the magnetic field inside the loop is increasing, a current will be induced that creates a magnetic field in the opposite direction, which will decrease the field. Similarly, if the magnetic field is decreasing in the loop, a current will be induced that adds to, or increases, the field.

This induced current is very important in electronics and especially for devices such as generators (discussed later in the text). There are two conceptual ways to induce current by changing the magnetic field. The first is to hold the loop of wire stationary (or many loops like in a solenoid) and to increase or decrease the strength of the magnetic field. This can be as simple as moving a magnet closer to and farther from a wire loop. The second is to have a stationary magnet and a moving coil of wire. This scenario is more

Light is made up of electric and magnetic fields that create each other as the wave moves, which is why light is called an electromagnetic wave.

common because magnets are usually much heavier than coils of wire. In this case, a loop of wire is usually rotated in a magnetic field. This is shown in Figure 6.15. If the magnetic field is pointing in a direction parallel to the center of the loop, then the strength of the field inside the loop is at a maximum. When the loop is perpendicular to the center of the loop, then the strength of the field is at a minimum.

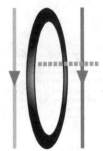

Parallel to center of circle

Maximum magnetic field strength

Perpendicular to center of circle

Minimum magnetic field strength

Figure 6.14. Magnetic Field Strength Inside a Wire Loop as the Loop Rotates in the Field

It is worth revisiting the capacitor. Because a capacitor is two conducting plates separated by an insulator, current (charge) never actually flows through the device. As the charge is building up on the plates, the electric field between the plates is changing, which creates a measurable magnetic field around the device. In fact, the magnetic field that is measured is exactly what would be measured if a current was flowing through the insulating material. In summary of this effect and this section, changing electric fields will create magnetic fields, and changing magnetic fields will create electric fields.

Examples

1. Which of the following will generate a magnetic field?

(A) a cucumber

(B) an electric alarm clock

(C) a mechanical alarm clock

(D) a chair

Answers:

(A) is incorrect. A cucumber does not create a magnetic field.

(B) is correct. Any electric circuit will have current flowing through it, and current creates a magnetic field.

(C) is incorrect. A mechanical alarm clock generally uses a wound spring for power and therefore has no magnets or current flow.

(D) is incorrect. A chair does not create a magnetic field.

2. If the north pole of a magnet is brought closer to the center of a wire loop, what direction will the current flow?

(A) The current will flow in the direction that opposes the change of the magnetic field.

(B) The current will flow in the direction that increases the change of the magnetic field.

(C) Current will not flow without a power supply.

(D) Current will not flow unless the magnet actually touches the wire.

Answers:

(A) is correct. Current will flow in the direction that opposes the change in magnetic field.

(B) is incorrect. Current will flow in the direction that opposes the change in magnetic field.

(C) is incorrect. In this case, the changing magnetic field induces an EMF that acts like a power supply to the wire.

(D) is incorrect. The magnet does not need to touch the wire to induce current.

Inductors and Transformers

An **INDUCTOR** is another energy storage device, but it stores its energy in the magnetic field (remember that the capacitor stores energy in the electric field). It is effectively a solenoid, and the coil of wire is usually readily seen.

The fundamental use of an inductor is to resist current change. If the current does change, the magnetic field within the inductor also changes. However, this change in magnetic field also leads to an induced current that resists the magnetic field change! Therefore, a change in current through an inductor will lead to a **SELF-INDUCED ELECTROMOTIVE FORCE** (EMF), which can be measured as a voltage across the inductor itself. This effect is called self-inductance, and the voltage is given by:

$$V_{ab} = L\frac{\Delta I}{\Delta t}$$

where V_{ab} is the voltage across the inductor, L is the inductance (in henrys, H), ΔI is the change in current, and Δt is the change in time.

This equation states that if the current is constant, then there is no voltage across the inductor. If the current is increasing through the inductor, then the self-induced EMF will move charges opposite to the current direction and create a voltage drop across the inductor. If current is decreasing through the inductor, the self-induced EMF will move charges in the same direction as the current and have a voltage increase. This is shown in Figure 10.16.

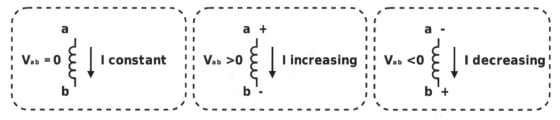

Figure 6.15. The Operation of an Inductor with Current Changes

Inductors are used in AC circuits primarily, as they only respond to changes in current. At low frequencies, the power source can be approximated as a DC source, and inductors can be approximated as a wire or short (there would be no voltage across the inductor, and it would not impact the rest of the circuit). At very high frequencies, the current change is so quick that the inductor can be approximated as an open circuit where current cannot flow through it.

A light will turn on immediately when the light switch is flipped. What would happen if an inductor was placed in the circuit?

If a solenoid is placed within a larger solenoid, their interaction leads to what is called mutual inductance. When current flows through the inner coil, a magnetic field is created that then induces a current in the outer coil. An EMF applied to the inner coil will induce an EMF in the outer coil, or vice versa. It is important to remember that induced current only works when current is changing, or in AC circuits.

A device called a TRANSFORMER uses this effect. An example transformer is shown in Figure 6.17. In this figure, there is an O-shaped iron core, with a loop of wire wrapped around the left side and another loop of wire wrapped around the right side. The iron core works to guide the magnetic field through both loops, and it increases the field itself. The loops either help create the field or have an induced current in response to the field.

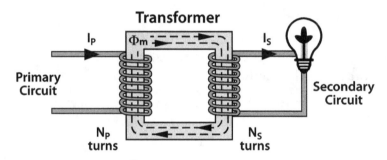

Figure 6.16. A Transformer

As discussed before, the magnetic field strength produced by a coil depends on the number of turns in that coil. In addition, the overall amount of current (or EMF) induced in a coil by a changing field also depends on the number of turns. In this way, a transformer can be designed to transform the voltage from a power supply to a lower or higher value simply by adjusting the number of turns in each coil. The equation is as follows:

$$\frac{V_{out}}{V_{input}} = \frac{N_{out}}{N_{input}}$$

Where V_{out} and V_{input} are the EMFs for the output and input, respectively. N_{out} and N_{input} are the number of turns in the output and input coils.

Example

If an inductor were connected in series with a light bulb, what would happen when the light switch is flipped?

(A) The inductor would have no effect.

(B) The light bulb would gradually turn on or off.

(C) The light bulb would stay off; it would never turn on.

(D) The light bulb would stay on; it would never turn off.

Motors and Generators

Electrical motors and generators are based on the principles explained in the previous section. An electric generator converts movement (mechanical power) into electrical power, while an electric motor converts electrical power into physical movement.

An AC generator is called an **ALTERNATOR**, which can be made in many different ways. A simple example is a stationary magnet (or electromagnet) that creates a constant magnetic field, and a coil of wire that is moved within the field. The stationary part of a generator or motor is called the **STATOR**, and the magnetic field is called the **STATOR FIELD**. The moving part is called the **ROTOR**, and the moving coil is called the **ARMATURE**. As the coil rotates, the strength and direction of the field through the coil changes, which results in a sinusoidal (AC) current through the coil.

Electric power can be created based on this basic core design. Hydroelectric power plants use water flowing over turbines to rotate the coil. Nuclear, coal, and natural gas power plants boil water into steam to turn turbines that rotate the coil. Automobile engines rotate the coil in the alternators in our cars.

One type of electric motor effectively works in reverse: an AC motor. Instead of using an outside force to rotate the coil, a current is instead sent through the coil. This current creates a magnetic field that reacts with the magnetic field from the stationary magnet and results in a rotational force (torque) on the coil (remember that like poles repel and opposite poles attract).

Another type of AC motor is called an **INDUCTION MOTOR**. In an induction motor, the armature is not connected to an external circuit. Instead, the stator consists of coils that can vary the magnetic field. This induces a current inside the armature, which creates a magnetic field that results in rotation. A **SYNCHRONOUS MOTOR** has the AC source current at the same frequency as the rotation.

There are also motors that run with DC sources. The stator is again either a permanent magnet or an electromagnet. And again, current is sent through the armature, which induces a magnetic field and therefore the torque that turns the motor. A DC motor, however, includes a **COMMUTATOR**, which will change the direction of the current (and the direction of the induced field in the armature) as it rotates.

Most DC motors use an electromagnet as the stator. There are three circuit configurations for a DC motor, where the stator and armature are configured as series, shunt, or compound motors. These are shown in Figure 6.18 on the following page.

The type of motor used depends on the application, especially the mechanical load that the motor is driving. A **SERIES MOTOR** (where the stator and armature coils are in series) is commonly used in applications that need large starting torques, like initially starting an electric train. A **SHUNT MOTOR** (where the stator and armature coils are in parallel) is used in applications where the rotation speed needs to be maintained with changing loads, like machine tools. A **COMPOUND MOTOR** is a combination of a series and a shunt motor. Therefore, it has both high starting torque and rotation speed regulation.

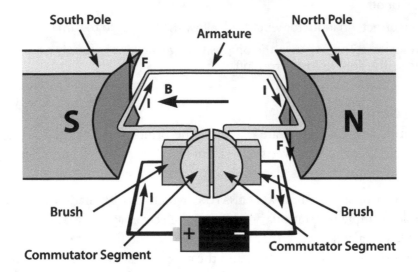

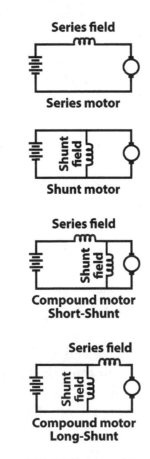

Figure 6.17. DC Motor and Configurations

A DC motor operated in reverse, where the armature is moved by external mechanical means to create current, is a DC generator, or **DYNAMO**. However, an AC generator is often used with a rectifier to produce DC power.

Example

What is one way to create a stator field?

(A) an electromagnet

(B) a permanent charge

(C) moving the stator

(D) There is no field from the stator.

Answers:

(A) is correct. An electromagnetic is a common way to create the stator magnetic field.

(B) is incorrect. A permanent charge will provide an electric field. The stator field is a magnetic field.

(C) is incorrect. The stator by definition does not move.

(D) is incorrect. The stator supplies a field that is critical to the operation of generators and motors.

7

AUTOMOTIVE INFORMATION

The Automotive Information section of the CAT-ASVAB includes eleven multiple-choice questions that cover the components and function of automotive systems, including the engine, chassis, and electrical systems. Test questions may include how an engine works, differences between engine components, proper engine maintenance, differences in how the vehicles moves, how electrical components monitor the vehicle, and proper safety precautions.

The paper-and-pencil ASVAB includes twenty-five multiple-choice questions on the combined Automotive and Shop Information section.

THE ENGINE

Internal Combustion Engines

Combustion is the process of burning an air-fuel mixture. In an **INTERNAL COMBUSTION ENGINE**, the ignition and combustion of the air-fuel mixture occurs within the engine's **COMBUSTION CHAMBER**. When this air-fuel mixture is burned, the mixture expands, creating a high-pressure gas that forces the piston's movement. Most engines used today are internal combustion engines and are used in automobiles, heavy machinery, generators, boats, airplanes, and commercial and recreational vehicles.

The main body of the engine is called the **ENGINE BLOCK,** which consists of a **CRANKCASE** and **CYLINDER**.

The cylinder is the main housing for the **PISTON**, which is connected to the crankshaft by a **CONNECTING ROD**. A **WRIST PIN** and retainers—circlips or snap rings—keep the piston mounted to the top of the connecting rod. As the crankshaft rotates, the piston will move in the cylinder.

The **CYLINDER HEAD** is mounted on top of the cylinder, and the **VALVE TRAIN** is located in the cylinder head. The main valve train components are **INTAKE VALVES**, **EXHAUST VALVES**, and a **CAMSHAFT**. The camshaft has an oval lobe—a cam—that rotates with the **CRANK-SHAFT**. In a four-stroke engine, the crankshaft rotates twice for every rotation of the camshaft. The camshaft and crankshaft may be connected by gears, chain, or belt. The motion of the camshaft causes other valve train components to function. When the oval lobe rotates, the intake and exhaust valves open and close during specific engine revolutions.

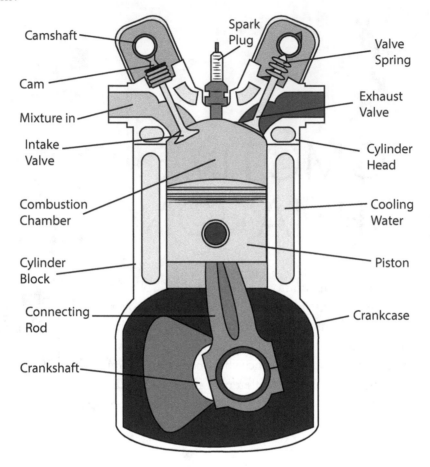

Figure 7.1. Engine

The cylinder is the main housing for the **PISTON**, which is connected to the crankshaft by a **CONNECTING ROD**. A **WRIST PIN** and retainers— circlips or snap rings—keep the piston mounted to the top of the connecting rod. As the crankshaft rotates, the piston moves in the cylinder.

The main body of the engine is called the **ENGINE BLOCK**. The engine block consists of a crankcase and cylinder.

The combustion process starts when an air-fuel mixture enters the **CYLINDER**. The air-fuel mixture is pressurized inside the cylinder by the momentum of the piston's movement. A timed spark causes this pressurized air-fuel mixture to burn inside the **COMBUSTION CHAMBER**.

Example

In which part of the engine does the piston move up and down?

(A) the engine block

(B) the cylinder head

(C) the cylinder

(D) the piston housing

Answers:

(A) is incorrect. The engine block is the crankcase and cylinder. The piston is located in the cylinder.

(B) is incorrect. The cylinder head contains the valve train components.

(C) is correct. The piston moves up and down in the cylinder.

(D) is incorrect. Piston housing is not the correct term.

The Four-Stroke Cycle

The first **FOUR-STROKE ENGINE** is credited to German engineer Nikolaus Otto, whose engine design is known as the **OTTO CYCLE**. That cycle process is the same in today's four-stroke engines.

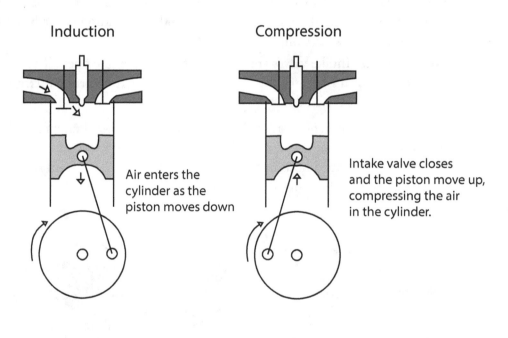

Induction — Air enters the cylinder as the piston moves down

Compression — Intake valve closes and the piston move up, compressing the air in the cylinder.

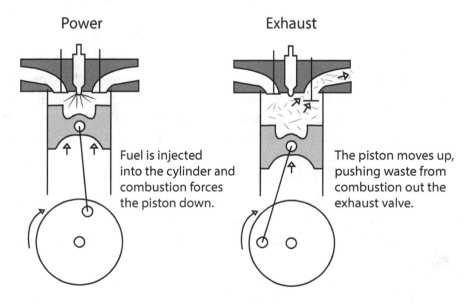

Power — Fuel is injected into the cylinder and combustion forces the piston down.

Exhaust — The piston moves up, pushing waste from combustion out the exhaust valve.

Figure 7.2. Four-Cycle Process

Top dead center (TDC) is when the piston is at the upper stroke, farthest from the crankshaft. Bottom dead center (BDC) is when the piston is at the bottom stroke, closest to the crankshaft. When describing the four-cycle process, the terms *stroke* and *cycle* may be interchanged.

A four-stroke cycle means that four strokes are required to complete a cycle. A four-stroke cycle has four distinct events:

1. **INTAKE STROKE:** Intake valves are open; exhaust valves are closed. When the intake valve is open, the air-fuel mixture enters the cylinder. The piston stroke is from top dead center (TDC) to bottom dead center (BDC).

2. **COMPRESSION STROKE:** All valves are closed. The piston stroke is from BDC to TDC. This stroke compresses the air-fuel mixture.

3. **POWER STROKE:** All valves are closed. During this stroke the compressed air-fuel mixture is ignited by heat, creating a rapidly expanding super-heated gas that forces the piston from TDC to BDC.

4. **EXHAUST STROKE:** Intake valves are closed; exhaust valves are open. The piston stroke is from BDC to TDC. During this stroke the burned mixture is discharged out of the cylinder.

Another internal combustion engine is the **WANKEL ROTARY ENGINE**, known simply as a rotary engine. Although the rotary engine is a different design, the principle is the same. A rotary engine has an oval-shaped housing with an oval-shaped cam. The cam rotates in a circular motion to complete the four-cycle process of intake, compression, power, and exhaust.

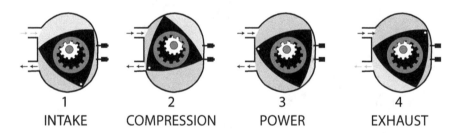

1	2	3	4
INTAKE	COMPRESSION	POWER	EXHAUST

Figure 7.3. Rotary Engine

Classifying Engines

Engine cylinders are laid out in different configurations. **INLINE** engines have two, three, four, or more cylinders side by side in a row. In **V-TYPE ENGINES,** two, four, or more cylinders are aligned in a *V*-shape. In **FLAT ENGINES** or **HORIZONTALLY OPPOSED ENGINES**, the cylinders are located on either side of the crankshaft. These engines are often called boxer engines because the pistons move in and out together horizontally rather than vertically, similar to the movements of boxers.

Engine cylinders have a specific **FIRING ORDER**. When there are multiple cylinders, there is a sequence of operation for the cylinders to fire. This sequence is controlled by a timed spark in a defined order. The firing order varies by engine and manufacturer.

🔒

In diesel engines the sequential firing order is determined by the fuel injection.

Engines in which the valve train and camshaft are located in the cylinder head are called **OVERHEAD VALVE** (OHV) or **OVERHEAD CAM** (OHC) engines. In some flat-head engines the valves are located next to the piston. In *V*-type engines and some inline engines, the camshaft is located in the block. As the camshaft rotates, the lobes operate lifters and pushrods.

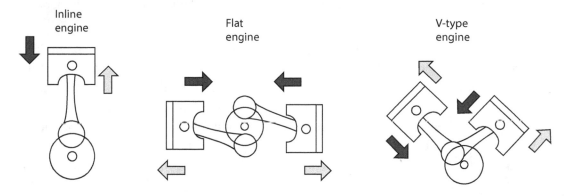

Figure 7.4. Types of Engines

As discussed previously, engines use valves in the cylinder head. There must be at least **TWO VALVES** per cylinder, one intake and one exhaust. The intake valve allows an air-fuel mixture to enter the cylinder and the exhaust valve allows the burned waste to exit the cylinder. A **FOUR-VALVE ENGINE** consists of two intake and two exhaust valves.

Example

In which type of engine are the valves located next to the piston?

(A) flat-head

(B) overhead valve

(C) overhead cam

(D) two-stroke

Answers:

(A) is correct. The valves in a flat-head engine are located next to the piston.

(B) is incorrect. The valves in an overhead-valve engine are located in the cylinder head, which is above the piston.

(C) is incorrect. The valves in an overhead-cam engine are located in the cylinder head. This is above the piston.

(D) is incorrect. Two-stroke engines do not use valves.

Cooling the Engine

Heat is produced during the combustion process. Some of the heat is used for the power stroke, but the remainder needs to be removed from the engine to avoid damaging internal parts. Two cooling systems that are typically used are **AIR-COOLED** and **LIQUID-COOLED**.

AIR-COOLED is the simpler design of the two, since the movement of air cools the cylinders. Some air-cooled engines use an integrated fan and shrouds to direct airflow over the fins while others rely on the momentum of the vehicle. Air-cooled cylinders have fins, which increase the surface area of the cylinder to help transfer heat away from the cylinder and into the air. If the engine is running and the vehicle is not moving, the engine will retain the extra heat. Damage may occur if the vehicle is left running in a stationary position for a long period of time.

LIQUID-COOLED ENGINES use a fluid known as COOLANT or ANTIFREEZE. The advantage of a liquid cooling system is that it maintains a constant operating temperature. Operating temperatures for air-cooled engines can fluctuate depending on the outside air temperature and airflow.

The liquid cooling system contains multiple components to help remove heat and keep the engine cool. A WATER PUMP is used to circulate fluid through the system. The fluid circulated through the system passes through hoses and internal passages located in the engine block known as a WATER JACKET. A THERMOSTAT controls the temperature and flow of the coolant. When the thermostat opens, hot coolant is sent to the radiator to be cooled.

⚠️ On a cold day, another set of hoses transfers coolant to the heater system where hot coolant is used to warm up the vehicle's interior.

The radiator is made up of tiny fins. A COOLING FAN located behind the radiator draws outside air toward the radiator to help with cooling in extreme conditions. If the coolant temperature is below what the thermostat is rated for, the thermostat will stay closed. Coolant will not be sent to the radiator, but will be redirected back to the engine through a BYPASS TUBE.

The system is pressurized; a RADIATOR CAP controls the pressure. If the pressure exceeds the radiator cap's rating, the excess pressurized fluid is sent to the COOLANT RECOVERY BOTTLE. An UPPER RADIATOR HOSE and a LOWER RADIATOR HOSE both connect to the engine.

Cooling system maintenance is very important to protect the engine and other parts of the cooling system. Visually inspect hoses, belts, and exterior components for damage. Hoses will often crack, bulge, or split. Belts may crack or start to lose material over time. Gaskets around the water pump and thermostat housing may dry out, causing the cooling system to leak. Water pumps should be inspected for excessive fluid leaking out around the weep hole; this is a sign that the internal seals or bearings have failed. It is also important to verify that the correct coolant type is being used. Some coolant brands come premixed

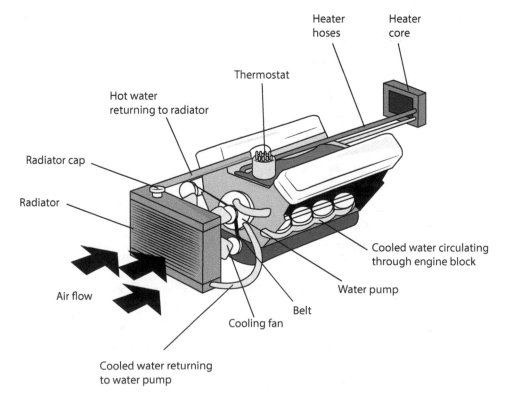

Figure 7.5. Automotive Cooling System

while others need to be mixed with water in a 50/50 mixture. Distilled water is recommended for use with the coolant.

Example

Where is the cooling fan located?

(A) behind the radiator

(B) in front of the radiator

(C) between the engine and interior of the vehicle

(D) mounted in the engine

Answers:

(A) is correct. The cooling fan is located behind the radiator to pull air over the radiator.

(B) is incorrect. The fan is not in front of the radiator.

(C) is incorrect. The heater core, not the cooling fan, is located between the engine and interior of the vehicle.

(D) is incorrect. The fan is located in the front area of the engine.

Lubricating the Engine

Engine lubrication is designed to decrease friction between the moving components. This friction can cause heat from metal-to-metal contact. Oil lubrication also helps to cool, clean, and seal internal engine components.

Engine lubrication in a two-stroke engine varies from that in a four-stroke engine. Two-stroke engines use a premixed concentration of fuel and oil that is burned during the combustion process. In one method, the oil and fuel can be mixed at a specific ratio and directly added to the fuel tank. The other method uses an oil-injection pump to deliver oil from an oil tank. Engine speed and load control the injection of oil to the fuel.

In a four-stroke engine design, lubrication is circulated throughout the engine to various internal components. Two main lubricating systems are WET SUMP and DRY SUMP.

WET SUMP engines contain oil in the OIL PAN, which is part of the engine. An oil pump provides the lubrication flow, drawing oil through the OIL PICK-UP TUBE AND SCREEN. The oil is then filtered by an OIL FILTER and distributed through OIL GALLEYS in the crankcase. The pressure is controlled by the OIL PRESSURE RELIEF VALVE, which opens if the pressure exceeds the valve's pressure rating. When the relief valve is closed, oil is directed through distribution galleys. The lower galleys supply oil to bottom-end engine components, while the upper galleys direct oil to the engine cylinder head and timing components.

DRY SUMP systems operate in much the same way as wet sumps but use an auxiliary oil tank to store oil. The oil then flows into the supply side of an OIL PUMP. After the oil circulates through the filtering components and engine, it is returned to the oil tank by the return side of the oil pump.

Engine oil is produced from a BASE OIL, a refined crude oil. Additives are added to improve the base oil's lubrication performance. Base oils are classified into five groups, based on how the oil is refined, the VISCOSITY, or resistance of fluid flow, and added contents such as sulfur and saturates.

"Wet" Sump System

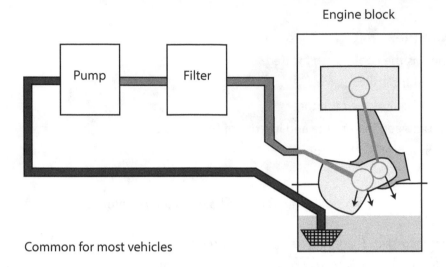

Common for most vehicles

"Dry" Sump System

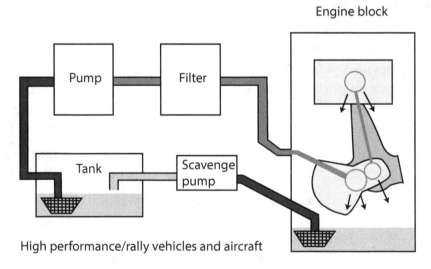

High performance/rally vehicles and aircraft

Figure 7.6. Sumps

Viscosity and **OIL WEIGHT** play a major role in keeping the engine in proper operating condition. Viscosity is the resistance of fluid flow. The lower the viscosity weight, the less resistance there will be to fluid flow. A 10w40 oil is thinner than a 20w50. A 10w40 oil may be recommended for winter conditions, and a 20w50 may be recommended for warmer conditions. The *w* indicates the winter weight, and it is the thinner property of the oil. The second number is the summer-rated weight, and is the thicker property of the oil.

Proper maintenance of the lubrication system is important for the engine's longevity. The use of incorrect oil weights can cause internal damage to the engine. If the oil is heavier than recommended, this can cause high engine loads and lead to a shortened engine life.

If the oil is lighter than recommended, this may result in premature mechanical wear and may also reduce the engine's life. If the engine oil level becomes low, friction between components may occur. Checking the oil level periodically is recommended to ensure the oil is clean and at the proper level. The oil and filter should be changed if the oil is very dark and almost like a thick sludge. Changing the oil and oil filter at the recommended maintenance period intervals will prevent long-term complications with the engine and internal components.

Example

What is viscosity?

(A) the type of oil rated to use in the summer

(B) the type of oil rated to use in the winter

(C) resistance of fluid flow

(D) the type of oil dry sumps use

Answers:

(A) is incorrect. Viscosity is not a type of oil rated for the summer.

(B) is incorrect. Viscosity is not a type of oil for the winter.

(C) is correct. Viscosity refers to the resistance of fluid flow.

(D) is incorrect. Viscosity does not refer to a type of oil for dry sumps.

Diesel Engines

Diesel engines and gasoline engines are very similar: They are both internal combustion engines; they have similar internal components such as pistons, crankshafts, piston rings, valves, camshafts; and they have both two-stroke and four-stroke designs.

One major difference between gasoline and diesel engines is how they ignite during the power stroke. In gasoline engines, a spark plug ignites the compressed air-fuel mixture, causing combustion to occur and forcing the piston to move.

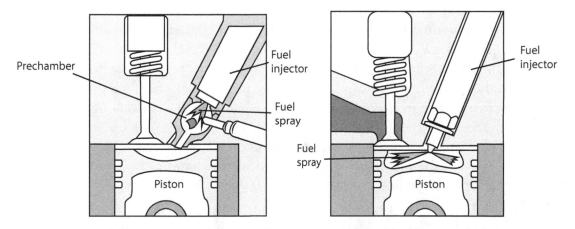

Figure 7.7. Diesel Engine Injection

Indirect Injection (IDI) diesel engines ignite in a **PRE-COMBUSTION CHAMBER**. This pre-chamber is where fuel is injected from the fuel injector, mixes with air, and then pre-ignites. This pre-ignition spark expands from the pre-chamber to the combustion chamber, then mixes fuel with the rest of the compressed air. Direct Injection (DI) diesel engines, in contrast, inject diesel fuel directly into the combustion chamber. Most diesel engines today are DI.

Gasoline engine compression is between 6:1 and 10:1. The diesel compression ratio can be between 15:1 and 23:1.

The **COMPRESSION RATIO** is much higher in a diesel engine than in a gasoline engine. When air enters the cylinder and is compressed, the highly compressed hot air is sprayed with a mist of diesel fuel from the fuel injectors, causing a controlled explosion. This explosion forces the piston to move, producing the power stroke that moves the vehicle or machine. When the piston moves through the cylinder, exhaust gases are discharged through the exhaust valve. This process repeats as the engine is running.

Example

Diesel engines use which type of spark plugs?

(A) None—diesel engines do not use spark plugs.

(B) Diesel engines use hot plugs.

(C) Diesel engines use cold plugs.

(D) The type varies by engine.

Answers:

(A) is correct. Diesel engines do not use spark plugs.

(B) is incorrect. A hot plug refers to the heat range of a spark plug.

(C) is incorrect. A cold plug refers to the heat range of a spark plug.

(D) is incorrect. Spark plug heat ranges vary in gasoline engines.

COMBUSTION

The Fuel-Injection System

The fuel system stores fuel, mixes the air and fuel to the proper ratio, and delivers this mixture to the engine. Fuel systems use **CARBURETORS** or fuel-injection for fuel delivery.

ELECTRONIC FUEL INJECTION (EFI) is more efficient than carburetors and earlier designs of fuel injection. EFI systems can precisely control the amount of fuel to a cylinder through the use of a **POWERTRAIN CONTROL MODULE (PCM)**. The fuel system consists of an **ELECTRIC FUEL PUMP**, **FUEL FILTER**, **PRESSURE REGULATOR**, **FUEL LINES**, **FUEL INJECTORS**, and a **FUEL TANK**. The fuel filter captures any contaminants in the fuel, and the fuel pump, usually located in the fuel tank, delivers fuel to the injectors. The pressure regulator keeps the fuel pressure at the specific pressure rating needed for the injectors to operate efficiently. The PCM sends an electronic **PULSE WIDTH MODULATING** (PWM) signal to the fuel injector.

The fuel injector sprays the proper amount of fuel into the **INTAKE MANIFOLD** or **COMBUSTION CHAMBER** where it mixes with air.

An intake air filter traps dirt and debris and prevents it from entering the engine's air intake and fuel system.

The **AIR-FUEL RATIO** depends on how long the injector is controlled to stay open. The ideal air-fuel ratio should be around 14.7:1 (14.7 parts of air to 1 part of fuel). However this ratio can vary depending on fuel systems and types of fuel used. A **LEAN MIXTURE** (15:1) contains more air and a **RICH MIXTURE** (13:1) contains less. Either can lead to problems with the engine. A lean mixture may cause internal damage to the engine, and a rich mixture may cause lower engine performance and poor fuel economy.

Oxygen (O_2) sensors are used to monitor the air-fuel ratio. Most systems have one sensor located before and another after the catalytic converter. The first sensor adjusts the air-fuel ratio while the second helps monitor the efficiency of the catalytic converter. A scan tool may be used to monitor the oxygen sensor. The sensor converts the burned exhaust gas into a voltage reading. A normal reading constantly fluctuates between high and low voltages.

THROTTLE BODY INJECTION (TBI) involves one or two injectors mounted at the **THROTTLE BODY** ports. The **THROTTLE PLATE** moves as fuel is injected into the cylinder. This was an early design, before manufacturers switched from carburetors to fuel injection.

MULTIPORT FUEL INJECTION uses separate fuel injectors for each cylinder. These injectors are mounted in the intake manifold. **DIRECT INJECTION** also uses a separate fuel injector for each cylinder, but the injector is mounted on the engine, in the cylinder head. The injector sprays fuel directly into the combustion chamber.

The carburetor is small and takes up much less space than the fuel injection system because a carburetor contains small jets and passageways internal to the carburetor body. The carburetor also requires more adjustments and maintenance than fuel injection. A **CHOKE PLATE** helps meter the air-fuel during cold starts. A closed choke plate restricts air flow and allows more fuel to enter the engine, resulting in a rich mixture. When the choke is off, the plate is open.

A **FORCED INDUCTION SYSTEM** may use either a **TURBOCHARGER** or **SUPERCHARGER** to increase power and efficiency by pressurizing air before it enters the engine's cylinder. A turbocharger uses the discharged exhaust gas to build boost pressure. Boost pressure is built from the turbine spinning from the exhaust flow. A supercharger uses a belt, chain, gear or shaft that operates on the engine's crankshaft to build pressure.

Vapor lock happens when liquid fuel is turned into gas. Fuel may vaporize in the heat produced by the engine. Vapor lock interrupts the fuel pump, causing a loss of fuel to the carburetor or fuel injection system. As a result, hard starting may occur.

Checking and maintaining the fuel system is important. If the fuel system is either too rich or too lean, the engine will have poor power output. A dirty air filter will restrict air into the system, causing a rich condition. A lean condition may cause difficulties in starting the vehicle. **VAPOR LOCK** interrupts fuel flow, and if this occurs in the fuel system, the engine may lose power or stall. Clogged or dirty injectors may cause engine hesitation, rough idling, and poor fuel economy. Fuel filters should be replaced according to the service interval recommendations.

Example

Which engine component uses exhaust gases to build up boost pressure?

(A) supercharger

(B) choke plate

(C) carburetor

(D) turbocharger

Answers:

(A) is incorrect. The supercharger uses the engine's mechanical rotation.

(B) is incorrect. The choke plate reduces air.

(C) is incorrect. The carburetor is used for fuel and air metering.

(D) is correct. Exhaust gases cause the turbine wheel to spin.

Ignition

The purpose of an ignition system is to start the controlled combustion process in the engine. The **PRIMARY IGNITION SYSTEM** is made up of a **BATTERY**, **IGNITION SWITCH**, **IGNITION MODULE** or contact points, and the ignition **COIL PRIMARY WINDING**. These components use battery voltage, which produces low voltage. When the ignition switch is placed in the on position, battery voltage is sent to the primary coil windings, creating a magnetic field. Contact points or the control module are used to make or break the primary coil circuit. When the contact points or control module interrupt the primary coil windings, the magnetic field collapses, causing voltage to be created to the secondary windings. This **STEP-UP EFFECT** creates a high voltage that is sent from the ignition coil secondary windings to the **DISTRIBUTOR CAP** or coil pack. The **SECONDARY IGNITION SYSTEM** is made up of the **IGNITION COIL'S SECONDARY WINDINGS**, **SPARK PLUG WIRE**, and **SPARK PLUG**.

In a **DISTRIBUTOR** system, the distributor delivers the secondary ignition current. The distributor contains a geared shaft driven by a gear on the camshaft. High voltage is sent from the coil's secondary windings through the **COIL WIRE** to the center of the **DISTRIBUTOR CAP**. The distributor cap has **SPARK PLUG WIRES** connected to **SPARK PLUGS**, and under the distributor cap is a shaft with a toothed gear, known as a **RELUCTOR**, and a **PICK-UP COIL**. The **PICK-UP COIL**, which contains a magnet, is placed close to the highest point of the reluctor tooth. A small air gap is needed between the pick-up coil and reluctor. AC voltage current is generated as the distributor shaft rotates and each tooth of the reluctor moves past the magnet of the pick-up. An AC voltage signal is sent to the **IGNITION MODULE,** where it is converted to an on/off digital signal that is used by the ignition module to open the primary circuit and determine engine speed.

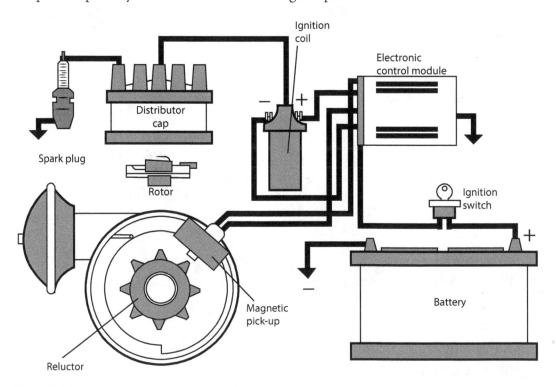

Figure 7.8. Distributor

A **DISTRIBUTOR-LESS IGNITION SYSTEM** has fewer components than a distributor system, and the spark plugs are connected directly to the ignition coil. Some systems may have one coil per cylinder or one coil for each pair of cylinders. Instead of using a pickup coil and reluctor under a distributor cap, a distributorless ignition system uses a crankshaft position sensor and camshaft sensor. Fewer mechanical adjustments are required in this style of ignition system.

Another style of distributor-less ignition system is called COIL-ON-PLUG IGNITION. In this type of system the ignition coil is on top of the spark plug, eliminating spark plug wires.

IGNITION TIMING refers to the crankshaft and piston position when the spark ignition happens. The measurement is in degrees of crankshaft rotation. Combustion must begin near the end of the compression stroke, and before the piston reaches top dead center (TDC). When ignition takes place, the compressed heat and gas mixture ignites, and the expanding pressure forces the piston's movement. Ignition timing can be ADVANCED or RETARDED in some systems. Timing that is advanced too much will cause the spark to happen before the piston has reached TDC, and will force the piston down too soon. If the ignition system is retarded, the spark will happen late, as the piston moves to bottom dead center (BDC), resulting in a lack of power on this stroke.

Incorrect timing and incorrect spark plug heat ranges may cause PRE-IGNITION and DETONATION in an engine. Pre-ignition is when the air-fuel mixture ignites before the spark has ignited. Detonation takes place after the spark has ignited the air-fuel mixture. The residual mixture is also heated up, causing abnormal combustion.

Spark plugs ranges are identified by letters and numbers. Verify what type of plug the vehicle uses and check the heat range with the spark plug manufacturer.

A spark plug's heat range is determined by its ability to transfer heat from the combustion chamber to the cylinder head. A HOT PLUG has a larger surface area exposed in the combustion chamber and slowly transfers heat away from the tip. A COLD PLUG has a smaller surface area exposed in the combustion chamber and quickly transfers heat away from the tip.

Example

What are cold plugs?

(A) spark plugs

(B) coil on plugs

(C) distributor-less plugs

(D) plugs on the side of the engine that keep coolant in

Answers:

(A) is correct. Cold plugs are a type of spark plug.

(B) is incorrect. Coil-on-plugs are a type of ignition coil.

(C) is incorrect. Distributor-less is a type of ignition system.

(D) is incorrect. These are called freeze plugs.

Emission Control

The engine's combustion process creates HYDROCARBON emissions of unburned raw fuel, carbon monoxide, and nitrogen dioxide. Federal government agencies require manufacturers to keep these emission levels to a minimum, and exhaust systems are designed to help eliminate these unwanted waste materials. When the exhaust valve is open, exhaust from the cylinder is discharged to the EXHAUST MANIFOLD or HEADER PIPES connected to the engine exhaust ports. The CATALYTIC CONVERTER, located between the exhaust manifold and the MUFFLER, contains catalyst elements. When the hot exhaust heat passes over these elements, the byproducts are water vapor, carbon dioxide, and oxygen. The exhaust flow passes through the muffler to quiet the noise, and finally out the TAILPIPE.

Some emission systems require a nitrogen oxide control. An EXHAUST GAS RECIRCULATION (EGR) SYSTEM allows part of the exhaust flow to be recirculated back into the engine to reduce combustion temperature and pressure to control nitrogen oxide.

A manifold is a collection of pipes that are formed together. Header pipes are individual pipes.

A failing exhaust system can cause carbon monoxide poisoning if the gases enter the vehicle. An exhaust leak can result from improper connections, cracks, or extreme rusting in the exhaust system. Gasket connections should be regularly checked for severe discoloration. If the gasket is cracked, missing or covered in soot, it should be replaced.

Example

Which part of the exhaust system quiets noise?

(A) catalytic converter

(B) header pipes

(C) muffler

(D) tailpipe

Answers:

(A) is incorrect. The catalytic converter converts toxic emissions to cleaner emissions.

(B) is incorrect. Header pipes are connected to the engine and help with exhaust flow.

(C) is correct. The purpose of a muffler is to quiet the exhaust noise.

(D) is incorrect. The tailpipe carries the clean exhaust gases away from the vehicle.

THE CHASSIS

The Frame and Body

The FRAME is the main structure of a vehicle. It provides attachment points for the engine and other components. In body-on-frame construction the frame is separate from the BODY. By contrast, in UNIBODY CONSTRUCTION the frame, floor panels, and chassis body are one piece. This type of construction is considered lighter and more rigid. The unibody structure is a load-carrying frame that handles all weight and movement of the vehicle.

MONOCOQUE CONSTRUCTION is similar to the unibody design, but the outer shell and panels are the main load-bearing sections to reinforce the body. This construction does not have an internal load-carrying frame. A STRESSED SKIN CONSTRUCTION is a solid outer shell supported by ribs or internal frame components.

Example

Which part of the frame does a monocoque body mount to?

(A) the floor pan

(B) the unibody

(C) the ribs of the frame

(D) Monocoque does not mount to a frame; its body and frame are one piece.

The Drivetrain

The drivetrain is made up of a series of components that transfer engine power to the vehicle's wheels to provide movement. The **TRANSMISSION** varies the engine power to drive the wheels.

An **AUTOMATIC TRANSMISSION** is a self-shifting geared transmission. A **TORQUE CONVERTER** engages and disengages power from the engine to the transmission using fluid and internal gears inside the converter housing. When the operator places the vehicle in gear from neutral, the converter engages and applies power to the transmission. When the operator brakes the vehicle while in gear, the converter disengages from the transmission and the vehicle stops while the engine is running.

A **MANUAL TRANSMISSION** has gears that need to be manually shifted to move the vehicle. A **CLUTCH** is used to engage and disengage power from the engine to the transmission. When the transmission is in gear and the clutch is engaged, the vehicle will move. As the vehicle gains momentum, the operator must shift up through the gears, each time disengaging the clutch before shifting. The clutch also needs to be disengaged when the operator needs to **DOWNSHIFT**, or shift from a higher gear to a lower gear. When the clutch is disengaged and held in place while the vehicle is in gear, the vehicle is in a neutral state.

The clutch is engaged when the pedal or hand lever is not being applied. This allows the clutch to transfer power from the engine to the transmission. The clutch disengages power from the transmission when the pedal or lever is held in.

A **CONTINUOUSLY VARIABLE TRANSMISSION** **(CVT)** operates like an automatic transmission, but instead of gears there are two pulleys and a belt. This system offers a smooth transition as the vehicle changes speed ratios. The pulleys are cone shaped. One pulley is connected to the engine, the other is connected to the transmission, and a belt connects the two. As the engine pulley rotates, the belt delivers power to the transmission pulley. As the vehicle speeds up or slows down, the pulleys change in size, and the belt slides between the smaller and larger ends of the pulleys.

A **DRIVE AXLE** is a shaft that receives the engine's rotational momentum through the transmission and delivers this power to the wheels. Different types of shafts deliver power to the wheels.

A **TRANSAXLE** combines the transmission and differential in one casing. The differential drives the **HALF SHAFTS**. One end of the half shaft is connected to the differential by an inner **CONSTANT VELOCITY** **(CV) JOINT**, and the other end is connected to the wheel assembly by an outer CV joint. CV joints are flexible and allow the shafts to move and pivot when turning.

The CVT belt will alternate between the large side and smaller side of the pulley when the vehicle is in operation.

Four-wheel or all-wheel drive vehicles use a **TRANSFER CASE**, which receives engine power from the transmission and delivers power to the rear or front axles through drive shafts. **Universal joints** connect the drive shafts from the transfer case to the differentials.

Shafts and joints should be visually inspected periodically to verify the maintenance intervals and proper fluid specifications for the transmission, differential, and transfer case fluids. The recommended maintenance intervals should be followed for greasing and lubricating universal joints and pivot points. Proper operation of the vehicle is important, since harsh conditions may decrease the life expectancy of these components.

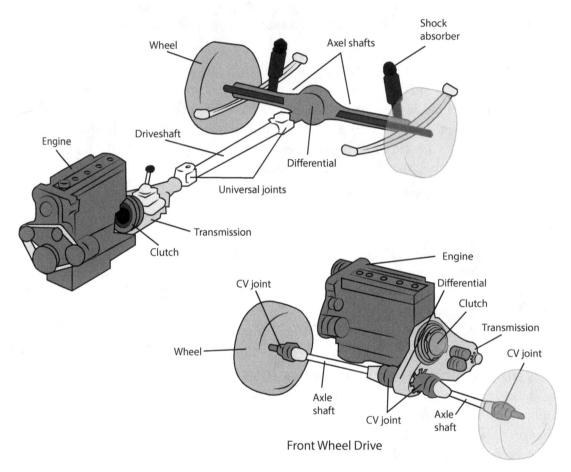

Figure 7.9. Drivetrain

Example

If the operator brakes to a complete stop in a vehicle with an automatic transmission and the engine is still running, what will happen?

(A) The vehicle will stall out.

(B) The vehicle will slow down, and the engine will keep the vehicle moving until the clutch is pressed.

(C) The vehicle will stop, and the engine will continue to run.

(D) Before the vehicle can be stopped, the operator must downshift.

Answers:

(A) is incorrect. The vehicle will continue to run.

(B) is incorrect. There is no clutch to press with an automatic transmission.

(C) is correct. The vehicle will stop moving and the engine will stay running.

(D) is incorrect. An automatic transmission automatically downshifts.

Suspension and Steering

The weight of the vehicle is carried by the suspension system, while the position and movement of the wheels is controlled through the steering.

The suspension system allows each wheel to adapt to various road conditions without affecting the opposite wheel. The system normally consists of **SHOCK ABSORBERS**, **SPRINGS**, and **UPPER** and **LOWER CONTROL ARMS**. Rough road conditions can cause a vehicle to **JOUNCE** and **REBOUND**, so the purpose of a shock absorber is to dampen these reactions. Coil springs provide proper ride height and maintain ride quality. The upper and lower control arms, which are bolted to the frame with bushings, help isolate movement and road noise. Control arms may also be called **A-ARMS**.

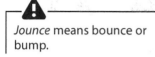

Jounce means bounce or bump.

The steering linkage usually consists of steering knuckles, ball joints, pitman arm, center link, idler arm, and tie rods. The **STEERING KNUCKLES** pivot on **UPPER** and **LOWER BALL JOINTS**. The **PITMAN ARM** is connected to the **STEERING BOX**, and when the steering moves, the pitman arm rotates and moves the center link right or left. An **IDLER ARM** is used to brace the center link to the frame. The **INNER TIE ROD** connects to the **CENTER LINK**, and the **OUTER TIE ROD** connects to the steering knuckle.

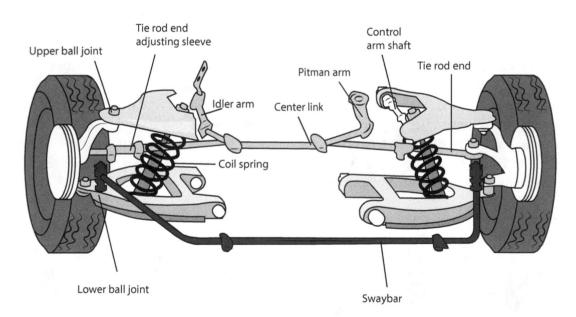

Figure 7.10. Steering Linkage

A **RACK AND PINION** system does not use a pitman arm, center link, or idler arm. The pinion is a gear that rotates over a rack, which has a long row of teeth across a bar. As the steering is turned, the pinion gear moves the rack back and forth.

A **WHEEL HUB** assembly is connected to the steering knuckle, and the **RIM** and **TIRE** are mounted to the wheel hub. Before removing a tire from the rim, the **BEAD** must first be broken or

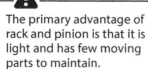

The primary advantage of rack and pinion is that it is light and has few moving parts to maintain.

unseated. The bead is the seal between the tire and rim. A **RADIAL TIRE** is constructed from **BODY PLIES**, an inner **LINER**, **TREAD**, and **SIDEWALL**.

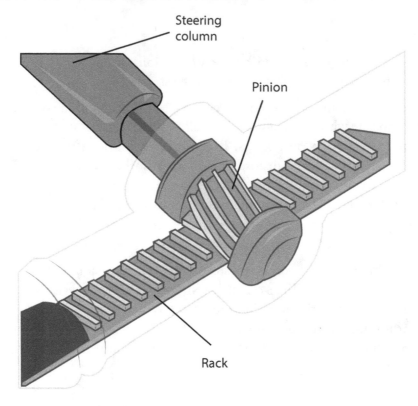

Figure 7.11. Rack and Pinion

Maintaining wheel alignment is important to prevent the failure of the suspension and steering system. **CAMBER** is the inward or outward tilt of the wheel from its centerline. **POSITIVE CAMBER** is when the wheel is tilted outward. **NEGATIVE CAMBER** is when the wheel is tilted inward (see Figure 7.12). **CASTER** is the forward or rearward tilt of the wheel from its center line. **NEGATIVE CASTER** is the forward tilt of the wheel and **POSITIVE CASTER** is the rearward tilt of the wheel (see Figure 7.13). Greasing and lubing the linkage and suspension points will keep these components from failing.

Figure 7.12. Camber

Periodically, visual inspections should be made to check for leaking shocks or worn-out components such as bushings, rubber covers, or busted tie rod ends.

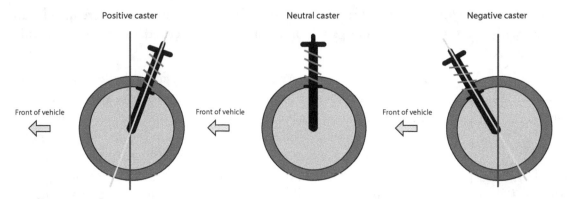

Positive caster   Neutral caster   Negative caster

Front of vehicle   Front of vehicle   Front of vehicle

Figure 7.13. Caster

Example

What needs to be broken to remove a tire from the rim?

(A) bead

(B) tread

(C) body ply

(D) liner

Answers:

(A) is correct. The bead, the seal between a tire and rim, must be broken to remove the tire.

(B) is incorrect. Tread is the pattern on the outside of the tire.

(C) is incorrect. Body ply is part of the tire.

(D) is incorrect. Liner is part of the tire.

Brakes

The vehicle's brake system absorbs the energy of the wheels to slow down or stop the vehicle. The typical **BRAKE ASSEMBLIES** are **DISC BRAKES** in the front and **DRUM BRAKES** in the rear. With disc brakes, when the **BRAKE PEDAL** is applied, a plunger presses into the **MASTER CYLINDER** and forces **BRAKE FLUID** through the **BRAKE LINES** to a caliper. As fluid pushes against a piston, the piston squeezes the brake pads against the disc, or rotor, attached to the wheel. The friction from the pads pressing into the rotor will slow or stop the wheel.

For drum brakes, the fluid enters the wheel cylinder and presses the **BRAKE SHOES** outward against the drum. The drum, attached to the wheel, forces the wheel to slow down or stop.

A **BRAKE BOOSTER** is located between the master cylinder and brake pedal. The booster helps to minimize pedal pressure needed when applying brakes.

An **ANTI-LOCK BRAKE SYSTEM (ABS)** improves braking and steering control during sudden stops, and on wet or slick surfaces. The ABS system components include wheel speed sensors, ABS control module, brake pressure regulator and the ABS light. When the ABS module senses that one wheel speed sensor is slowing down faster than another, the computer will reduce brake pressure to that wheel. Once the pressure has been isolated to that wheel, pressure is applied and

 Drum brakes can be hydraulically or mechanically actuated. Look for the type of hoses or cables connected to the drums.

released rapidly until the wheel regains traction. If the ABS light is on, there may be an issue with the system. The emergency brake should be checked to ensure it is fully disengaged.

If the ABS light is on, it does NOT mean the ABS is active. There may be a system fault like low brake fluid. The ABS system is disabled when the light is on.

Brake maintenance is very important since a failing brake system could result in serious injury or death. The **BRAKE FLUID RESERVOIR** should be checked periodically to make sure it is full and that the fluid is not dark; if it is, the fluid should be changed and the system flushed. Furthermore, using the correct brake fluid is essential. Improper brake fluid may damage seals and cause the system to lose braking power. Brake pads have a wear indicator that shows the life expectancy of the pads. When working on the brake system, it is important not to let air enter the system. Anytime a brake line is disconnected or the reservoir cap is off, the brake pedal should not be pressed. If the brakes feel spongy or soft, there may be air in the system. The system should be bled to remove air.

Example

The master cylinder does what?

(A) presses the brake shoe into the drum

(B) supplies fluid to the brake lines

(C) makes it easier to apply force to the brake pedal

(D) presses against the brake pads

Answers:

(A) is incorrect. A wheel cylinder presses the brake shoes into the drum.

(B) is correct. When pressure is applied to the master cylinder, fluid is forced into the brake lines.

(C) is incorrect. A brake booster makes it easier to step on the brake pedal.

(D) is incorrect. A piston presses against the brake pads.

ELECTRICAL SYSTEMS

The electrical system consists of a **BATTERY**, wires, and other electronic components to start, charge, and operate the vehicle. Most vehicles today use a 12-volt system, although some heavy machinery uses a 24-volt system. The electrical system can be broken down into a few sections.

A **LEAD-ACID BATTERY** is the vehicle's primary source for voltage and electrical current. The lead plates in the battery are soaked with sulfuric acid. Some batteries require maintenance of the fluid level. Most batteries used today, however, are sealed and require only charging maintenance.

The charging system consists of a battery, **IGNITION**, **ALTERNATOR** or generator, **VOLTAGE REGULATOR**, and a **BRIDGE RECTIFIER**. The ignition turns the charging system on and off. When the engine is running, a belt between the alternator pulley and the engine pulley will drive the alternator and generate current to keep the battery charged. When the vehicle is running, current and electricity are supplied throughout the electrical system. The voltage regulator controls the voltage output. A **BRIDGE RECTIFIER** is a series of diodes that converts alternating current (AC) to direct current (DC) in the electrical system.

The exterior and interior lights receive voltage from the electrical system. The **HEADLIGHTS** are located at the front of the vehicle and the **TAIL LIGHTS** are located in the rear. These exterior lighting systems provide vehicle visibility at night. The **INTERIOR LIGHTING** system ensures the operator can see the vehicle gauges and provides lighting to see the vehicle interior.

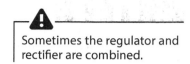

Sometimes the regulator and rectifier are combined.

Maintaining the electrical systems involves visually inspecting the battery, battery cables, terminal connections, and alternator belt. Dirty or corroded electrical connections should be carefully cleaned. Faulty wiring or connections may cause issues with ignition and battery charging. The battery should have a standing voltage of 12.6 volts. If the battery is not used for a long period of time, the battery should be maintained on a battery charger. If the battery is not sealed and caps are located on top, check the acid level. If the acid level is low, fill the battery with distilled water; do not use new acid. When the vehicle is running, the battery output should be between 13 and 14.5 volts. If the voltage is incorrect, the alternator or voltage regulator may be failing. The alternator belt should be inspected for cracks and wear. A loose alternator belt will cause improper charging to the battery.

Example

If the battery has caps on top and the fluid is low, what should you fill it with?

(A) lead acid

(B) tap water

(C) oil

(D) distilled water

Answers:

(A) is incorrect. Acid is used only if the battery is new.

(B) is incorrect. Tap water is not recommended.

(C) is incorrect. Oil is not to be used to fill a battery.

(D) is correct. Distilled water should be used to fill a vehicle battery.

VEHICLE COMPUTER SYSTEM

The computer system of the vehicle may contain one or multiple modules. The vehicle electrical system may contain a **POWERTRAIN CONTROL MODULE (PCM)**, electronic control module (ECM), engine control unit (ECU), body control module, transmission control module or an ABS module. The purpose of these modules is to monitor sensor inputs, control outputs, and monitor and adjust the fuel system and ignition timing.

The term *computer* broadly describes the electronic boxes in the vehicle's electrical system.

When the control unit sends an output signal to the **ACTUATOR**, the actuator moves. An electric motor or electronic solenoid valve is considered an actuator.

Sensors monitor certain functions of the vehicle and send a signal back to the control module. One example is the camshaft sensor that monitors the movement of the camshaft. The sensor picks up the shaft's rotation and sends a signal to the control module, which can determine cylinder and spark ignition. An **ACTIVE SENSOR** monitors and responds to movement but requires a power source to operate. A **PASSIVE SENSOR** monitors and responds to movement; however it does not require a power source to operate.

Several sensors work in the vehicle, measuring temperature, pressure, positioning, and other indicators. The **INTAKE AIR TEMPERATURE SENSOR** monitors the air temperature in the intake stream. It sends the air temperature value to the control module so the engine can adjust the air-fuel ratio. A different sensor located in the engine block or cylinder head, the **ENGINE COOLANT TEMPERATURE SENSOR** monitors the engine's coolant temperature. It is a thermistor-style sensor that changes resistance; the lower the temperature, the higher the resistance value, and vice versa.

The **AMBIENT AIR PRESSURE SENSOR** monitors outdoor air. As air pressure changes, the air-fuel mixture must adjust to the engine for proper performance. Meanwhile, the **MANIFOLD ABSOLUTE PRESSURE SENSOR** monitors the difference between the intake manifold and outside air pressure.

Also important to maintaining proper air-fuel ratio, the **THROTTLE POSITION SENSOR** monitors the position of the throttle opening. It sends a signal back to the control module, which uses this information to adjust air-fuel mixture. Another position sensor, the **CRANK-SHAFT POSITION SENSOR** monitors the rotation of the crankshaft; it sends a sensor signal to the control module to control ignition timing and the fuel delivery system. Meanwhile, the **KNOCK SENSOR** monitors for engine detonation or *knock*.

Finally, the **IMPACT SENSOR** is a safety sensor that detects when the vehicle has been in a crash or has been hit hard. The sensor will send a signal to the inflatable restraint module, which in turn will activate the individual airbags as necessary.

A **POWERTRAIN CONTROL MODULE** may have two electronic connections. One side may be used for engine control information, while the other may be for transmission or body control information. The **ENGINE CONTROL UNIT** itself monitors and regulates functions of the engine, including ignition spark timing, emission monitoring, and fuel delivery. Briefly discussed below, the **SCAN TOOL** is a diagnostic tool that reads fault codes, which are fault numbers stored in the control module. Some scan tools can monitor sensor data and other system functions.

Cold air is denser than hot air. If cold air enters the engine, what does adding more air do to the air-fuel mixture?

When the brake pedal is applied, another safety indicator, the **BRAKE SWITCH** signal, will turn the rear brake lights on.

The vehicle's computer system continually monitors the vehicle engine and the vehicle's sensor inputs. If the vehicle is not operating properly or a component fails, a "check engine" dashboard light will automatically switch on, warning the driver to use the scan tool to diagnose which component or system may be failing. Faulty wiring or dirty sensors may also cause the light to switch on. The operator manual includes diagnostic procedures for in-depth troubleshooting to correct the fault or failure.

Example

What does a scan tool do?

(A) It adjusts the air-fuel mixture.

(B) It detects engine knock.

(C) It reads fault codes.

(D) It checks the position of the throttle valve.

Answers:

(A) is incorrect. A control module adjusts the air-fuel mixture.

(B) is incorrect. A knock sensor detects engine knock.

(C) is correct. Scan tools can read fault codes; some can monitor data.

(D) is incorrect. A throttle position sensor checks the position of the throttle valve.

SAFETY SYSTEMS

A vehicle's safety system prevents injury to the operator in an accident or when a malfunction occurs. A **SEAT BELT'S** function is to keep the operator secure during a violent movement or collision. Today's vehicles are equipped with **AIRBAG** systems. If the vehicle is involved in a crash, the impact sensors will activate the **FRONT** or **SIDE AIRBAGS,** depending on the point of impact. Some vehicles have a **DUAL-STAGE FRONT AIR BAG** that deploys in two stages to better protect the driver. In a low-speed crash, only the first stage of the airbag will deploy, but in a high-speed crash, both stages could deploy.

A **ROLLOVER PROTECTION SYSTEM (ROPS)** is found on various sizes of vehicles, from small cars up to heavy machinery. The ROPS consists of roll-cages or roll-bars fitted around the frame of the vehicle. If the vehicle were to roll over, this system would keep the upper frame from collapsing on the operator.

The **TIRE PRESSURE MONITORING SYSTEM** uses sensors incorporated into the valve stem in the wheel. If one or more tires have low air pressure, creating unsafe driving conditions, a light will notify the operator.

TRACTION CONTROL is a system that helps improve the handling and stability of the vehicle during acceleration on wet, icy, or gravel surfaces. If the system's wheel sensor detects a wheel spinning, engine power is reduced. The system will temporarily apply brake pressure to the spinning wheel and allow the vehicle to accelerate smoothly.

ELECTRONIC STABILITY CONTROL is the updated version of traction control. If the wheel sensor senses that a wheel or wheels are slipping, the system will apply brake pressure. The system can brake one, two, or three wheels to maneuver the vehicle in the direction the operator is trying to compensate to. Engine power may even be cut off to help the vehicle maneuver.

The **LOWER ANCHORS AND TETHERS FOR CHILDREN (LATCH)** system was designed to enable the proper installation of child safety seats. Prior to this system, seat belts held child seats in place. The LATCH system consists of anchored hardware points located in the rear passenger seats.

Example

What does ROPS do?

(A) It helps to deploy the airbag system.

(B) It keeps the top of the vehicle from collapsing.

(C) It prevents the rear of the vehicle from being smashed in.

(D) It keeps the operator still during a violent crash.

Answers:

(A) is incorrect. Impact sensors help to deploy the airbag system.

(B) is correct. The roll cage or roll bars keep the top of the vehicle from collapsing.

(C) is incorrect. The roll bars do not offer protection for this.

(D) is incorrect. Seat belts keep the operator in place.

8

SHOP INFORMATION

INTRODUCTION

Working in a shop environment requires the knowledge of and proper use of each tool and its associated fastener. Tools and fasteners are defined in each section, listed below:

- measuring tools
- cutting tools
- drilling tools
- striking tools
- turning tools

- fasteners
- soldering and welding tools
- gripping tools
- finishing tools

Example questions are located at the end of each section. Use the questions as a review for the associated section.

A sample test is located at the end of the chapter. The test consists of twenty-five multiple-choice questions.

MEASURING TOOLS

Measuring length, level, and diameter are common tasks a technician performs. Each task requires a different tool. See Figure 8.1., Measuring Tools.

- **TAPE MEASURE:** This is a retractable steel tape in metal or plastic housing. Available in various lengths, most are incremented in both inches and millimeters.
- **CALIPER:** This tool is used for taking inside- and outside-diameter measurements.
- **INSIDE CALIPER:** The technician adjusts the caliper until ends touch the inside bearing housing, then measures the distance of the caliper ends.
- **OUTSIDE CALIPER:** The technician adjusts the clapper until the ends touch the outside diameter of the shaft, then measures the distance of the caliper ends.

- **VERNIER CALIPER:** This caliper provides inside- and outside-diameter measurements, and is available in scale or digital readout. The technician uses the thumbwheel on both versions to adjust the size.
- **MICROMETER:** This tool is used for taking critical shaft measurements and is the most accurate outside-diameter measuring tool. The technician adjusts the thumbwheel to make measurements.
- **LEVEL:** This tool is used to level machinery and frameworks.
- **TUBULAR SPIRIT LEVEL:** A bubble inside the tube moves to indicate the amount of level. This style is generally used in framework or linear leveling activities.
- **BULLSEYE SPIRIT LEVEL:** A bubble is located in a circular housing. The bubble in the center of the bullseye indicates level. Common uses are tripod and spot level points.
- **STEEL SQUARE:** Squares are used to square framework. There are various increments available. Often squares are used to aid in marking straight cuts.

Figure 8.1. Measuring Tools

Example

Which of the following can be used for inside- and outside-diameter measurements?

(A) inside caliper

(B) outside caliper

(C) Vernier caliper

(D) micrometer

Answers:

(A) is incorrect. An inside caliper is used only for inside measurements.

(B) is incorrect. An outside caliper is used only for outside measurements.

(C) is correct. A Vernier caliper is used for both inside and outside measurements.

(D) is incorrect. This caliper is used only for outside measurements.

CUTTING TOOLS

Cutting tools can be used to cut wood, metal, or composites. See Figure 8.2., Cutting Tools. The blade installed onto the tool defines the material it can cut.

- **SAW:** This is a device used for cutting wood, steel, or composite material.

- **CROSS-CUT SAW:** This saw is hand-operated with saw teeth arranged in the most aggressive pattern for removing wood and is used when cutting against the grain on a board.

- **RIPSAW:** This saw is hand-operated with saw teeth arranged in a less aggressive pattern for removing wood and is used for cutting with the grain of wood.

- **COPING SAW:** A coping saw is hand-operated with a fine sawtooth pattern. The saw's blade is flexible and is designed to cut shapes or curves.

- **BACKSAW:** A backsaw is any saw with a reinforced back edge, which keeps the saw from bending during use. This saw is hand-operated and available in different tooth patterns.

- **HACKSAW:** This saw is hand-operated with a fine-tooth pattern and is used to cut metal.

- **CIRCULAR SAW:** A circular saw is composed of a circular blade operated with an electric motor. Cross-cut, ripping, metal, and masonry blades are available for this saw.

- **MITER SAW:** This saw is made up of a circular blade operated with an electric motor, mounted on a stationary table. The saw table will adjust to various angles.

Back Saw   Rip Saw   Miter Saw

Hack Saw   Coping Saw   Circular Saw

Cross Cut Saw   Band Saw   Table Saw

Figure 8.2. Cutting Tools

- **TABLE SAW:** A table saw is composed of a circular blade operated with an electric motor. The table is equipped with guides for ripping the wood.

- **BAND SAW:** A band saw has an electric motor that drives a circular metal blade. Band saws are used to cut irregular shapes and curves into wood, metal, and composite materials.

- **MITER BOX:** This is a box sized to various board widths with grooves precut at precise angles. The selected board is placed into the box and cut to the desired angle with a hand-operated saw.

- **KERF CUT:** This term refers to placing individual cuts across the grain of a board at predetermined distances. When all cuts are completed, the board can be bent.

Example

Which handsaw can be used to cut metal?

(A) coping saw

(B) band saw

(C) cross-cut saw

(D) hacksaw

DRILLING TOOLS

Drilling tools are used when a hole needs to be bored into wood, metal, or composite materials. See Figure 8.3., Drilling Tools. Drill bits provide a means of boring small holes, while hole saws offer the ability to cut larger holes.

- **HAND DRILL:** This drill can be battery-operated or plug-in style. A drill chuck can accommodate drill bits or hole saws.

- **DRILL BITS:** All drill bits are heat-treated and used to bore holes into various materials. The metal and heat treatments determine the material the bit is used on.

- **RIGHT-HAND DRILL BITS:** This is the most common bit, used to bore holes in desired materials.

- **LEFT-HAND DRILL BITS:** This drill bit is designed for counterclockwise operation and is used to remove studs and broken bolts.

- **HOLE SAW:** These saws attach to a drill-bit assembly and are used to bore larger holes in materials.

- **CHUCK:** Drill bits, hole saws, or accessories are secured into this component.

- **CHUCK KEY:** A key is inserted into a hole in the chuck. Turning the key clockwise or counterclockwise allows installation or removal of the bit.

- **KEYLESS CHUCK:** A chuck key is not needed for this chuck. It is knurled to allow users to hand-tighten the bit.

- **REVERSIBLE DRILL:** This refers to any drill with the ability to turn the chuck clockwise and counterclockwise. Drill rotation must be stopped to change directions.

- **VARIABLE SPEED DRILL:** This is a drill with the ability to change speed chuck turns. To change the speed of a drill press, the belt is moved from one set of pulleys to another. Hand drills offer directional speed switches.

- **DRILL PRESS:** This is a stationary drill driven by an electric motor, pulley, and belt arrangement. A drill press allows for the use of various chucks.

Figure 8.3. Drilling Tools

- TAP: Taps are made from hardened steel. They are used to insert threads into holes in steel.
- HAND TAP: Taps are used to thread holes. The square end is inserted into the hand-tapping device.

Example

What is a left-hand drill bit used for?

(A) normal drilling operations

(B) removing studs and broken bolts

(C) tapping holes

(D) installing left-handed threaded studs

Answers:

(A) is incorrect. Right-hand bits are used for normal drilling operations.

(B) is correct. Left-hand bits rotate counterclockwise. This turns the object out of the threads.

(C) is incorrect. Taps are used to thread holes.

(D) is incorrect. Pliers are used to install studs.

STRIKING TOOLS

These tools supply force to align, trim, and mark components and materials. See Figure 8.4., Striking Tools.

- HAMMER: A hammer supplies impact force to tools and components. Many styles are available to accommodate all shop needs, including:
- BALL-PEEN HAMMER: A flat and rounded metal head is attached to a handle. This hammer is used with chisels, center punches, and other metal tools.
- RUBBER MALLET: A rubber head is attached to a handle. Mallets are used to align components without causing impact damage.
- WOODEN MALLET: A wood head is attached to a handle. Wooden mallets are used to align wooden pieces.
- CLAW HAMMER: The hammer head is made of metal, with a driving head on one side and a claw on the other. This is used to drive and pull nails.

Figure 8.4. Striking Tools

- **SLEDGEHAMMER:** A large metal dual-sided head is attached to a handle. These hammers are used to align large metal components.
- **PUNCH:** The most common uses for punches are to drive, align, and mark materials.
- **PIN PUNCH:** The head of a punch is designed to fit roll pins. Each punch is sized to a roll pin and is used to remove and install roll pins.
- **CENTER PUNCH:** A hardened punch head is ground to a point. Center punches are used to mark the location of holes for drilling.
- **DRIFT:** A drift is commonly a long shaft with a rounded head that is chamfer-ground. Drifts are used to align holes in components for assembly.
- **CHISEL:** Metal and wood chisels are among the most common tools of this type. The hardened ground cutting edge allows for impact cutting use.
- **NAIL GUN:** This can be operated from a battery or pneumatic supply. Each nail gun is designed to use a certain nail.

Example

Which tool is used to drive and pull nails?

(A) nail gun

(B) ball-peen hammer

(C) wooden mallet

(D) claw hammer

Answers:

(A) is incorrect. A nail gun will only drive nails.

(B) is incorrect. A ball-peen hammer will not remove nails.

(C) is incorrect. A wooden mallet will not remove nails.

(D) is correct. A claw hammer can drive and remove nails.

TURNING TOOLS

Screwdrivers

Screwdrivers are made in many lengths, head styles, and sizes. They are used to remove threaded fasteners. See Figure 8.5., Screwdrivers. Some screw heads are designed to prevent easy removal.

- **SCREWDRIVER:** A screwdriver is a hardened metal shaft inserted into a wood, plastic, or composite handle. The tip of the shaft is machined into various shapes, including:
- **FLAT-TIP/SLOTTED SCREWDRIVER:** This screwdriver is used with fasteners that have a slot in the head.

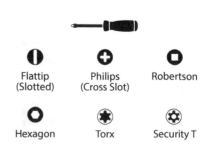

Figure 8.5. Screwdrivers

- **PHILLIPS/CROSS-SLOT SCREWDRIVER:** This tool comes with fasteners that have a cross slot in the head.
- **ROBERTSON SCREWDRIVER:** These screwdrivers are used with fasteners that have a square hole in the head.
- **TORX SCREWDRIVER:** This screwdriver has fasteners with a star hole in the head.
- **SECURITY T SCREWDRIVER:** This is used with fasteners that have a star hole and rod insert in the head.
- **HEXAGON SCREWDRIVER:** This tool comes with fasteners that have a hexagon hole in the head.

Example

Which tool is used to remove a threaded fastener with a head that has a star hole with a rod insert?

(A) Security T

(B) Torx

(C) Robertson

(D) Phillips/cross-slot

Answers:

(A) is correct. A Security T screwdriver has a star hole and rod insert in the head.

(B) is incorrect. A Torx fastener does not have a rod insert in the head.

(C) is incorrect. A Robertson fastener does not have a square hole in the head.

(D) is incorrect. This does not have a cross-slot in the head.

Wrenches

End wrench and socket wrenches are used in shop functions. See Figure 8.6., Wrenches. Each style is developed to remove hexagon head fasteners. Socket wrenches, often called ratchets, allow for quick removal of fasteners. The larger design of a ratchet prohibits use in confined areas. Wrenches are used for tight areas.

- **WRENCH:** A wrench is created by stamping metal from stock, then heat treating. Various styles are listed below:
- **OPEN-END WRENCH:** Both ends of this wrench are open. This wrench fits on hexagon head fasteners and is used in areas in which a box-end wrench will not fit.
- **BOX-END WRENCH:** Both ends of the wrench are closed in a six- or twelve-point configuration. This is used in areas where a ratchet or socket will not fit.
- **COMBINATION WRENCH:** This wrench is constructed with a box end on one side and an open end on the other. Open and box ends are generally the same size.

Figure 8.6. Wrenches

- **ADJUSTABLE WRENCH:** A thumbwheel adjusts the jaw of the wrench to change sizes.
- **RATCHET:** This tool has a reversible ratcheting device installed to allow for quick fastener installation and removal.
- **DRIVE SIZE:** The square drive on the ratchet is commonly available in $\frac{1}{4}$-inch, $\frac{3}{8}$-inch, $\frac{1}{2}$-inch, $\frac{3}{4}$-inch, and 1-inch sizes.
- **SIX-POINT SOCKET:** This socket is developed with six points and fits over hexagon head fasteners.
- **TWELVE-POINT SOCKET:** This is made with twelve points and fits over hexagon head fasteners.
- **IMPACT SOCKETS:** These sockets are created from softer steel and are designed for use with an impact wrench. Impact wrench and socket combinations are the quickest way to remove a nut or bolt.

Example

Which tool(s) is/are used to remove a threaded fastener quickly?

(A) ratchet and socket

(B) socket

(C) end wrench

(D) combination wrench

Answers:

(A) is correct. Both ratchet and socket are used for removal.

(B) is incorrect. A socket must be used with a ratchet.

(C) is incorrect. Any type of wrench is a slower method for use in confined areas.

(D) is incorrect. Any type of wrench is a slower method for use in confined areas.

FASTENERS

Fasteners are used in a variety of applications, listed below:

- **NAILS:** This fastener is most commonly used to fasten two pieces of wood together.
- **SCREWS:** This fastener can be used to attach wood or dissimilar materials.
- **NUTS AND BOLTS:** These are commonly used to attach components.
- **RIVETS:** These are used to fasten sheet metal to metal framework.

Each type of fastener has different designs and classifications.

Nails

Nails are created from wire stock, which is then formed into individual nails. Each style of nail is available in different lengths and sizes depending on the application. See Figure 8.7., Nails.

Commonly used styles of nails include:

- **FRAMING**: These nails are robust and are available in various sizes. They are commonly used to attach boards in construction.
- **MASONRY**: This nail is created with a vertical spiral shank and is mostly used to attach materials or components to stone or brickwork.
- **ROOFING**: This is a thick-body nail with a large wide head made of zinc or that has been galvanized. It is used to attach shingles to a roof.
- **DRYWALL**: This is a thin-body nail with horizontal extrusions on the shank and is used to attach drywall to wood framework.
- **FINISH**: This is a thin-shank nail with a small head containing a counter sunk hole. These nails are used in furniture applications.

The nail is divided into the following areas:

- **HEAD**: Force is applied to the head of the nail to drive into the desired material.
- **SHANK**: The nail shank is the material between the head and the point.
- **POINT**: The shank is tapered into a point that allows for ease of insertion into materials.

Framing Nail   Masonry Nail   Roofing Nail   Drywall Nail   Finish Nail

Figure 8.7. Nails

Example

Which nail is used to attach two boards together in construction applications?

(A) finish

(B) framing

(C) drywall

(D) roofing

Answers:

(A) is incorrect. Finish nails are used in furniture applications.

(B) is correct. Framing nails are used to attach boards in construction applications.

(C) is incorrect. These nails are used to attach drywall to wood framing.

(D) is incorrect. Roofing nails are used to attach shingles to roof boarding.

Screws

Screws start as wire stock. A machining process creates the head and threads on wire stock. Many styles of screws are available in different lengths and thread sizes, depending on the application. See Figure 8.8., Screws. Common styles of screws include:

- **WOOD**: This type of screw is created with a minimum of hardening and is threaded to a tapering fine point.
- **SHEET METAL**: This screw is harder than a wood screw and is threaded to a tapering fine point. A pilot hole must be drilled before using this screw.

- **MACHINE:** The threaded shaft on this screw is not tapered. It is developed to be used with a nut and washer combination, or to be used in a threaded hole.
- **SELF-DRILLING:** The point on this screw resembles a drill-bit point. These screws are used with metal and do not require a pilot hole.
- **MASONRY:** This screw is developed for masonry applications and has a second set of threads.

Wood   Sheet Metal Machine   Masonry   Self Drilling
Screw   Screw   Screw   Screw   Screw

Figure 8.8. Screws

Example

Which screw does NOT need a pilot hole and is used for metal applications?

(A) sheet metal

(B) self-drilling

(C) machine

(D) wood

Answers:

(A) is incorrect. This screw must have a pilot hole.

(B) is correct. This is used for metal and does not need a pilot hole.

(C) is incorrect. A machine screw is used with a washer and nut combination or with a threaded hole.

(D) is incorrect. This screw is used for wood applications only.

Nuts and Bolts

Nuts and bolts are used to attach one component to another. See Figure 8.9., Nuts and Bolts. Nuts can be threaded onto a stud or used in combination with a bolt, flat washer, or lock washer. Bolts are also used in threaded holes. Both nuts and bolts are available in various materials, sizes, and thread pitch.

A list of definitions of nuts and bolts and commonly used terms follows:

- **NUT:** A nut consists of a six-sided fastener with internal threads. Nuts are available in various sizes, thread pitches, and hardness ratings.
- **BOLT:** This fastener is a threaded shaft with a six-sided head. Bolts are available in multiple sizes, lengths, thread pitches, and hardness ratings.
- **WASHER:** Flat washers and lock washers are the most common types. When a flat-and-lock-washer combination is used, nuts will not loosen.
- **EXTERNAL THREAD:** This refers to any component with threads cut onto the outside diameter (bolt).
- **INTERNAL THREAD:** This refers to any component with threads cut into the inside diameter (nut).
- **THREAD PITCH:** Part of the sizing requirement for metric nuts and bolts is thread pitch, which refers to the distance between threads.

- **WING NUT:** This nut is designed with thumb tabs to allow for quick removal.
- **CASTLE NUT:** This nut is designed for use on components that require play for operation. Vehicle front-end components often require castle nut and cotter pin installation. The nut is installed on a component stud and is adjusted to specification. A cotter pin is inserted through the stud and nut.
- **LOCK NUT:** These nuts have an insert that locks into the threads of a bolt or stud. Applications using lock nuts do not need a lock washer.
- **THREAD-PITCH GAUGE:** These gauges are used to measure the pitch of a thread on a bolt or threaded hole.
- **UNIFIED NATIONAL COARSE (UNC):** This is the English standard for inside and outside coarse-threaded fasteners, which are classified in amount of threads per inch.
- **UNIFIED NATIONAL FINE (UNF):** This is the English standard for inside and outside fine-threaded fasteners, which are classified in amount of threads per inch.

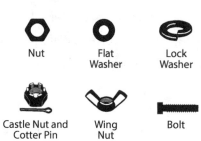

Figure 8.9. Nuts and Bolts

Example

Which fastener uses a cotter pin to secure it in place?

(A) wing nut

(B) bolt

(C) lock nut

(D) castle nut

Answers:

(A) is incorrect. Wing nuts are designed to be removed quickly and often.

(B) is incorrect. Standard bolts are not drilled for a cotter pin.

(C) is incorrect. Lock nuts are constructed with an insert and cannot use a cotter pin.

(D) is correct. Castle nuts use a cotter pin.

Snap Rings

Snap rings are constructed from hardened spring steel. See Figure 8.10., Snap Rings. They are designed to secure components inside a cylinder or on a shaft. Special tools are required to remove both types of snap rings. The snap ring styles and associated tools are as follows:

- **EXTERNAL SNAP RING:** These snap rings expand to fit over a shaft. They are often used in shaft and bearing assemblies.
- **INTERNAL SNAP RING:** These snap rings compress to fit inside a bore. They often secure bearings inside housings.
- **SNAP-RING PLIERS:** These pliers are available in internal, external, and both styles. The tool ends move inward or outward.

Figure 8.10. Snap Rings

Example

Internal snap rings are used for which application(s)?

(A) securing a bearing to a shaft

(B) securing a bearing inside a bore

(C) joining two pieces of metal

(D) both A and C

Answers:

(A) is incorrect. Internal snap rings do not expand; they contract.

(B) is correct. Internal snap rings are compressed to be inserted into a bore.

(C) is incorrect. Welding joins two pieces of metal together.

(D) is incorrect. B is only correct answer.

Rivets

A rivet is a hollow, short metal cylinder with a pin inserted through the middle. See Figure 8.11., Rivets and Rivet Gun. Rivets are used to fasten two pieces together. One end of the cylinder has a large flat head, and the other end is the size of the hole in metal pieces. Rivets are inserted into gun, and the small end is expanded after insertion into metal pieces. Rivets must be drilled to be removed.

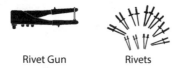

Rivet Gun   Rivets

Figure 8.11. Rivet Gun and Rivets

Example

What application are rivets used for?

(A) attaching wood pieces

(B) attaching metal pieces

(C) boring holes in metal

(D) threading drilled holes

Answers:

(A) is incorrect. Wood screws are used for wood applications.

(B) is correct. Rivets are used for connecting pieces of metal.

(C) is incorrect. Drill bits bore holes.

(D) is incorrect. A tap is used to thread holes.

SOLDERING AND WELDING TOOLS

There are two forms of attaching metallic components. Soldering uses direct heat from a soldering iron or gun. Welding uses electrical current to melt the rod between two pieces of metal. See Figure 8.12., Soldering and Welding Tools. The tools and accessories necessary to complete various soldering and welding operations are listed below:

- **SOLDERING:** This is the process that joins electrical components or wires in electrical applications. Direct heat is used with flux or rosin to melt a lead acid solder that joins different components or wire.

- **SOLDERING IRON:** This is an electrically operated tool that is commonly used in circuit card repair.

- **SOLDERING GUN:** This is an electrically operated tool that is commonly used to join large electrical wires.

- **ROSIN-CORE SOLDER:** This solder has a rosin core that melts when heated, eliminating the need for applying external rosin.

- **WELDING:** This is the process of joining metal pieces or components together without the use of fasteners. Electric welders are plugged into an electrical supply, and the ground lead is connected to one of the pieces of metal to be welded. Unlike soldering, the base metal itself is melted, not a filler metal or solder that connects different items.

- **OXYACETYLENE WELDING:** This operation is performed with an oxyacetylene torch set, which is composed of gauges, an oxygen tank, an acetylene tank, and a torch with a rosebud end installed. This type of welding is most commonly used on soft-metal applications.

- **FILLER ROD:** This is constructed from different metals, with brass as the most common. The rods are used to attach softer metals in oxyacetylene welding operations.

- **ELECTRIC-ARC WELDING:** This type of welder uses electricity to melt a metal rod joining metal pieces. The welder plugs into supply voltage, and ground lead is connected to metal to weld.

- **STINGER:** This is a connector that holds welding in electric-arc welding operations.

- **WELDING ROD:** The rod is coated with flux and inserted into a stinger to attach metal pieces.

- **MIG WELDING:** Wire is routed through the stinger in these applications. The operator can continuously weld until the wire roll is exhausted.

Figure 8.12. Soldering and Welding Tools

⟶
CONTINUE

Example

Which welder(s) uses/use a wire feed to attach metal pieces?

(A) MIG welder

(B) electric-arc welder

(C) oxyacetylene welder

(D) Both MIG and arc welder

Answers:

(A) is correct. The MIG welder uses wire feed.

(B) is incorrect. The electric-arc welder uses welding rod.

(C) is incorrect. The oxyacetylene welder uses fill rod.

(D) is incorrect. A is the only correct answer.

GRIPPING TOOLS

Gripping tools are designed to cut, squeeze, and lock onto various-size objects. See Figure 8.13., Gripping Tools. Some tools are designed to grip small objects, while others can lock onto rounded nuts or studs. Common gripping tools include:

- **PLIERS**: These do not have adjustable jaws. The jaw opening limits the objects that can be gripped.
- **COMBINATION SLIP-JOINT PLIERS**: The jaws of these pliers are milled so that the pliers can adjust to one size larger.
- **ADJUSTABLE-JOINT PLIERS**: The jaws of these pliers are milled so that they can adjust to many sizes.
- **LINEMAN PLIERS**: These pliers have jaws capable of cutting and gripping. They are commonly used by electricians in wiring applications.
- **DIAGONAL CUTTERS**: The jaws of this tool are designed for cutting wire.
- **NEEDLE-NOSE PLIERS**: These pliers are designed to grip small components in tight areas.
- **LOCKING PLIERS**: These pliers have a thumbscrew on the back handle, which is adjusted to vary the size of locking jaws.

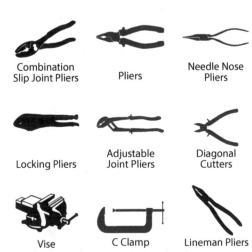

Figure 8.13. Gripping Tools

- **C-CLAMP**: These clamps are available in various sizes and have many applications, including using with steel in metalworking projects.
- **VISE**: A vise is commonly mounted on a sturdy shop bench. The jaws are adjusted by turning the T-handle.

Example

Which gripping tool is used to grip small objects in a confined area?

(A) needle-nose pliers

(B) adjustable-joint pliers

(C) lineman pliers

(D) locking pliers

Answers:

(A) is correct. Needle-nose pliers are designed for work on small components in small areas.

(B) is incorrect. The ends of these pliers do not allow access into small areas.

(C) is incorrect. Lineman pliers are used for electrical work and are too large.

(D) is incorrect. These pliers are used to lock onto objects and are not designed for small-area work.

FINISHING TOOLS

Finishing tools are used to apply finish to a wood or metal project. See Figure 8.14., Finishing Tools. The finish on the product depends largely on the tool used to apply the finish and can vary from a rough to a fine finish on wood or metal. Common hand tools for applying finish include:

- **PLANE:** A plane is used to level a wooden surface prior to the sanding and finishing process.

- **JACK PLANE:** This tool requires two hands to operate. An adjustable blade allows the operator to determine the amount of wood to be removed in a single pass.

- **WOOD CHISEL:** This chisel is designed to remove wood in small amounts. Impact force is applied by a hammer to remove desired material.

- **FILE:** This is an instrument made from steel flat bar stock. Cutting design implication and heat treatment finish the tool. The file has multiple uses that are determined by design and hardness. Common files include:

- **FLAT FILE:** Both surfaces are flat on this file. It is commonly used for filing flat surfaces.

- **HALF-ROUND FILE:** This file is constructed with a flat surface on one side and a half-round surface on the other. It is commonly used for filing curved surfaces.

- **TRIANGULAR FILE:** The file is created with three equal surfaces and is used to remove material on internal surfaces.

- **RASP:** This file is a coarse-tooth file used in wood and soft-material applications.

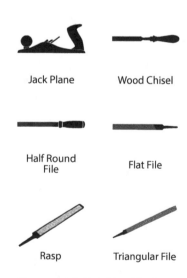

Jack Plane   Wood Chisel

Half Round File   Flat File

Rasp   Triangular File

Figure 8.14. Finishing Tools

Example

What tool is used to remove material on internal surfaces?

(A) triangular file

(B) flat file

(C) rasp

(D) miter saw

Answers:

(A) is correct. A triangular file is used to remove material on internal surfaces.

(B) is incorrect. A flat file is used to remove material on flat surfaces.

(C) is incorrect. A rasp is used to remove large amounts of material on flat and curved surfaces.

(D) is incorrect. A miter saw is used to cut boards at various angles.

MECHANICAL COMPREHENSION

The Mechanical Comprehension section of the ASVAB tests candidates' understanding of the basic principles of physics and how those principles are applied to real-world situations. Topics include Newton's laws of motion, work and energy, and simple machines. The CAT-ASVAB includes sixteen mechanical comprehension questions to be answered in twenty minutes. The paper-and-pencil ASVAB includes twenty-five questions to be answered in nineteen minutes.

FORCES

Newton's Laws

A fundamental concept of mechanics is INERTIA, which states that an object has a tendency to maintain its state of motion. An object at rest will stay at rest, and an object moving at constant velocity will continue to move at that velocity, unless something pushes or pulls on it. This push or pull is called a FORCE. The newton (N) is the SI unit for force (1 newton is 1 kg m/s^2).

MASS is a fundamental property of matter and is a measure of the inertia of an object. The kilogram (kg) is the SI unit for mass. An object with a larger mass will resist a change in motion more than an object with a smaller mass will. For example, it is harder to throw an elephant than it is to throw a baseball (the elephant has much more mass than a baseball).

> ⚠️
> A **system** is a collection of particles or objects that is isolated from its surroundings. All forces within a system are called internal forces, and forces outside the system are called external forces.

In 1687, Isaac Newton published three laws of motion that describe the behavior of force and mass. Newton's first law is also called the law of inertia. It states that an object will maintain its current state of motion unless acted on by an outside force.

Newton's second law is an equation,

$$F = ma$$

where F is the sum of the forces on an object (also called the net force), m is the mass of the object, and a is the acceleration. The law states that the net force on an object will lead to an acceleration. Also, if an object has an acceleration, there must be a force that is causing it. Extending the previous example, if the same amount of force is applied to an elephant and a baseball, the baseball will have a much larger acceleration than the elephant (and so it is easier to throw).

An object in EQUILIBRIUM is either at rest or is moving at constant velocity; in other words, the object has no acceleration, or $a = 0$. Using Newton's second law, an object is in equilibrium if the net force on the object is 0, or $F = 0$ (this is called the equilibrium condition).

Newton's third law states that for every action (force), there will be an equal and opposite reaction (force). For instance, if a person is standing on the floor, there is a force of gravity pulling him toward the earth. However, he is not accelerating toward the earth; he is simply standing at rest on the floor (in equilibrium). So, the floor must provide a force that is equal in magnitude and in the opposite direction to the force of gravity.

Newton's second law, $F = ma$, can be used to remember all three laws.

If there is no outside force ($F = 0$), the object will not accelerate and thus will stay at rest or at a constant velocity (Newton's first law).

If an object is resting on the floor, it is not moving, and $a = 0$. To maintain this equilibrium, the weight of the object must be matched by the force pushing up from the floor (Newton's third law).

Another example is a person kicking a wall. While it may seem like kicking a wall would only damage the wall, the force applied to the wall from the person's foot is identical to the force applied to the person's foot from the wall.

Examples

1. When a car moving forward stops abruptly, which of the following describes what happens to the driver if she is wearing a seat belt?

   (A) The driver's body will continue to move forward due to inertia, and the seat belt will apply the required force to keep her in her seat.

   (B) The driver is inside the car, so she will stop with the car whether or not she is wearing a seat belt.

   (C) Due to inertia, the driver's body wants to be at rest, so she will stop automatically once the car stops moving.

   (D) The driver's body will slow down because inertia is passed from the seat belt in the car to the driver.

   Answers:

   (A) is correct. The driver's body will continue moving forward due to inertia. A force is required to slow the driver down (Newton's first law).

   (B) is incorrect. Being inside the car does not matter; a force is required to slow the driver down.

   (C) is incorrect. Inertia states that an object will remain at rest or at constant velocity.

   (D) is incorrect. Inertia is not passed between objects; it is a property of matter stating that objects have a tendency to remain at rest or at constant velocity.

2. Which example describes an object in equilibrium?

    (A) a parachutist after he jumps from an airplane

    (B) an airplane taking off

    (C) a person sitting still in a chair

    (D) a soccer ball when it is kicked

Answers:

(A) is incorrect. The parachutist will accelerate toward the earth.

(B) is incorrect. The airplane is accelerating to take off.

(C) is correct. The person is not accelerating.

(D) is incorrect. During a kick, the soccer ball is accelerating.

Types of Forces

There are four **FUNDAMENTAL FORCES** that form the basis for all other forces. The **GRAV-ITATIONAL** force is the force that pulls mass together. It is an attractive force and is what holds stars and planets together as spheres and keeps them in orbit. It also keeps humans on the surface of the earth. The **WEAK** force is beyond the scope of this text, but it plays a role in nuclear reactions (like those in stars). The **ELECTROMAGNETIC** force is the force between electric charges. It is repulsive when the charges are the same sign (positive-positive or negative-negative) and is attractive when the charges are the opposite sign (positive-negative). This force holds the positive nuclei and negative electrons of atoms together. Finally, the **NUCLEAR** (or strong) force is so named because it holds together the nucleus in an atom. The nuclear force has a larger magnitude than the electromagnetic force that pushes protons (positive charges) away from each other in the nucleus.

Non-fundamental forces are defined as forces that can be derived from the four fundamental forces. These forces include tension, friction, the normal force, and the buoyant force. **TENSION** (F_T or T) is found in ropes pulling or holding up an object, and **FRICTION** (F_f) is created by two objects moving against each other. The **NORMAL FORCE** (F_N or N) occurs when an object is resting on another object. The normal force is always equal and opposite to the force pushing onto the surface. The **BUOYANT** force (F_B) is the upward force experienced by floating objects. Finally, an **APPLIED FORCE** (F_A) is any force applied to an object by another object.

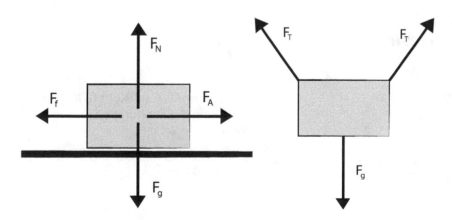

Figure 9.1. Free-Body Diagrams

When working with forces, it is helpful to draw a **FREE-BODY DIAGRAM**, which shows all the forces acting on an object. Because forces are vectors, it is important to consider the direction of the force when drawing a diagram.

Example

Which of the following forces causes oppositely charged ions to attract?

(A) nuclear

(B) electromagnetic

(C) tension

(D) gravitational

Answers:

(A) is incorrect. The nuclear force holds together the subatomic particles in an atom's nucleus.

(B) is correct. The electromagnetic force is the force between charged particles that causes them to attract or repel each other.

(C) is incorrect. Tension is a force that results from an object being pulled or hung from a rope or chain.

(D) is incorrect. The gravitational force is the attractive force between masses.

Weight

The gravitational force felt by an object on the surface of the earth is called the object's **WEIGHT**. The acceleration due to gravity on the surface of the earth is $g = 9.8$ m/s^2 and always points toward the center of the earth. Using Newton's second law, the weight W of an object of mass m is

$$W = mg$$

Example

An object with a weight of 32 N on the moon is brought to Earth. If the acceleration due to gravity on the moon is 1.6 m/s^2, what is the weight of the object on Earth?

(A) 1.96 N

(B) 19.6 N

(C) 196 N

(D) 1,960 N

Answer:

$W = mg$ $32 = m(1.6)$ $m = 20$ kg	Use the formula for weight to find the object's mass using the acceleration due to gravity on the moon.
$W = mg$ $W = 20(9.8) =$ **196 N (C)**	Use the object's mass to find its weight on Earth using $g = 9.8$ m/s^2.

Tension

A common type of applied force is **TENSION**, the force applied by a rope or chain as it pulls on an object. In a free-body diagram, the vector for tension always points along the rope away from the object. Tension plays an important role in pulley systems, as shown in the figure below. The tension in the pulley's rope acts against the mass's weight, and the magnitude of the two forces determines whether the mass moves up or down.

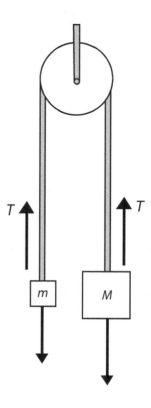

Example

In the figure on the right, if mass *M* is much greater than mass *m*, what direction do both masses move?

(A) Mass *M* will move down, and mass *m* will move up.

(B) Mass *M* will move up, and mass *m* will move down.

(C) Neither mass will move; the system is in equilibrium.

(D) Both masses will move down.

Answers:

(A) is correct. If mass *M* is larger, then the weight of mass *M* will produce a larger force than the weight of mass *m*. The larger force will move mass *M* down and mass *m* up.

(B) is incorrect. If mass *M* is larger, then the weight of mass *M* will produce a larger force than the weight of mass *m*. The larger force will move mass *M* down and mass *m* up.

(C) is incorrect. The forces are not balanced. Mass *M* will have a larger weight, so the system is not in equilibrium.

(D) is incorrect. A pulley will not allow the masses to move in this way.

Friction

Microscopically, no surface is perfectly smooth. The irregular shape of the surfaces in contact will lead to interactions that resist movement. The resulting force is **FRICTION**. Friction opposes motion and describes the resistance of two surfaces in contact as they move across each other. On a free-body diagram, friction always points in the direction opposite the object's motion.

There are two types of friction: static and kinetic. **STATIC FRICTION** is applicable to an object that is not moving and is always equal to the force applied to the object. In other words, it is the amount of force that needs to be overcome for an object to move. For example, a small force applied to a large rock will not move the rock because static friction will match the applied force in the opposite direction. However, when enough force is applied, static friction can be overcome, and an object will begin moving. When this happens, the moving object experiences **KINETIC** friction.

The size of the friction force is dependent on an object's weight. Think of a couch being slid across a carpet. The couch becomes much harder to move if a person sits on the couch, and harder still if more people are added. This effect is written mathematically in terms of the normal force from the surface:

$$f_s \leq \mu_s N \qquad\qquad f_k = \mu_k N$$

where f_s and f_k are the static and kinetic forces of friction, μ_s and μ_k are the static and kinetic coefficients of friction, and N is the normal force.

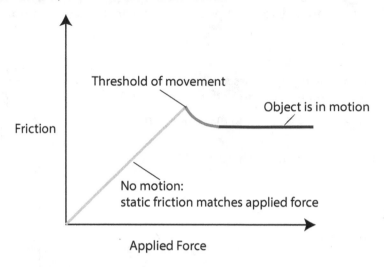

Figure 9.2. Static and Kinetic Friction

Examples

1. If a block is sliding down an inclined plane, in what direction will the friction vector point?

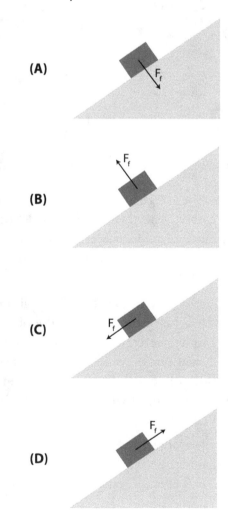

Answers:

(A) is incorrect. This describes the direction of the component of the block's weight into the plane.

(B) is incorrect. This describes the direction of the normal force.

(C) is incorrect. The force of friction will always oppose motion.

(D) is correct. If the block is moving down the plane, the force of friction points up the plane.

2. In which of the following situations is an object experiencing static friction?

   (A) an ice skater skating around a rink

   (B) a person in a moving car slamming on the brakes

   (C) a refrigerator that slides down a ramp

   (D) a person leaning against a car

Answers:

(A) is incorrect. Kinetic friction will be in effect because the ice skater is moving.

(B) is incorrect. Kinetic friction will be in effect because the car is moving.

(C) is incorrect. Kinetic friction will be in effect because the refrigerator is moving.

(D) is correct. The person is applying a force to the car, and static friction is keeping the car from moving.

Buoyant Force

When a boat or object is floating or under water or another liquid, the BUOYANT FORCE pushes vertically against the weight of the object. The magnitude of this force is calculated by considering the volume of the object that is submerged in the fluid. The object displaces a volume of liquid equal to its own volume, and the liquid pushes back by an amount that is exactly equal to the weight of the liquid that would exist in that volume. The buoyant force (always a vector pointing up), is given by

$$F_{buoyant} = m_{fluid}g = \rho V$$

where m_{fluid} is the mass of the fluid displaced, ρ is the density of the fluid, V is the volume of fluid that is displaced by the object, and g is the acceleration due to gravity.

Example

Which object will experience the largest buoyant force when fully submerged?

(A) a marble

(B) a golf ball

(C) a baseball

(D) a basketball

Answers:

(A) is incorrect. Of the five, the marble does not have the largest volume.

(B) is incorrect. Of the five, the golf ball does not have the largest volume.

(C) is incorrect. Of the five, the baseball does not have the largest volume.

(D) is correct. A basketball will have the largest volume and will displace the most water. This will lead to the largest buoyant force of the five.

Torque

TORQUE is the force required to rotate an object. The units for torque are N m (newton meters), and the equation is:

$$\tau = rF$$

where r is the radius (the distance from the axis of rotation to the location of F), and F is the force. It is important to understand that r and F are vectors and that the equation is valid only in the case where r and F are perpendicular to each other.

 Boats float by using the buoyant force. Ships that hold very large loads need a large buoyant force and so need to displace a large amount of water.

Remember that mass is measure of inertia, where a larger mass is harder to accelerate with a force. MOMENT OF INERTIA is similarly used when discussing a rotating object to describe the object's inertia, or, its resistance to being rotated. A large amount of mass far away from the axis of rotation will have a larger moment of inertia than a smaller mass closer to the axis of rotation. For a single mass m at a distance r from a rotation axis, the moment of inertia is given by

$$I = mr^2$$

For an object to be truly in equilibrium in terms of energy, it must not only be at rest or at constant velocity ($F = 0$); it must also not be rotating ($\tau = 0$). The object is then in ROTATIONAL EQUILIBRIUM.

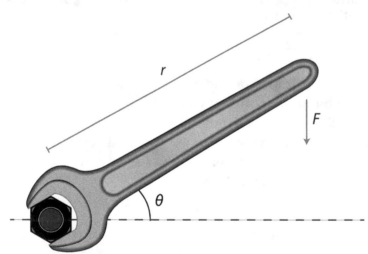

Figure 9.3. Torque

Example

Of the choices below, which object has the highest moment of inertia?

(A)

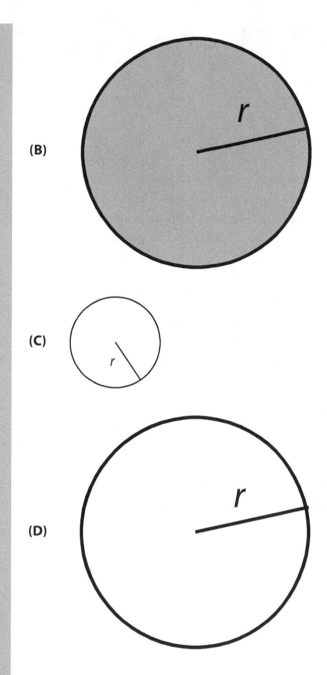

(B)

(C)

(D)

Answers:

(A) is incorrect. An object's moment of inertia is largest when it has mass that is located far away from the axis of rotation. Compared to object D, the mass in this disk is closer to the axis of rotation.

(B) is ncorrect. Compared to object D, most of the mass in this disk is closer to the axis of rotation.

(C) is incorrect. The mass of this object is located at a smaller distance from the axis of rotation than object D.

(D) is correct. This object has identical mass to the other objects, but all the mass is located at a larger distance from the axis of rotation than the other objects.

WORK, ENERGY, AND POWER

Work

WORK is a scalar value that is defined as the application of a force over a distance. The SI unit for work is joule (J). The equation for work is

$$W = Fd$$

where F is the force and d is the distance.

One example is a person lifting a book off the ground. As she lifts the book, the book has a weight, and her hand and arm are producing a force that is larger than that weight to make the book rise. In terms of work, the person's hand is doing work on the book to lift the book from the ground to its final position. If she drops the book, the force of gravity will push the book back to the ground. So, during a drop, gravity (the earth) is doing work on the book.

Another example is a person holding the book steady. Neither his hand nor gravity are doing work on the book because the book is not moving any distance. However, it is interesting to note that the person's hand and arm will get tired holding a book in the air. This is due to work that is done inside his body to keep his hand at its position while holding the book.

The sign of the work done is important. In the example of lifting a book, the person's hand is doing positive (+) work on the book. However, gravity is always pulling the book down, which means that during a lift, gravity is doing negative (–) work on the book. This can be expressed as such: If the force and the displacement are in the same direction, then the work is positive (+). If the force and the displacement are in opposite directions, then the work is negative (–). In the case of lifting a book, the net work done on the book is positive.

Example

Which situation requires the most work done on a car?

(A) pushing on the car, but it does not move

(B) towing the car up a steep hill for 100 meters

(C) pushing the car 5 meters across a parking lot

(D) painting the car

Answers:

(A) is incorrect. If the car does not move, then no work is done on the car.

(B) is correct. A steep hill requires a large force to counter the gravitational force. The large distance will also lead to a large amount of work done.

(C) Is incorrect. Work will be done, but much less than in case B.

(D) is incorrect. Painting the car is "work," but this is not the proper definition of *work* in mechanics. The car is not moving while being painted, so no work is done on the car.

Energy

ENERGY is an abstract concept, but everything in nature has an energy associated with it. There are many types of energy, including mechanical, chemical, thermal, nuclear, electric, magnetic, and so on. The **MECHANICAL ENERGY** of an object is due to its motion (kinetic energy) and position (potential energy). Energy is a scalar and is given in the SI unit of joules (J).

There is an energy related to movement called the **KINETIC ENERGY**. Any object that has mass and is moving will have a kinetic energy. The equation for kinetic energy is

$$KE = \frac{1}{2}mv^2$$

where m is the mass and v is the speed.

POTENTIAL ENERGY is understood as the potential for an object to gain kinetic energy. This can also be seen as energy stored in a system. There are several types of potential energy. **ELECTRIC POTENTIAL ENERGY** is derived from the interaction between positive and negative charges. Because opposite charges attract each other, and like charges repel, energy can be stored when opposite charges are moved apart or when like charges are pushed together. Similarly, compressing a spring stores **ELASTIC POTENTIAL ENERGY**. Energy is also stored in chemical bonds as **CHEMICAL POTENTIAL ENERGY**.

The energy stored in a book placed on a table is **GRAVITATIONAL POTENTIAL ENERGY**; it is derived from the pull of the earth's gravity on the book. The equation for gravitational potential energy is given by

$$PE_g = mgh$$

where m is the mass, g is 9.8 m/s^2 (remember mg is an object's weight), and h is the height.

A simple way to understand gravitational potential energy is to consider an object's initial height. The speed of an object at a moment just before hitting the ground (and therefore the kinetic energy difference just before hitting the ground) after falling from a short stool to the ground may be compared to the speed of an object falling from the roof of a house to the ground. The jump from the roof will lead to a much higher kinetic energy, so the potential energy is higher on the roof.

Energy can be converted into other forms of energy, but it cannot be created or destroyed. This principle is called the **CONSERVATION OF ENERGY**. A swing provides a simple example of this principle. Throughout the swing's path, the total energy of the system remains the same. At the highest point of a swing's path, it has potential energy but no

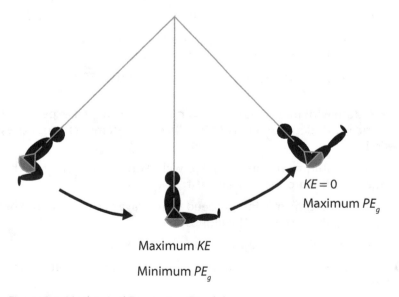

$KE = 0$
Maximum PE_g

Maximum KE

Minimum PE_g

Figure 9.4. Mechanical Energy in a Pendulum

kinetic energy (because it has stopped moving momentarily as it changes direction). As the swing drops, that potential energy is converted to kinetic energy, and the swing's velocity increases. At the bottom of its path, all its potential energy has been converted into kinetic energy (meaning its potential energy is zero). This process repeats as the swing moves up and down. At any point in the swing's path, the kinetic and potential energies will sum to the same value.

> Electrical power plants are energy converters. A hydroelectric plant converts gravitational energy (from water falling through the dam) into electrical energy. A nuclear power plant converts nuclear energy into electrical energy. Coal and gas power plants convert chemical energy into electrical energy. Solar panels convert light energy into electrical energy.

In reality, there is air resistance against the swing, and there is friction between the swing's chain and the bar that holds the swing. Friction (and air resistance) convert mechanical energies into heat (thermal energy). This is why a swing will gradually slow down and reach lower heights with each back-and-forth motion. Energy loss through heat also occurs in electronics and motors.

Revisiting the concept of work, a change in position with the application of a force will necessarily lead to a velocity and therefore to kinetic energy. So, work is effectively an energy and can be related to kinetic energy with the following equation:

$$W = \Delta KE = \frac{1}{2}mv_2^2 - \frac{1}{2}mv_1^2$$

Examples

1. Imagine a roller coaster that does not have its own power and starts on a hill at a height of 100 meters. There is no air resistance or friction. It falls down to a height of 50 meters in the first dip and begins to move up the next hill that is 200 meters high. What will happen to the coaster on the next hill?

    (A) It will slow down but will make it over the 200 m hill.

    (B) It will make it up to 150 m up the hill and move back down to the first dip.

    (C) It will make it up to 100 m up the hill and move back down to the first dip.

    (D) It will make it up to 75 m up the hill and move back down to the first dip.

    Answers:

    (A) is incorrect. It will not have enough energy to make it over the hill.

    (B) is incorrect. It will not have enough energy to make it to 150 m.

    (C) is correct. Its maximum energy is from its starting point, the potential energy at 100 m, so it can never move higher than 100 m.

    (D) is incorrect. It has enough energy to make it past 75 m.

2. A pendulum with mass *m* is swinging back and forth. If it experiences both air resistance and friction, which of the following statements about the pendulum's speed is true?

    (A) The pendulum's maximum speed will always occur where the height of the mass off the ground is the lowest.

    (B) The pendulum's maximum speed will always occur where the height of the mass off the ground is the highest.

    (C) The mass will always travel at the same speed.

    (D) The pendulum's maximum speed will be at a height that is half of the maximum height.

Answers:

(A) is correct. When the height is the lowest, the potential energy is a minimum, and so the kinetic energy is at its maximum.

(B) is incorrect. When the height is the highest, the potential energy is a maximum, and so the kinetic energy is at its minimum.

(C) is incorrect. The kinetic energy will change during the path.

(D) is incorrect. At half the maximum height, the kinetic energy will be less than it is at the lowest height.

Power

As stated before, energy cannot be created or destroyed but can only change forms. A measure of this transfer of energy is called **POWER**, which is the rate of work done or energy conversion per time. The SI unit for power is a watt, W. Because work is defined as a force applied along a distance, power can also be written as a force multiplied by a speed. Power is a scalar with an equation that is given by

$$P = \frac{W}{t} = Fv$$

where W is the work done (or energy converted) over an amount of time t, F is a force, and v is the speed.

Power is a commonly used measure of electrical devices. For example, light bulbs are labeled in terms of their wattage (40 W, 60 W, etc.). A 60 W light bulb will use 60 joules of electrical energy per second, and this energy will be converted into light energy (that is the light bulb's purpose), but also a great deal of that energy is converted into thermal energy (heat). The heat from light bulbs is wasted energy.

Electrical power from power companies is commonly charged in terms of kilowatt hours (kWh). From the equation for power above, the energy used during a time period can be calculated by multiplying the power by time. As an example, the energy used can be expressed as the amount kilowatts used multiplied by the number of hours. So, kilowatt hours is a unit of energy (1kWh = 3,600,000 J).

Examples

1. Which of the following is NOT a unit of energy?

    (A) joule

    (B) kilowatt hour

    (C) watt second

    (D) newton

Answers:

(A) is incorrect. A joule is the unit for energy.

(B) is incorrect. Any form of watt multiplied by an amount of time is suitable for representing energy.

(C) is incorrect. Any form of watt multiplied by an amount of time is suitable for representing energy.

(D) is correct. A newton is the unit for force.

2. A constant external force of 10 N is applied to an object to keep it moving at a constant speed of 10 m/s. Which of the following statements about the object is true?

(A) No power is used to move the object.

(B) The external force supplies power to keep the object moving at 10 m/s.

(C) The object is not accelerating, so no power is used.

(D) There is no work done on the object.

Answers:

(A) is incorrect. Power is the result of a constant force on an object moving at constant speed, so power is used to move the object.

(B) is correct. One definition for power is force multiplied by speed, so the external force is supplying power.

(C) is incorrect. The object does not need to accelerate to use power.

(D) is incorrect. There is an external force and distance traveled by the object, so there is work done on the object.

MOMENTUM AND COLLISIONS

The term **MOMENTUM** is a common one in the English language, but it has a specific meaning in mechanics: the mass of an object multiplied by its velocity. Any object that has mass and is also moving has momentum. Momentum is a vector and is given by the equation

$$p = mv$$

where m is the mass and v is the velocity.

The concept of momentum can be used to describe a change in motion. For example, a baseball has a certain momentum when it is traveling through the air, but it has zero momentum once it has been caught. A change in velocity requires a force to cause an acceleration over a period of time, t. The change in momentum is called the **IMPULSE** and can be written as

$$I = \Delta p = mv_2 - mv_1 = Ft$$

where p is the momentum; m and v are mass and speed, respectively; and F is the force over a time, t.

The relationship for impulse has interesting implications. If an object has a momentum change, then there was a force applied over a time t to cause that change. So, for an identical impulse value, a longer time requires less force to be used. Similarly, a shorter time requires more force. This is why a baseball catcher will wear a thick mitt and other padding to increase the interaction time that slows the ball. As a result, the catcher's hand feels a much smaller force than it would without the glove. Using the same reasoning, but in reverse, a baseball bat has no padding, which decreases the interaction time and relatively increases the force applied to the ball.

You are an astronaut in space and are holding a baseball in your hand. If you make the motion to throw the ball but never actually throw it, will you still move away as if you did?

Like energy, **MOMENTUM IS CONSERVED**. However, momentum is conserved only when there are no outside forces on the system. Conservation of momentum states that if an object in a system is given momentum, then all the other objects in the system will have a net momentum that will be opposite to the object. The total momentum of the system remains unchanged. For example, the sidebar on the previous page addresses an astronaut is at rest in space. If she throws an object to her right, her body will also move to the left in response.

Examples

1. Modern cars are designed to crumple during a collision. Using the concept of impulse, how does this protect the passengers?

   (A) By decreasing the interaction time, the crumple maximizes the force felt by the passengers.

   (B) By decreasing the interaction time, the crumple minimizes the force felt by the passengers.

   (C) By increasing the interaction time, the crumple maximizes the force felt by the passengers.

   (D) By increasing the interaction time, the crumple minimizes the force felt by the passengers.

   Answers:

   (A) is incorrect. The crumple will increase the interaction time. A decrease in interaction time will increase the amount of force felt by the passengers.

   (B) is incorrect. The crumple will increase the interaction time. A decrease in interaction time will increase the amount of force felt by the passengers.

   (C) is incorrect. The crumple does increase the time of interaction, but this decreases the force felt by the passengers.

   (D) is correct. The crumple increases the time of interaction and so decreases the force felt by the passengers.

2. A man is sitting in a boat next to a dock and decides to jump from the boat to the dock. The boat is much lighter than the man. Using conservation of momentum, what will be the most likely result?

   (A) The man will most likely fall into the water.

   (B) The man will reach the dock with no problem.

   (C) The boat will not move.

   (D) The man will remain in the boat.

   Answers:

   (A) is correct. The boat will move behind the man at high speed, while the man will move forward at low speed. He will most likely end up falling in the water.

   (B) is incorrect. The boat will move behind the man at high speed, while the man will move forward at low speed. He will most likely end up falling in the water.

   (C) is incorrect. If the man jumps toward the dock, the boat will move away from the dock.

   (D) is incorrect. If the man jumps toward the dock, the boat will move away from the dock. So, the man and the boat will separate.

CONTINUE

SIMPLE MACHINES

A simple machine changes the magnitude or direction of an applied force, with the result leading to a MECHANICAL ADVANTAGE for the user. This advantage is the ratio of force that is output from the machine relative to the force input. The equation for mechanical advantage is given by

$$MA = \frac{F_{output}}{F_{input}}$$

A LEVER is a simple machine based on the concept of torque. The axis of rotation and also where the lever rests is called the FULCRUM. Using the figure as a guide, $r_{input} F_{input} = r_{output} F_{output}$. Using the previous definition for mechanical advantages gives

$$MA = \frac{r_{input}}{r_{output}}$$

There are three types of levers. A FIRST-CLASS LEVER has the fulcrum between the input and output forces, and the input force is in the opposite direction of the output force. A SECOND-CLASS LEVER has the input and output forces on one common side of the fulcrum, and both are in the same direction. The output force is closer to the fulcrum than the input force is. Like the second-class lever, a THIRD-CLASS LEVER has the input and output forces on one common side of the fulcrum, and both are in the same direction. The input force is closer to the fulcrum than the output force is.

The idea of simple machines was invented by Archimedes in the third century BCE.

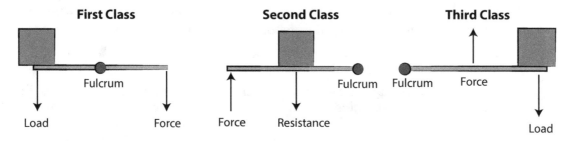

Figure 9.5. Types of Levers

An INCLINED PLANE is a simple machine (a ramp) that reduces the amount of force needed to raise a mass to a certain height. Earlier in this text it was shown that the weight of a mass on an inclined plane has a portion that pushes into the plane. Only a fraction of the weight is in the direction down the plane. This is the operating principle for this simple machine. In terms of work, the input work to move an object up an inclined plane of length L is $W_{in} = F_{input} \times L$. The output work is what is required to lift the object up to a height h, $W_{output} = F_{output} \times h$, where F_{output} is the object's weight. Combining these gives the mechanical advantage

$$MA = \frac{L}{h}$$

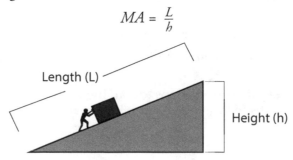

Figure 9.6. An Inclined Plane

where L is the length of the inclined plane and h is the height.

A **PULLEY** is a simple machine that redirects force by supporting a rope that can move freely by rotating the pulley. A single pulley lifting a weight will have a mechanical advantage of 1. When a second pulley is added in a block-and-tackle configuration, the input force required to lift the weight is halved, and so the mechanical advantage is 2. Similarly, a three-pulley system will have a mechanical advantage of 3.

$$MA = \text{number of pulleys}$$

A **WEDGE** is a simple machine that converts an input force onto one surface into a force that is perpendicular to its other surfaces. A wedge is often used to separate material; common examples are an ax or knife. Using the same reasoning as used for an inclined plane (a wedge is effectively two inclined planes on top of each other), the mechanical advantage is

Figure 9.7. A Three-Pulley System

$$MA = \frac{L}{W}$$

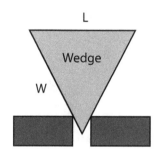

Figure 9.8. A Simple Wedge

where L is the length of the inclined plane on the wedge, and W is the width (the length of the back edge).

A **WHEEL AND AXLE** is a simple machine that has a rotating structure with two different radii. The larger radius is the wheel, and the smaller radius is the axle. It is similar conceptually to a lever, where the different radii convert the torque on the wheel into a torque on the axle (or vice versa). The mechanical advantage is the same as for the lever:

$$MA = \frac{r_{input}}{r_{output}}$$

where r_{input} is the radius of the input, and r_{output} is the radius of the output.

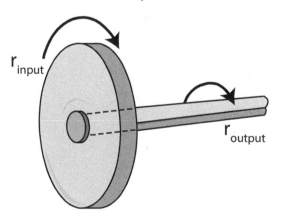

Figure 9.9. Wheel and Axle

GEARS are simple machines that are circular and have notches or teeth along the outer edge. Several gears in contact form a gear train. Again, the force applied along a gear train is related to the torque, where a large-radius gear will apply a large torque to a smaller gear on the train. The number of teeth on a gear is directly related to the radius of the gear, allowing the mechanical advantage to be written as

$$MA = \frac{\tau_{output}}{\tau_{input}} = \frac{N_{output}}{N_{input}}$$

where τ are the torques from each gear, and N is the number of teeth on each gear.

Another concept for a gear train is the **GEAR RATIO**, or speed ratio, which is a ratio of the angular velocity of the input gear to the angular velocity of the output gear. At the point of contact, the linear velocity must be the same, so $v = \omega_{input}\, r_{input} = \omega_{output}\, r_{output}$. So, the gear ratio is

$$\frac{\omega_{input}}{\omega_{output}} = \frac{r_{output}}{r_{input}} = \frac{N_{output}}{N_{input}}$$

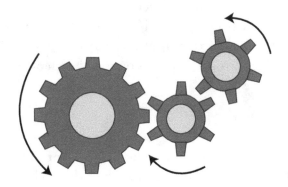

Figure 9.10. Gear Train

A **SCREW** is a simple machine that converts rotational motion into linear motion. In general, a screw is a cylinder with an inclined plane wrapped around it. The wrapped incline plane is called the thread, while the distance between the planes is called the pitch. The pitch is directed along the length of the screw. Again considering the work done, $W_{input} = F_{input}\, 2\pi r$, where r is the radius of the screw; and $W_{output} = F_{output}\, h$, where h is the pitch. The mechanical advantage then becomes

$$MA = \frac{2\pi r}{h}$$

where r is the radius of the screw, and h is the pitch.

Examples

1. Which is an example of a first-class lever?

    (A) crowbar

    (B) wheelbarrow

    (C) scissors

    (D) tweezers

Answers:

(A) is incorrect. This is a second-class lever.

(B) is incorrect. This is a second-class lever.

(C) is correct. This is a first-class lever.

(D) is incorrect. This is a third-class lever.

2. Which mechanical advantage is the best for the user?

(A) 10

(B) 5

(C) 2

(D) 1

Answers:

(A) is correct. The highest mechanical advantage is the best for the user.

(B) is incorrect. The highest mechanical advantage is the best for the user.

(C) is incorrect. The highest mechanical advantage is the best for the user.

(D) is incorrect. The highest mechanical advantage is the best for the user.

10

ASSEMBLING OBJECTS

The Assembling Objects chapter of the test measures a candidate's ability to understand spatial relationships between shapes. The CAT exam includes sixteen questions to be answered in sixteen minutes. The pen-and-paper exam includes twenty-five questions to be answered in fifteen minutes.

There are two types of questions on this test: connecting shapes and puzzles.

CONNECTING SHAPES

Connecting Shapes questions show two shapes and a connecting line. One shape will have a dot labeled **A**, and the other will have a dot labeled **B**. The line will be labeled **A** on one end and **B** on the other. The correct answer choice will show what the two shapes would look like if properly joined by the connecting line (**A** to **A** and **B** to **B**). The shapes may be rotated, but they will not be reflected or flipped over.

The best way to attack these problems is to compare the location of the dots in the question to the location of the dots on answer choices. In the incorrect answer choices, the **A** and **B** dots will be in the wrong spot on the shapes. Each question should be approached methodically. Candidates should first mark where **A** should be on the first shape in each answer choice and eliminate any incorrect answers. Then, they should mark where **B** should be in the second shape in each answer choice. The correct answer will be the only choice with **A** and **B** in the correct location.

PUZZLES

Puzzle questions show four shapes that can be put together like a jigsaw puzzle. The correct answer choice will show how the shapes fit together correctly.

As with Connecting Shapes questions, Puzzle questions can be solved by eliminating wrong answers. Incorrect answer choices will be missing one of the shapes from the question, or they will include a shape that is not part of the question. Starting with choice

A, candidates will compare the four shapes in the answer with the four shapes in the question for each answer choice until the right one is found.

Examples

1.

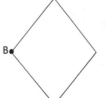

(A)

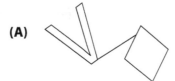

(B)

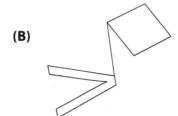

(C)

(D)

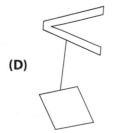

2.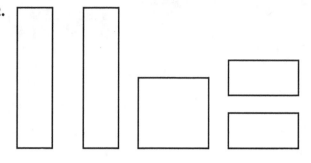

(A)

(B)

(C)

(D)

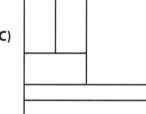

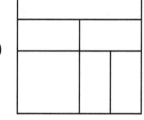

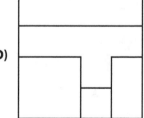

Answers:

1.   (C)

2.   (B)

PRACTICE TEST

GENERAL SCIENCE

This part of the test measures your knowledge in the area of science. Each of the questions or incomplete statements is followed by four choices. You are to decide which one of the choices best answers the question or completes the statement.

1. Bone is composed primarily of which inorganic material?
   (A) calcium
   (B) phosphorus
   (C) collagen
   (D) potassium

2. Which of these is a biome?
   (A) a desert
   (B) a cornfield
   (C) a herd of bison
   (D) a beehive

3. Which planet orbits closest to Earth?
   (A) Mercury
   (B) Venus
   (C) Jupiter
   (D) Saturn

4. What is the name of the phenomenon when a star suddenly increases in brightness and then disappears from view?
   (A) aurora
   (B) galaxy
   (C) black hole
   (D) supernova

5. Which organism has cells that contain mitochondria?
   (A) whale
   (B) mushroom
   (C) tulip
   (D) all of the above

6. Isotopes of an element will have the same number of _____ and different numbers of _____.
   (A) electrons; neutrons
   (B) neutrons; electrons
   (C) protons; neutrons
   (D) protons; electrons

7. Which condition can be diagnosed by an electrocardiogram (EKG)?
    (A) diabetes
    (B) torn ligaments
    (C) cancer
    (D) tachycardia

8. What are the negatively charged particles inside an atom?
    (A) protons
    (B) neutrons
    (C) electrons
    (D) ions

9. Which organism regulates its body temperature externally?
    (A) lobster
    (B) dolphin
    (C) whale
    (D) pelican

10. A box sliding down a ramp experiences all of the following forces EXCEPT
    (A) tension.
    (B) friction.
    (C) gravity.
    (D) normal.

11. Which organism is a decomposer?
    (A) apple trees
    (B) mushrooms
    (C) goats
    (D) lions

12. Which pH level is classified as a base?
    (A) 1
    (B) 4
    (C) 6
    (D) 8

13. Which body system is responsible for the release of growth hormones?
    (A) digestive system
    (B) endocrine system
    (C) nervous system
    (D) circulatory system

14. What is the term for the top layer of the earth's surface?
    (A) exosphere
    (B) lithosphere
    (C) atmosphere
    (D) biosphere

15. Which of the following describes a physical change?
    (A) Water becomes ice.
    (B) Batter is baked into a cake.
    (C) An iron fence rusts.
    (D) A firecracker explodes.

16. Which energy source is nonrenewable?
    (A) water
    (B) wind
    (C) coal
    (D) sunlight

17. How long does it take the earth to rotate on its axis?
    (A) one hour
    (B) one day
    (C) one month
    (D) one year

18. During what process do producers make sugars and release oxygen?
    (A) digestion
    (B) chloroplast
    (C) decomposition
    (D) photosynthesis

19. $2C_6H_{14} + 19O_2 \rightarrow 12CO_2 + 14H_2O$
What type of reaction is shown above?

(A) substitution reaction

(B) acid-base reaction

(C) decomposition reaction

(D) combustion reaction

20. Which factor is an abiotic part of an ecosystem?

(A) producers

(B) consumers

(C) water

(D) decomposers

21. What is the primary function of the respiratory system?

(A) to create sound and speech

(B) to take oxygen into the body while removing carbon dioxide

(C) to transport nutrients to the cells and tissue of the body

(D) to act as a barrier between the body's organs and foreign pathogens

22. The process of organisms with advantageous traits surviving more often and producing more offspring than organisms without these advantageous traits describes which basic mechanism of evolution?

(A) gene flow

(B) genetic drift

(C) mutation

(D) natural selection

23. Which muscular organ processes food material into smaller pieces and helps mix it with saliva?

(A) pharynx

(B) tongue

(C) diaphragm

(D) stomach

24. Which of the following correctly describes a strong acid?

(A) A strong acid completely ionizes in water.

(B) A strong acid donates more than one proton.

(C) A strong acid has a pH close to 7.

(D) A strong acid will not ionize.

25. Which action is an example of mechanical weathering?

(A) Calcium carbonate reacts with water to form a cave.

(B) An iron gate rusts.

(C) Tree roots grow under the foundation of a house and cause cracks.

(D) Bananas turn brown after they are peeled.

ARITHMETIC REASONING

This part of the test measures your ability to use arithmetic to solve problems. Each problem is followed by four possible answers. You are to decide which one of the four choices is correct.

1. A high school cross country team sent 25 percent of its runners to a regional competition. Of these, 10 percent won medals. If 2 runners earned medals, how many members does the cross country team have?

   (A) 8
   (B) 10
   (C) 80
   (D) 125

2. Convert 55 meters to feet (round to the nearest tenth of a foot).

   (A) 16.8 feet
   (B) 21.7 feet
   (C) 139.7 feet
   (D) 180.4 feet

3. If a person reads 40 pages in 45 minutes, approximately how many minutes will it take her to read 265 pages?

   (A) 202
   (B) 236
   (C) 265
   (D) 298

4. If three burgers and two orders of fries costs $26.50 and a burger costs $6.50, how much does one order of fries cost?

   (A) $1.75
   (B) $3.50
   (C) $6.75
   (D) $7.00

5. A worker was paid $15,036 for 7 months of work. If he received the same amount each month, how much was he paid for the first 2 months?

   (A) $2,148
   (B) $4,296
   (C) $5,137
   (D) $6,444

6. The average speed of cars on a highway (s) is inversely proportional to the number of cars on the road (n). If a car drives at 65 mph when there are 250 cars on the road, how fast will a car drive when there are 325 cars on the road?

   (A) 50 mph
   (B) 55 mph
   (C) 60 mph
   (D) 85 mph

7. The probability of drawing a blue marble from a bag of marbles is $\frac{1}{20}$ and the probability of drawing a red marble from the same bag is $\frac{7}{20}$. What is the probability of drawing a blue marble or a red marble?

   (A) $\frac{1}{10}$
   (B) $\frac{3}{10}$
   (C) $\frac{7}{20}$
   (D) $\frac{2}{5}$

8. The population of a town was 7,250 in 2014 and 7,375 in 2015. What was the percent increase from 2014 to 2015 to the nearest tenth of a percent?

(A) 1.5%

(B) 1.6%

(C) 1.7%

(D) 1.8%

9. Lynn has 4 test scores in science class. Each test is worth 100 points, and Lynn has an 85% average. If Lynn scored 100% on each of the first 3 tests, what did she score on her 4th test?

(A) 40%

(B) 55%

(C) 60%

(D) 85%

10. Allison used $2\frac{1}{2}$ cups of flour to make a cake, and $\frac{3}{4}$ of a cup of flour to make a pie. If she started with 4 cups of flour, how many cups of flour does she have left?

(A) $\frac{3}{4}$

(B) 1

(C) $\frac{5}{4}$

(D) $\frac{5}{2}$

11. Alex cleans houses and charges $25 per bedroom, $35 per bathroom, and $40 per kitchen. If he cleans a house with 4 bedrooms, 2 bathrooms, and 1 kitchen, how much will he be paid?

(A) $205

(B) $210

(C) $215

(D) $230

12. Juan plans to spend 25% of his workday writing a report. If he is at work for 9 hours, how many hours will he spend writing the report?

(A) 2.25

(B) 2.50

(C) 2.75

(D) 3.25

13. Valerie receives a base salary of $740 a week for working 40 hours. For every extra hour she works, she is paid at a rate of $27.75 per hour. If Valerie works t hours in a week, which of the following equations represents the amount of money, A, she will receive?

(A) $A = 740 + 27.75(t - 40)$

(B) $A = 740 + 27.75(40 - t)$

(C) $A = 740 - 27.75(40 - t)$

(D) $A = 27.75t - 740$

14. If $\triangle ABD \sim \triangle DEF$ and the similarity ratio is 3:4, what is the measure of DE if $AB = 12$?

(A) 6

(B) 9

(C) 12

(D) 16

15. Justin has a summer lawn care business and earns $40 for each lawn he mows. He also pays $35 per week in business expenses. Which of the following expressions represents Justin's profit after x weeks if he mows m number of lawns?

(A) $40m - 35x$

(B) $40m + 35x$

(C) $35x(40 + m)$

(D) $35(40m + x)$

16. Micah has invited 23 friends to his house and is having pizza for dinner. If each pizza feeds 4 people, how many pizzas should he order?

(A) 4
(B) 5
(C) 6
(D) 7

17. In the fall, 425 students pass the math benchmark. In the spring, 680 students pass the same benchmark. What is the percentage increase in passing scores from fall to spring?

(A) 37.5%
(B) 55%
(C) 60%
(D) 62.5%

18. Maria paid $24.65 for her meal at a restaurant. If that price included a tax of 8.25 percent, what was the price of the meal before tax?

(A) $22.61
(B) $22.68
(C) $22.77
(D) $22.82

19. A high school football team played 12 games in a season. If they won 75 percent of their games, how many games did they lose?

(A) 3
(B) 4
(C) 6
(D) 9

20. A fruit stand sells apples, bananas, and oranges at a ratio of 3:2:1. If the fruit stand sells 20 bananas, how many total pieces of fruit does the fruit stand sell?

(A) 10
(B) 30
(C) 40
(D) 60

21. Aprille has $50 to buy the items on her shopping list. Assuming there is no sales tax, about how much change will Aprille receive after buying all the items on her list?

Aprille's List

ITEM	PRICE
Hammer	$13.24
Screwdriver	$11.99
Nails	$4.27
Wrench	$5.60

(A) $12
(B) $13
(C) $14
(D) $15

22. A company interviewed 21 applicants for a recent opening. Of these applicants, 7 wore blue and 6 wore white, while 5 applicants wore both blue and white. What is the number of applicants who wore neither blue nor white?

(A) 1
(B) 6
(C) 8
(D) 13

23. In the sequence below, each term is found by finding the difference between the previous two numbers and multiplying the result by −3. What is the 6th term of the sequence?

{3, 0, −9, −36, ... }

(A) −81
(B) −135
(C) 45
(D) 81

24. If the length of a rectangle is increased by 40% and its width is decreased by 40%, what is the effect on the rectangle's area?

(A) The area is the same.

(B) It increases by 16%.

(C) It increases by 20%.

(D) It decreases by 16%.

25. If a plane travels 2,775 miles in 3 hours, how far will it travel in 5 hours?

(A) 1,665 miles

(B) 3,475 miles

(C) 4,625 miles

(D) 5,550 miles

26. A theater has 180 rows of seats. The first row has 10 seats. Each row has 4 seats more than the row in front of it. How many seats are in the entire theater?

(A) 18,000

(B) 20,000

(C) 36,200

(D) 66,240

27. Erica is at work for $8\frac{1}{2}$ hours a day. If she takes one 30-minute lunch break and two 15-minute breaks during the day, how many hours does she work?

(A) 6 hours, 30 minutes

(B) 6 hours, 45 minutes

(C) 7 hours, 15 minutes

(D) 7 hours, 30 minutes

28. At the grocery store, apples cost $1.89 per pound and oranges cost $2.19 per pound. How much would it cost to purchase 2 pounds of apples and 1.5 pounds of oranges?

(A) $6.62

(B) $7.07

(C) $7.14

(D) $7.22

29. A car traveled at 65 miles per hour for $1\frac{1}{2}$ hours and then traveled at 50 miles per hour for $2\frac{1}{2}$ hours. How many miles did the car travel?

(A) 190.5 miles

(B) 215.0 miles

(C) 222.5 miles

(D) 237.5 miles

30. What is the square root of 169?

(A) 9

(B) 13

(C) 16

(D) 19

WORD KNOWLEDGE

This part of the test measures your knowledge of words and their meanings. For each question, you are to choose the word below that is closest in meaning to the capitalized word above.

1. Pacify most nearly means
   (A) soothe.
   (B) transport.
   (C) bathe.
   (D) motivate.

2. The judge ruled that certain facts were immaterial to the case, so she would not allow the prosecutor to use those facts as evidence.
   (A) invisible
   (B) opposed
   (C) offensive
   (D) inconsequential

3. The man flagrantly broke several laws, so he was easily convicted and sent to prison.
   (A) joyously
   (B) unashamedly
   (C) incautiously
   (D) mistakenly

4. Indolence most nearly means
   (A) serenity.
   (B) bliss.
   (C) laziness.
   (D) tolerance.

5. When a strange dog ran into the room, the cat made the judicious decision to jump onto the top of the bookcase.
   (A) wise.
   (B) quick.
   (C) weird.
   (D) brave.

6. Pragmatic most nearly means
   (A) accurate.
   (B) tedious.
   (C) realistic.
   (D) imaginative.

7. Countenance most nearly means
   (A) total amount.
   (B) fancy clothing.
   (C) body language.
   (D) facial expression.

8. Cacophony most nearly means
   (A) harsh sound.
   (B) melodious music.
   (C) synthetic product.
   (D) artificial flavor.

9. Charisma most nearly means
   (A) love.
   (B) motion.
   (C) sneakiness.
   (D) attractiveness.

10. My aunt has a capricious nature, so we never know whether she will or will not show up at family celebrations.
    (A) voluminous
    (B) materialistic
    (C) unreliable
    (D) intolerable

11. Daunt most nearly means
    (A) thrill.
    (B) shove.
    (C) intimidate.
    (D) encourage.

12. The theater's new production received great <u>acclaim</u> from newspaper critics.
    (A) pity.
    (B) praise.
    (C) notoriety.
    (D) interest.

13. <u>Credulous</u> most nearly means
    (A) naïve.
    (B) amazing.
    (C) tedious.
    (D) optimistic.

14. Rotary telephones are <u>obsolete</u>, and almost no one uses them anymore.
    (A) unsafe
    (B) old-fashioned
    (C) too bulky
    (D) too heavy

15. <u>Labyrinth</u> most nearly means
    (A) maze.
    (B) dungeon.
    (C) workshop.
    (D) basement.

16. <u>Sacrosanct</u> most nearly means
    (A) handy.
    (B) quiet.
    (C) secure.
    (D) holy.

17. My sister has an <u>effervescent</u> personality, so everyone invites her to their parties to liven them up.
    (A) jumpy
    (B) vivacious
    (C) eternal
    (D) suspicious

18. <u>Rudimentary</u> most nearly means
    (A) impolite.
    (B) basic.
    (C) juvenile.
    (D) innovative.

19. Showing deep emotion, the conductor flourished his baton, directing the orchestra with <u>fervor</u>.
    (A) indifference
    (B) swiftness
    (C) grace
    (D) eagerness

20. To <u>cajole</u> most nearly means to
    (A) persuade.
    (B) cheer up.
    (C) imprison.
    (D) compel.

21. <u>Impartial</u> most nearly means
    (A) fond.
    (B) incomplete.
    (C) objective.
    (D) mathematical.

22. A mountain peak may seem <u>immutable</u>, but erosion may wear it down over thousands of years.
    (A) gigantic
    (B) awesome
    (C) unalterable
    (D) insensible

23. <u>Reiterate</u> most nearly means
    (A) recite.
    (B) repeat.
    (C) reunite.
    (D) reread.

24. The politician gave a long, <u>bombastic</u> speech that was full of pretentious language.
    (A) folksy
    (B) exploding
    (C) pompous
    (D) eloquent

25. <u>Precedent</u> most nearly means
    (A) event.
    (B) birth.
    (C) idea.
    (D) model.

26. <u>Prudent</u> most nearly means
    (A) sensible.
    (B) inquisitive.
    (C) terrified.
    (D) squeamish.

27. The office is organized in a <u>haphazard</u> manner, so it is next to impossible to find anything quickly.
    (A) dangerous
    (B) precise
    (C) chaotic
    (D) cautious

28. <u>Figurative</u> most nearly means
    (A) lofty.
    (B) lengthy.
    (C) nonliteral.
    (D) uncooperative.

29. <u>Innocuous</u> most nearly means
    (A) susceptible.
    (B) sickly.
    (C) bland.
    (D) cautious.

30. Shelby *is* the club president, but I sometimes wish she were not so <u>officious</u>—I get tired of her bossy manner.
    (A) resourceful
    (B) emotional
    (C) detail-oriented
    (D) overbearing

31. <u>Negligence</u> most nearly means
    (A) malice.
    (B) immorality.
    (C) inattention.
    (D) nothingness.

32. <u>Lax</u> most nearly means
    (A) decorative.
    (B) malicious.
    (C) meddlesome.
    (D) permissive.

33. My dog is always <u>meandering</u> around the yard, smelling every scent she can detect.
    (A) digging
    (B) relaxing
    (C) sprinting
    (D) wandering

34. <u>Ardent</u> most nearly means
    (A) silvery.
    (B) stubborn.
    (C) metallic.
    (D) passionate.

35. Whenever she wears a certain jacket, my sister <u>garners</u> compliments from everyone she meets.
    (A) awards
    (B) enjoys
    (C) collects
    (D) improves

PARAGRAPH COMPREHENSION

This part of the test measures your ability to read and understand written material. Each passage is followed by a multiple-choice question. You are to choose the option that best answers the question based on the passage. No additional information or specific knowledge is needed.

In December of 1945, Germany launched its last major offensive campaign of World War II, pushing through the dense forests of the Ardennes region of Belgium, France, and Luxembourg. The attack, designed to block the Allies from the Belgian port of Antwerp and to split their lines, caught the Allied forces by surprise. Due to troop positioning, the Americans bore the brunt of the attack, incurring 100,000 deaths, the highest number of casualties of any battle during the war. However, after a month of grueling fighting in the bitter cold, a lack of fuel and a masterful American military strategy resulted in an Allied victory that sealed Germany's fate.

1.   In the last sentence, the word *grueling* most nearly means

   (A) exhausting.

   (B) costly.

   (C) intermittent.

   (D) ineffective.

The social and political discourse of America continues to be permeated with idealism. An idealistic viewpoint asserts that the ideals of freedom, equality, justice, and human dignity are the truths that Americans must continue to aspire to. Idealists argue that truth is what should be, not necessarily what is. In general, they work to improve things and to make them as close to ideal as possible.

2.   The primary purpose of the passage is to

   (A) advocate for freedom, equality, justice, and human rights.

   (B) explain what an idealist believes in.

   (C) explain what's wrong with social and political discourse in America.

   (D) persuade readers to believe in certain truths.

The greatest changes in sensory, motor, and perceptual development happen in the first two years of life. When babies are first born, most of their senses operate in a similar way to those of adults. For example, babies are able to hear before they are born; studies show that babies turn toward the sound of their mothers' voices just minutes after being born, indicating they recognize the mother's voice from their time in the womb.

   The exception to this rule is vision. A baby's vision changes significantly in its first year of life; initially it has a range of vision of only 8–12 inches and no depth perception. As a result, infants rely primarily on hearing; vision does not become the dominant sense until around the age of 12 months. Babies also prefer faces to other objects. This preference, along with their limited vision range, means that their sight is initially focused on their caregiver.

3.   Which of the following senses do babies primarily rely on?

   (A) vision

   (B) hearing

   (C) touch

   (D) smell

Tourists flock to Yellowstone National Park each year to view the geysers that bubble and erupt throughout it. What most of these tourists do not know is that these geysers are formed by a caldera, a hot crater in the earth's crust, that was created by a series of three eruptions of an ancient supervolcano. These eruptions, which began 2.1 million years ago, spewed between 1,000 to 2,450 cubic kilometers of volcanic matter at such a rate that the volcano's magma chamber collapsed, creating the craters.

4. The main idea of the passage is that

(A) Yellowstone National Park is a popular tourist destination.

(B) The geysers in Yellowstone National Park rest on a caldera in the earth's crust.

(C) A supervolcano once sat in the area covered by Yellowstone National Park.

(D) The earth's crust is weaker in Yellowstone National Park.

In 1989, almost a million Chinese university students descended on central Beijing, protesting for increased democracy and calling for the resignation of Communist Party leaders. For three weeks, they marched, chanted, and held daily vigils in the city's Tiananmen Square. The protests had widespread support in China, particularly among factory workers who cheered them on. For Westerners watching, it seemed to be the beginning of a political revolution in China, so the world was stunned when, on July 4, Chinese troops and security police stormed the square, firing into the crowd. Chaos erupted with some students trying to fight back by throwing stones and setting fire to military vehicles. Tens of thousands more attempted to flee. While official numbers were never given, observers estimated anywhere from 300 to thousands of people were killed, while 10,000 were arrested.

5. It can be inferred from the passage that after July 4

(A) the protest movement in China gained increasing support.

(B) Western countries intervened on behalf of the university protestors.

(C) factory workers took action in defense of the protestors.

(D) the movement for increased democracy in China fell apart.

The Battle of Little Bighorn, commonly called Custer's Last Stand, was a battle between the Lakota, the Northern Cheyenne, the Arapaho, and the Seventh Calvary Regiment of the US Army. Led by war leaders Crazy Horse and Chief Gall and the religious leader Sitting Bull, the allied tribes of the Plains Indians decisively defeated their US foes. Two hundred and sixty-eight US soldiers were killed, including General George Armstrong Custer, two of his brothers, his nephew, his brother-in-law, and six Indian scouts.

6. What is the main idea of this passage?

(A) Most of General Custer's family died in the Battle of Little Bighorn.

(B) The Seventh Calvary regiment was formed to fight Native American tribes.

(C) Sitting Bull and George Custer were fierce enemies.

(D) The Battle of Little Bighorn was a significant victory for the Plains Indians.

At first glance, the landscape of the northern end of the Rift Valley appears to be a stretch of barren land. Paleoanthropologists, however, have discovered an abundance of fossils just beneath the dusty surface. They believe this area once contained open grasslands near lakes and rivers, populated with grazing animals. Forty miles from this spot, in 1974, scientists uncovered a 3.2 million-year-old non-human hominid they nicknamed "Lucy." And, in 2013, researchers found the oldest fossil in the human ancestral line. Before this, the oldest fossil from the genus

Homo—of which *Homo sapiens* are the only remaining species—dated only back to 2.3 million years ago, leaving a 700,000 gap between Lucy's species and the advent of humans. The new fossil dated back to 2.75 and 2.8 million years ago, pushing the appearance of humans back 400,000 years.

7. According to the passage, the discovery of Lucy

    (A) gave scientists new information about the development of humans.

    (B) provided evidence of a different ecosystem in the ancient Rift Valley.

    (C) supported the belief that other hominids existed significantly before humans.

    (D) closed the gap between the development of other hominids and humans.

In its most basic form, geography is the study of space; more specifically, it studies the physical space of the earth and the ways in which it interacts with, shapes, and is shaped by its habitants. Geographers look at the world from a spatial perspective. This means that at the center of all geographic study is the question, *where?* For geographers, the *where* of any interaction, event, or development is a crucial element to understanding it.

This question of *where* can be asked in a variety of fields of study, so there are many sub-disciplines of geography. These can be organized into four main categories: 1) regional studies, which examine the characteristics of a particular place; 2) topical studies, which look at a single physical or human feature that impacts the whole world; 3) physical studies, which focus on the physical features of Earth; and 4) human studies, which examine the relationship between human activity and the environment.

8. A researcher studying the relationship between farming and river systems would be engaged in which of the following geographical sub-disciplines?

    (A) regional studies

    (B) topical studies

    (C) physical studies

    (D) human studies

Researchers at the University of California, Berkeley, decided to tackle an age-old problem: why shoelaces come untied. They recorded the shoelaces of a volunteer walking on a treadmill by attaching devices to record the acceleration, or g-force, experienced by the knot. The results were surprising. A shoelace knot experiences more g-force from a person walking than any rollercoaster can generate. However, if the person simply stomped or swung their feet—the two movements that make up a walker's stride—the g-force was not enough to undo the knots. Researchers also found that while the knot loosened slowly at first, once it reached a certain laxness, it simply fell apart.

9. The author includes a comparison to rollercoasters in order to

    (A) illustrate the intensity of force experienced by the knots.

    (B) describe an experiment undertaken by researchers.

    (C) critique a main finding of the experiment.

    (D) provide further evidence to support the study's conclusion.

In 1953, doctors surgically removed the hippocampus of patient Henry Molaison in an attempt to stop his frequent seizures. Unexpectedly, he lost the ability to form new memories, leading to the biggest breakthrough in the science of memory. Molaison's long-term memory—of events more than a year before his surgery—was unchanged as was his ability to learn physical skills. From this, scientists learned that different types of memory are handled by different parts of the brain, with the hippocampus responsible for *episodic memory*, the short-term recall of events. They have since discovered that some memories are then channeled to the cortex, the outer layers of the brain that handle higher functions, where they are gradually integrated with related information to build lasting knowledge about our world.

10. The main idea of the passage is that
    (A) Molaison's surgery posed significant risk to the functioning of his brain.
    (B) short-term and long-term memory are stored in different parts of the brain.
    (C) long-term memory forms over a longer period than short-term memory.
    (D) memories of physical skills are processed differently than memories of events.

After World War I, powerful political and social forces pushed for a return to normalcy in the United States. The result was disengagement from the larger world and increased focus on American economic growth and personal enjoyment. Caught in the middle of this was a cache of American writers, raised on the values of the prewar world and frustrated with what they viewed as the superficiality and materialism of postwar American culture. Many of them, like Ernest Hemingway and F. Scott Fitzgerald, fled to Paris, where they became known as the "lost generation," creating a trove of literary works criticizing their home culture and delving into their own feelings of alienation.

11. In the third sentence, the word *cache* most nearly means
    (A) a group of the same type.
    (B) a majority segment.
    (C) an organization.
    (D) a dispersed number.

When the Spanish-American War broke out in 1898, the US Army was small and understaffed. President William McKinley called for 1,250 volunteers primarily from the Southwest to serve in the First US Volunteer Calvary. Eager to fight, the ranks were quickly filled by a diverse group of cowboys, gold prospectors, hunters, gamblers, Native Americans, veterans, police officers, and college students looking for an adventure. The officer corps was composed of veterans of the Civil War and the Indian Wars. With more volunteers than it could accept, the army set high standards: all the recruits had to be skilled on horseback and with guns. Consequently, they became known as the Rough Riders.

12. According to the passage, all the recruits were required to
    (A) have previously fought in a war.
    (B) be American citizens.
    (C) live in the Southwest.
    (D) ride a horse well.

It could be said that the great battle between the North and South we call the Civil War was a battle for individual identity. The states of the South had their own culture, one based on farming, independence, and the rights of both man and state to determine their own paths. Similarly, the North had forged its own identity as a center of centralized commerce and manufacturing. This clash of lifestyles was bound to create tension, and this tension was bound to lead to war. But people who try to sell you this narrative are wrong. The Civil War was not a battle of cultural identities—it was a battle about slavery. All other explanations for the war are either a direct consequence of the South's desire for wealth at the expense of her fellow man or a fanciful invention to cover up this sad portion of our nation's history. And it cannot be denied that this time in our past was very sad indeed.

13. What is the main idea of the passage?

(A) The Civil War was the result of cultural differences between the North and South.

(B) The Civil War was caused by the South's reliance on slave labor.

(C) The North's use of commerce and manufacturing allowed it to win the war.

(D) The South's belief in the rights of man and state cost the war.

When a fire destroyed San Francisco's American Indian Center in October of 1969, American Indian groups set their sights on the recently closed island prison of Alcatraz as a site of a new Indian cultural center and school. Ignored by the government, an activist group known as Indians of All Tribes sailed to Alcatraz in the early morning hours with eighty-nine men, women, and children. They landed on Alcatraz, claiming it for all the tribes of North America. Their demands were ignored, and so the group continued to occupy the island for the next nineteen months, its numbers swelling up to 600 as others joined. By January of 1970, many of the original protestors had left, and on June 11, 1971, federal marshals forcibly removed the last residents.

14. The main idea of this passage is that

(A) the government refused to listen to the demands of American Indians.

(B) American Indians occupied Alcatraz in protest of government policy.

(C) few people joined the occupation of Alcatraz, weakening its effectiveness.

(D) the government took violent action against protestors at Alcatraz.

The Bastille, Paris's famous historical prison, was originally built in 1370 as a fortification, called a *bastide* in Old French, to protect the city from English invasion during the Hundred Years' War. It rose 100 feet into the air, had eight towers, and was surrounded by a moat more than eighty feet wide. In the seventeenth century, the government converted the fortress into an elite prison for upper-class felons, political disruptors, and spies. Residents of the Bastille arrived by direct order of the king and usually were left there to languish without a trial.

15. In the first sentence, the word *fortification* most nearly means

(A) royal castle.

(B) national symbol.

(C) seat of government.

(D) defensive structure.

MATH KNOWLEDGE

This part of the test measures your knowledge of mathematical terms and principles. Each problem is followed by four possible answers. You are to decide which one of the four choices is correct.

1. Which of the following is equivalent to $z^3(z + 2)^2 - 4z^3 + 2$?

   (A) 2

   (B) $z^5 + 4z^4 + 4z^3 + 2$

   (C) $z^6 + 4z^3 + 2$

   (D) $z^5 + 4z^4 + 2$

2. Simplify: $\frac{(3x^2y^2)^2}{3^3x^{-2}y^3}$

   (A) $3x^6y$

   (B) $\frac{x^6y}{3}$

   (C) $\frac{x^4}{3y}$

   (D) $\frac{3x^4}{y}$

3. What is the value of $\left(\frac{1}{2}\right)^3$?

   (A) $\frac{1}{8}$

   (B) $\frac{1}{6}$

   (C) $\frac{1}{4}$

   (D) $\frac{3}{8}$

4. How many cubic feet of soil would be required to cover a circular garden with a diameter of 8 feet if the soil needs to be 0.5 feet deep (use $\pi = 3.14$)?

   (A) 6.28 ft^3

   (B) 12.56 ft^3

   (C) 25.12 ft^3

   (D) 100.48 ft^3

5. Which of the following sets of shapes are NOT all similar to each other?

   (A) right triangles

   (B) spheres

   (C) 30–60–90 triangles

   (D) squares

6. The line of best fit is calculated for a data set that tracks the number of miles that passenger cars traveled annually in the US from 1960 to 2010. In the model, $x = 0$ represents the year 1960, and y is the number of miles traveled in billions. If the line of best fit is $y = 0.0293x + 0.563$, approximately how many additional miles were traveled for every 5 years that passed?

   (A) 0.0293 billion

   (B) 0.1465 billion

   (C) 0.5630 billion

   (D) 0.7100 billion

   (E) 2.9615 billion

7. Simplify: $\sqrt[3]{64} + \sqrt[3]{729}$

   (A) 13

   (B) 15

   (C) 17

   (D) 31

8. What is the remainder when 397 is divided by 4?

   (A) 0

   (B) 1

   (C) 2

   (D) 3

9. If the surface area of a cylinder with radius of 4 feet is 48π square feet, what is its volume?

   (A) $1\pi \text{ ft.}^3$

   (B) $16\pi \text{ ft.}^3$

   (C) $32\pi \text{ ft.}^3$

   (D) $48\pi \text{ ft.}^3$

10. Which expression is equivalent to $(x + 3)(x - 2)(x + 4)$?

(A) $x^3 - 2x + 24$

(B) $x^3 + 5x - 24$

(C) $x^3 + 9x^2 - 24$

(D) $x^3 + 5x^2 - 2x - 24$

11. Which of the following is a solution of the given equation?

$4(m + 4)^2 - 4m^2 + 20 = 276$

(A) 3

(B) 4

(C) 6

(D) 12

12. What is the x-intercept of the given equation?

$10x + 10y = 10$

(A) $(1, 0)$

(B) $(0, 1)$

(C) $(0, 0)$

(D) $(1, 1)$

13. Which of the following is closest in value to $129,113 + 34,602$?

(A) 162,000

(B) 163,000

(C) 164,000

(D) 165,000

14. Solve for x: $x^2 - 3x - 18 = 0$

(A) $x = -3$

(B) $x = 2$

(C) $x = -3$ and $x = 6$

(D) $x = 2$ and $x = 3$

15. The coordinates of point A are $(7, 12)$ and the coordinates of point C are $(-3, 10)$. If C is the midpoint of $\overline{AB}$, what are the coordinates of point B?

(A) $(-13, 8)$

(B) $(-13, 11)$

(C) $(2, 11)$

(D) $(2, 14)$

16. Which of the following could be the perimeter of a triangle with two sides that measure 13 and 5?

(A) 24.5

(B) 26.5

(C) 36

(D) 37

17. What is $\frac{5}{8}$ as a percent?

(A) 1.6%

(B) 16%

(C) 0.625%

(D) 62.5%

18. What is the value of z in the following system?

$z - 2x = 14$

$2z - 6x = 18$

(A) -7

(B) -2

(C) 3

(D) 24

19. What is the value of the expression $15m + 2n^2 - 7$ if $m = 3$ and $n = -4$?

(A) -49

(B) -31

(C) 6

(D) 70

20. Which number has the greatest value?

(A) 9,299 ones

(B) 903 tens

(C) 93 hundreds

(D) 9 thousands

21. Which of the following is an equation of the line that passes through the points $(4, -3)$ and $(-2, 9)$ in the xy-plane?

(A) $y = -2x + 5$

(B) $y = -\frac{1}{2}x - 1$

(C) $y = \frac{1}{2}x - 5$

(D) $y = 2x - 11$

22. W, X, Y, and Z lie on a circle with center A. If the diameter of the circle is 75, what is the sum of $\overline{AW}$, $\overline{AX}$, $\overline{AY}$, and $\overline{AZ}$?

(A) 75

(B) 100

(C) 125

(D) 150

23. Which inequality is equivalent to $10 \leq k - 5$?

(A) $k \leq 15$

(B) $k \geq 15$

(C) $k \leq 5$

(D) $k \geq 5$

24. Rectangular water tank A is 5 feet long, 10 feet wide, and 4 feet tall. Rectangular tank B is 5 feet long, 5 feet wide, and 4 feet tall. If the same amount of water is poured into both tanks and the height of the water in Tank A is 1 foot, how high will the water be in Tank B?

(A) 1 foot

(B) 2 feet

(C) 3 feet

(D) 4 feet

25. The inequality $2a - 5b > 12$ is true for which values of a and b?

(A) $a = 2$ and $b = 6$

(B) $a = 1$ and $b = -3$

(C) $a = -1$ and $b = 3$

(D) $a = 7$ and $b = 2$

ELECTRONICS

This part of the test measures your knowledge of electronics. Each of the questions or incomplete statements is followed by four choices. You are to decide which one of the choices best answers the question or completes the statement.

1. An atom has 5 electrons and 12 protons. What is the total charge of the atom?

    (A) −17e

    (B) −7e

    (C) +7e

    (D) +17e

2. Power is measured in

    (A) watts.

    (B) amperes.

    (C) joules.

    (D) ohms.

3. Valence electrons are important in a circuit because they

    (A) can easily change between positive and negative charge.

    (B) allow protons to flow through the circuit, creating current.

    (C) are stored in the circuit's voltage source.

    (D) carry the charge in conducting materials.

4. Conventional current is

    (A) a naming convention that states that current is in the same direction as the movement of electrons.

    (B) a naming convention that states that current is in the same direction as the movement of positive charge, or holes.

    (C) another name for direct current.

    (D) another name for alternating current.

5. A circuit with one 5 Ω resistor has a current of 0.5 A. How much voltage is being applied to the circuit?

    (A) 0.1 V

    (B) 2.5 V

    (C) 10 V

    (D) 25 V

6. What is the source of the electromotive force, EMF, in a battery?

    (A) The is no EMF from a battery.

    (B) mechanical movement

    (C) changing magnetic field

    (D) chemical reactions

7. If the current flowing through a fuse is too high, how does a fuse protect a circuit?

    (A) The metal element in the fuse will overheat and vaporize, breaking the circuit.

    (B) The metal element in the fuse will overheat and oxidize, leading to a higher and higher resistance in the fuse.

    (C) The fuse has a built-in switch that will flip to break the circuit. The switch needs to be manually flipped back to reconnect the circuit.

    (D) The fuse will automatically lower the current value to an acceptable level if it gets too high.

8. The symbol below is used to represent which part of a circuit?

(A) diode
(B) switch
(C) fuse
(D) battery

9. If a voltmeter measures 10 V across a resistor and an ammeter measures 5 mA going through it, what would an ohmmeter measure as the resistance of the resistor?

(A) 500 Ω
(B) 1 kΩ
(C) 1.5 kΩ
(D) 2 kΩ

10. Find the equivalent resistance, R_{eq}, for the circuit in the figure below.

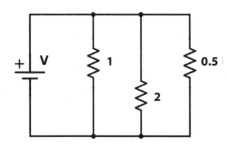

(A) 0.3 kΩ
(B) 0.5 kΩ
(C) 2 kΩ
(D) 3.5 kΩ

11. What application would use a variable resistor?

(A) a dimmer for a light bulb
(B) a regular switch for a light bulb
(C) a doorbell button
(D) a key on a computer keyboard

12. What is the basic function of a capacitor?

(A) It acts as a switch.
(B) It stores energy.
(C) It only allows current in one direction.
(D) It is the heating element in an oven.

13. What is the most common use of a transistor?

(A) a solid-state switch
(B) a solid-state capacitor
(C) a solid-state solenoid
(D) a solid-state laser

14. Which application would be a proper use of a rectifier circuit?

(A) transforming a 100 V signal into a 200 V signal
(B) transforming a 200 V signal into a 100 V signal
(C) converting the AC output from an alternator into a DC signal
(D) converting the DC output from a dynamo into an AC signal

15. How does an inductor behave in a circuit?

(A) It acts as an antenna.
(B) It produces sound.
(C) It resists a change in current.
(D) It converts AC into DC.

16. A customer needs a motor that rotates in a full circle 60 times per second (60 Hz). The motor will be connected to an AC power supply that has a frequency of 60 Hz. What type of motor is it?

(A) synchronous motor
(B) asynchronous motor
(C) high-speed motor
(D) low-torque motor

17. What is the stator field?

    (A) the magnetic field created by permanent magnets or electromagnets in the stator

    (B) the electric field created by permanent charges or electromagnets in the stator

    (C) the magnetic field created by permanent magnets in the rotor

    (D) the electric field created by permanent charges in the rotor

18. Electrical power suppliers produce power at high voltage to transfer power over long distances, and the voltage is reduced to the value (120 V) used in homes and offices. What device is used to make this reduction?

    (A) alternator

    (B) transformer

    (C) rectifier

    (D) capacitor

19. What is the current flowing through a 15 Ω resistor when 120 V is applied to the circuit?

    (A) 80 mA

    (B) 125 mA

    (C) 8 A

    (D) 12.5 A

20. All of the following store energy EXCEPT

    (A) capacitor.

    (B) battery.

    (C) inductor.

    (D) transformer.

Automotive and Shop Information

This part of the test measures your knowledge of automotive and shop information. Each of the questions or incomplete statements is followed by four choices. You are to decide which one of the choices best answers the question or completes the statement.

1. When does combustion happen?
   (A) when air enters the cylinder
   (B) when the air and fuel mixture has cooled down
   (C) when a mixture of air and fuel is pressurized and burned
   (D) when the fuel has been pressurized

2. Which of the following can be used for inside- and outside-diameter measurements?
   (A) tape measure
   (B) outside caliper
   (C) Vernier caliper
   (D) level

3. Which valves are open during the power stroke?
   (A) just the intake valve
   (B) the intake and exhaust valves
   (C) just the exhaust valve
   (D) no valves

4. Which handsaw is used to cut shapes or curves in wood?
   (A) coping saw
   (B) band saw
   (C) cross-cut saw
   (D) hacksaw

5. What is a tap used for?
   (A) normal drilling operations
   (B) removing studs and broken bolts from threaded holes
   (C) threading holes in metal
   (D) boring tapered holes in metal

6. The compression stroke occurs when
   (A) all valves are closed. The piston stroke is from BDC to TDC.
   (B) all valves are closed. The piston stroke is from TDC to BDC.
   (C) the intake valve is closed. The exhaust valve is open.
   (D) the intake valve is open. The exhaust valve is closed.

7. What is the firing order of an engine?
   (A) intake, compression, power, and exhaust
   (B) when the valves are opening and closing
   (C) timed spark in a defined order
   (D) follows the camshaft rotation

8. Which tool is used with chisels and punches?
   (A) nail gun
   (B) ball-peen hammer
   (C) wooden mallet
   (D) claw hammer

9. What is exposed to direct heat and pressure during combustion?
   (A) the cylinder head
   (B) the piston
   (C) air
   (D) fuel

10. Which tool is used to remove a threaded fastener with a head that has a star hole?

(A) Security T

(B) Torx

(C) Robertson

(D) Phillips/cross-slot

11. When does the thermostat open?

(A) when the engine is cold

(B) when the engine is hot

(C) during acceleration

(D) at start-up

12. Which tool(s) has/have an open-end wrench on one end and a box end on the other?

(A) ratchet and socket

(B) socket

(C) end wrench

(D) combination wrench

13. What indicates a defective water pump?

(A) an empty coolant recovery bottle

(B) the cooling fan not operating

(C) coolant leaking out of the water pump weep hole

(D) a leaking bypass tube

14. Which screw can be used with a nut and washer combination?

(A) sheet metal

(B) self-drilling

(C) machine

(D) wood

15. What does engine lubrication do?

(A) cools, cleans, seals, and lubricates parts of the engine

(B) carries away heat from the engine

(C) helps decrease friction between the exhaust valve and intake valve

(D) keeps the cylinder cool during combustion

16. The access panel for a piece of equipment has been placed on the mounting studs. The panel is removed often. Which fastener is used to secure the panel?

(A) wing nut

(B) bolt

(C) lock nut

(D) castle nut

17. What do dry sumps use?

(A) a premixed oil and fuel ratio

(B) an oil tank

(C) a fan

(D) a thermostat

18. The shop pressed a bearing into a brake rotor assembly. Which fastening device is used to secure the bearing in the rotor bore?

(A) inside snap ring

(B) outside snap ring

(C) internal/external snap-ring pliers

(D) locking nut

19. Compression ratios in a diesel engine are

(A) lower than gasoline engines.

(B) equal to gasoline engines.

(C) variable depending on engine sizes.

(D) higher than gasoline engines.

20. Which nail is used to attach shingles to a roof board?

    (A) finish

    (B) framing

    (C) drywall

    (D) roofing

21. What is the purpose of the fuel pressure regulator?

    (A) deliver fuel from the tank to the fuel system

    (B) regulate the injector's injection process

    (C) regulate fuel pressure in the fuel system for the injectors

    (D) adjust the air-fuel ratio

22. What application are rivets used for?

    (A) in combination with a jack plane

    (B) attaching metal pieces

    (C) boring holes in metal

    (D) attaching wood pieces

23. A lean mixture is what ratio?

    (A) 15:1

    (B) 13:1

    (C) 14.7:1

    (D) 50:50

24. Which welder(s) uses/use a stinger and welding rod to attach metal pieces?

    (A) MIG welder

    (B) arc welder

    (C) oxyacetylene welder

    (D) both MIG and arc welder

25. What is pre-ignition?

    (A) a part located under the distributor cap

    (B) a distributor-less ignition system

    (C) when the air-fuel mixture ignites early

    (D) when spark happens as the piston reaches BDC

MECHANICAL COMPREHENSION

This part of the test measures your knowledge of mechanics. Each of the questions or incomplete statements is followed by four choices. You are to decide which one of the choices best answers the question or completes the statement.

1. What is the net force acting on the block below? (Assume positive is to your right.)

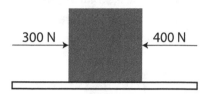

(A) −100 N

(B) 0 N

(C) 700 N

(D) 120,000 N

2. A person starts from rest and increases his velocity to 5 m/s over a time period of 1 s. What is his acceleration?

(A) −5 m/s²

(B) 0 m/s²

(C) 5 m/s²

(D) 10 m/s²

3. What is the mechanical advantage of the system of pulleys shown below?

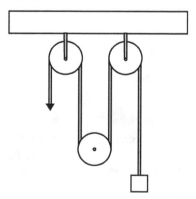

(A) 0

(B) 2

(C) 3

(D) 6

4. Which of these objects would be the hardest for an astronaut to move in outer space?

(A) a wrench

(B) another astronaut

(C) a screwdriver

(D) the International Space Station

5. Which of the following terms defines a force?

(A) a push or pull

(B) a measure of inertia

(C) a change in speed

(D) a change in acceleration

6. If the coefficient of kinetic friction between an object and the floor is $\mu_s = 0.5$, and the weight of the object is 10 N, what is the magnitude of the force of kinetic friction?

(A) 1 N

(B) 2 N

(C) 4 N

(D) 5 N

7. Which of the following describes what will happen when positive work is done on an object?

(A) The object will gain energy.

(B) The object will lose energy.

(C) The object will increase its temperature.

(D) The object will decrease its temperature.

8. What is the potential energy of a person who weighs 150 N when she is on a stool 1 m in the air?

    (A) 15 J

    (B) 30 J

    (C) 150 J

    (D) 300 J

9. A ramp has a length of 20 m, and the top end is rested on a ridge that is 5 m high. What is the mechanical advantage for this ramp?

    (A) 2

    (B) 3

    (C) 4

    (D) 5

10. What is the unit for power?

    (A) watt (W)

    (B) joule (J)

    (C) newton (N)

    (D) coulomb (C)

11. What is the momentum of a mass of 100 kg that is traveling at 2 m/s?

    (A) 50 kg m/s

    (B) 100 kg m/s

    (C) 200 kg m/s

    (D) 400 kg m/s

12. A car wheel has a radius of 1 m and applies a torque of 100 Nm to the road. What is the force applied to the road from the wheel?

    (A) 1 N

    (B) 10 N

    (C) 100 N

    (D) 1,000 N

13. In terms of moment of inertia, which example would be the most difficult for a person to spin in a circle?

    (A) a basketball at half an arm's length

    (B) a bowling ball at half an arm's length

    (C) a basketball at arm's length

    (D) a bowling ball at arm's length

14. What is the best explanation of what a pulley does?

    (A) changes the direction of an input force by supporting a rope that has a tension

    (B) applies an output force with a motor that drives the pulley

    (C) changes the angle of the input force by using an inclined plane

    (D) provides rotational force by friction to increase the output force of the pulley

15. A single pulley is attached to the ceiling. If the pulley is holding a rope that is attached to the floor on one side and a person of weight 100 N on the other, what is the tension in the rope?

    (A) 0 N

    (B) 50 N

    (C) 100 N

    (D) 200 N

16. A screw in a block of wood is rotated exactly once around its axis. What is another name for the distance it moves into the wood?

    (A) impulse

    (B) torque

    (C) wedge

    (D) pitch

17. Two ropes are connected on either side of a mass of 100 kg resting on a flat surface. Each rope is pulling on the mass with 50 N of force, parallel to the ground. What can be said about the motion of the mass?

(A) The mass will accelerate to left.

(B) The mass is in equilibrium.

(C) The mass will accelerate to the right.

(D) The mass will be lifted up.

18. Two masses each have a mass of 1 kg and are 1 m apart as shown below. Where is the center of mass of the two masses located?

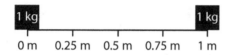

(A) 0 m

(B) 0.25 m

(C) 0.5 m

(D) 0.75 m

19. Why is it so difficult to hold a beach ball under water?

(A) The ball is full of air, which is much less dense than water.

(B) The ball shrinks under water, making it harder to hold.

(C) The ball expands under water, so it rises faster.

(D) The cool water will cool the air in the ball, making it rise.

20. How much energy is used by a 60 W light bulb that has been on for 100 s?

(A) 0.6 J

(B) 6 J

(C) 60 J

(D) 6,000 J

21. In the gear train shown below, Gear B will move _____ and Gear C will move _____.

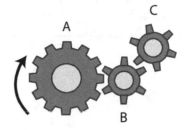

(A) clockwise; clockwise

(B) clockwise; counterclockwise

(C) counterclockwise; counterclockwise

(D) counterclockwise; clockwise

22. The arrow labeled F in the diagram of a box on an incline below represents

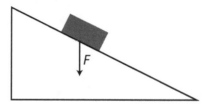

(A) normal force

(B) gravity

(C) friction

(D) tension

23. Which object will weigh the most?

(A) an object with mass = 10 kg

(B) an object with mass = 100 kg

(C) an object with mass = 1,000 kg

(D) an object with mass = 10,000 kg

24. Which of the following is a measure of the inertia of an object?

(A) mass

(B) speed

(C) acceleration

(D) force

25. A pendulum is swinging as shown in the figure below. At which point does the pendulum have the maximum amount of kinetic energy?

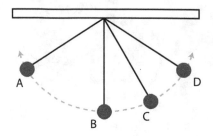

(A) Point A

(B) Point B

(C) Point C

(D) Point D

ASSEMBLING OBJECTS

Given a set of objects, your task is to determine which answer choice shows how the objects will look once the parts are put together.

1.

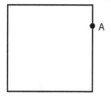

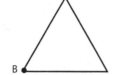

(A)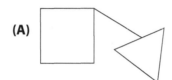

(B)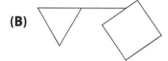

(C)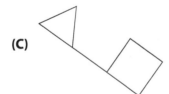

(D)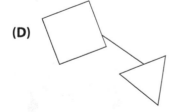

2.

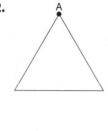

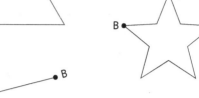

(A)

(B)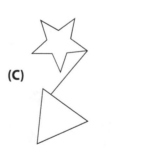

(C)

(D)

3.

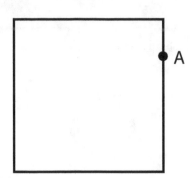

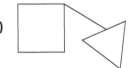
(A)

(C)

(B)

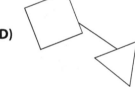
(D)

4.

(A)

(C)

(B)

(D)

5.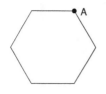

(A)

(B)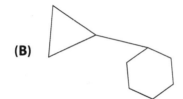

(C)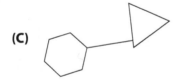

(D)

6.

(A)

(B)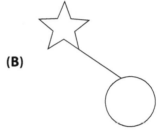

(C)

(D)

7.

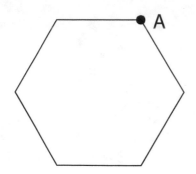

(A)

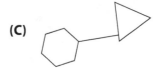

(C)

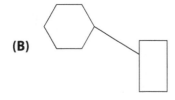

(B)

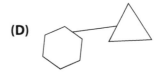

(D)

8.

(A)

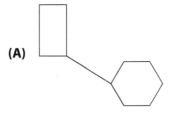

(C)

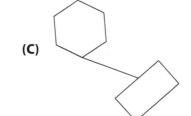

(B)

(D)

9.

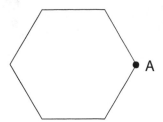

(A)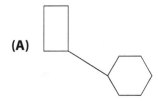

(C)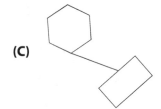

(B)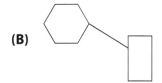

(D)

10.

(A)

(C)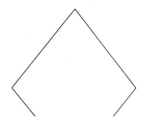

(B)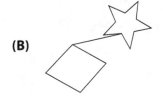

(D)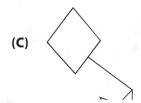

11.

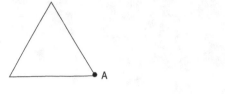

(A)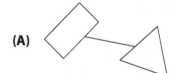

(B)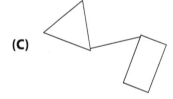

(C)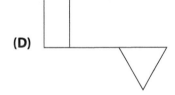

(D)

12.

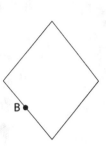

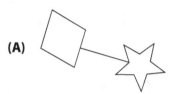

(A)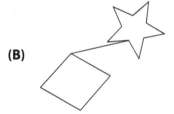

(B)

(C)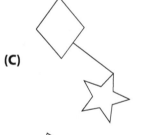

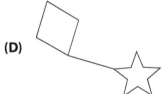

(D)

13.

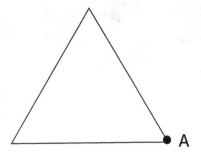

 **(A)** 　　　**(C)**

 **(B)** 　　　**(D)**

14.

 (A) 　　　**(C)**

 (B) 　　　**(D)**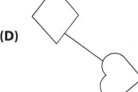

15.

 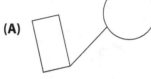 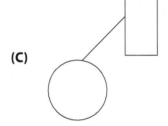 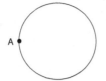

(A)

(B)

(C)

(D)

16.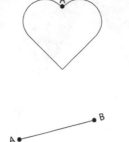

(A)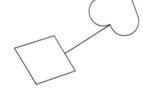

(B)

(C)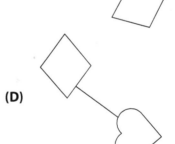

(D)

17.

(A)

(C)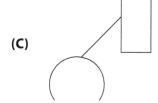

(B)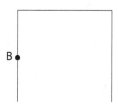

(D)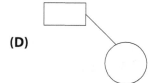

18.

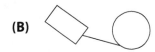

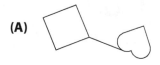

(A)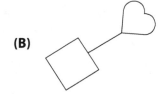

(C)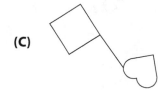

(B)

(D)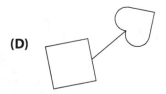

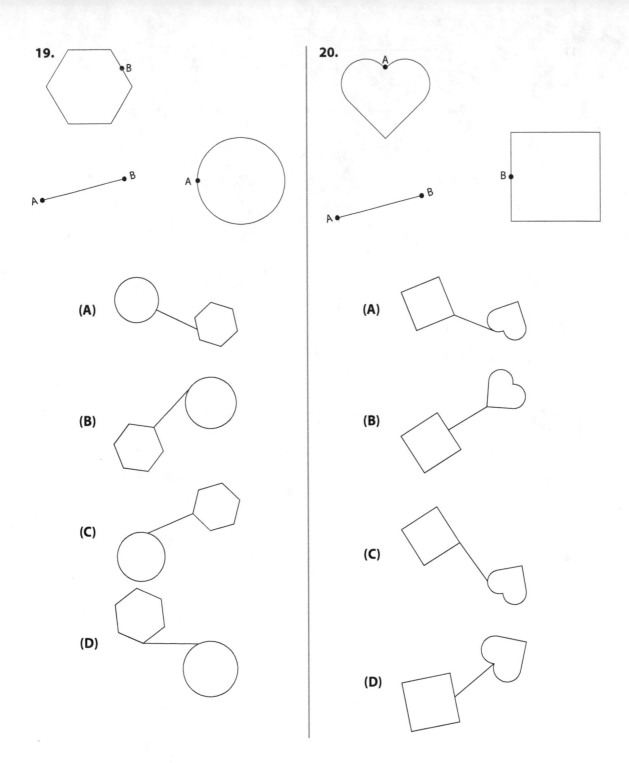

19.

(A)

(B)

(C)

(D)

20.

(A)

(B)

(C)

(D)

21.

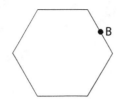

(A)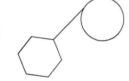

(C)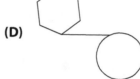

(B)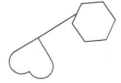

(D)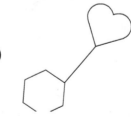

22.

(A)

(C)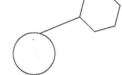

(B)

(D)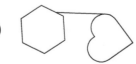

23.

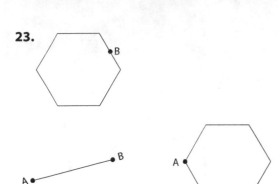

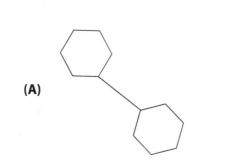

(A)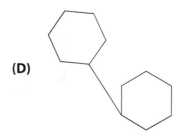

(B)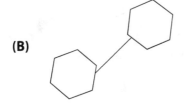

(C)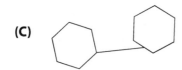

(D)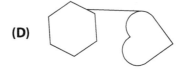

24.

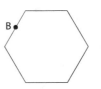

(A)

(B)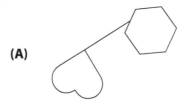

(C)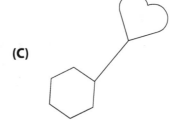

(D)

25.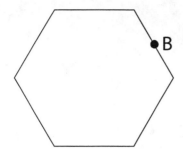

(A)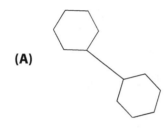

(C)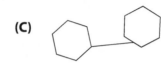

(B)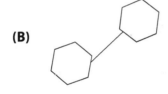

(D)

ANSWER KEY

GENERAL SCIENCE

1. **(A)**

   (A) is correct. Calcium is the most abundant mineral found in bones, as well as in the entire body.

   (B) is incorrect. Phosphorus is the second-most common material found in bones.

   (C) is incorrect. Collagen is a protein found in connective tissue.

   (D) is incorrect. Potassium is not found in high quantities in bone.

2. **(A)**

   (A) is correct. A biome is a large ecological community that includes specific plants and animals, such as a desert.

   (B) is incorrect. A cornfield is a part of a prairie biome.

   (C) is incorrect. Animals are part of a biome.

   (D) is incorrect. A beehive is part of a biome.

3. **(B)**

   (A) is incorrect. Mercury is the planet closest to the sun. Venus orbits between Mercury and Earth.

   (B) is correct. Venus's orbit is closest to Earth. Venus is the second planet

   from the sun, and Earth is the third planet from the sun.

   (C) is incorrect. Jupiter is the fifth planet from the sun.

   (D) is incorrect. Saturn is the sixth planet from the sun.

4. **(D)**

   (A) is incorrect. *Aurora* is the phenomenon of colored lights that appear in the sky near the North and South Poles.

   (B) is incorrect. The galaxy is a large group of stars held together by gravity.

   (C) is incorrect. Black holes are collapsed stars whose gravitational pull is so strong that light cannot escape.

   (D) is correct. Before a star collapses, the star burns brighter for a period of time and then fades from view. This is a supernova.

5. **(D)**

   (A) is incorrect. Mitochondria are not found only in animal cells.

   (B) is incorrect. Mitochondria are not found only in fungi cells.

   (C) is incorrect. Mitochondria are not found only in plant cells.

(D) is correct. Plant, animal, and fungi cells have mitochondria.

6. **(C)**

(A) is incorrect. Isotopes must have the same number of protons, not electrons.

(B) is incorrect. Isotopes are defined as having different numbers of neutrons, not the same number.

(C) is correct. Isotopes are atoms of the same element with the same number of protons but different numbers of neutrons.

(D) is incorrect. Isotopes have the same number of protons but can also have the same number of electrons.

7. **(D)**

(A) is incorrect. Blood tests are used to diagnose diabetes.

(B) is incorrect. Magnetic resonance imaging (MRI) is used to see soft tissue damage, such as torn ligaments.

(C) is incorrect. There are a variety of tests that diagnose cancer, such as blood tests, magnetic resonance imaging (MRI), and ultrasounds.

(D) is correct. Tachycardia is an abnormally fast heart rate, and electrocardiograms show the electrical activity of the heart.

8. **(C)**

(A) is incorrect. Protons are positively charged particles in the nucleus.

(B) is incorrect. Neutrons are particles in the nucleus that have no charge.

(C) is correct. Electrons are negatively charged particles in an atom; electrons orbit the nucleus.

(D) is incorrect. Ions are atoms that have lost or gained electrons and have a charge.

9. **(A)**

(A) is correct. The metabolic rate of crustaceans is too low to regulate their temperature. Crustaceans use behavioral techniques, such as

moving to shallow water, to maintain body temperature.

(B) is incorrect. Dolphins are mammals. Mammals are endothermic, meaning they have a mechanism to regulate body temperature internally.

(C) is incorrect. Whales are mammals, and so are endothermic.

(D) is incorrect. Birds are endothermic.

10. **(A)**

(A) is correct. Tension is the force that results from objects being pulled or hung.

(B) is incorrect. The box experiences friction as it slides against the ramp.

(C) is incorrect. Gravity is the force pulling the box down the ramp.

(D) is incorrect. The normal force is the upward force of the ramp on the box.

11. **(B)**

(A) is incorrect. Plants produce their own food through photosynthesis, making them producers.

(B) is correct. Mushrooms are fungi. Fungi break down organic material left by dead animals and plants, making them decomposers.

(C) is incorrect. Goats eat producers, such as grass, making them primary consumers.

(D) is incorrect. Lions are carnivorous animals that feed on primary consumers and secondary consumers, making them secondary or tertiary consumers.

12. **(D)**

(A) is incorrect. Acids have a pH between 0 and 7.

(B) is incorrect. Acids have a pH between 0 and 7.

(C) is incorrect. Acids have a pH between 0 and 7.

(D) is correct. Bases have a pH between 7 and 14.

13. (B)

(A) is incorrect. The digestive system turns food into energy.

(B) is correct. The endocrine system releases hormones, including growth hormones.

(C) is incorrect. The nervous system is a network of communication cells.

(D) is incorrect. The circulatory system delivers nutrients to cells and removes wastes from the body.

14. (B)

(A) is incorrect. The exosphere is the outermost layer of the earth's atmosphere.

(B) is correct. The lithosphere is the top layer of the earth's surface.

(C) is incorrect. The atmosphere refers to the layer of gases that surrounds the earth.

(D) is incorrect. The biosphere is the part of Earth where life exists; the biosphere includes the atmosphere, the oceans, and the life-supporting areas above and below Earth's surface.

15. (A)

(A) is correct. When water changes form, it does not change the chemical composition of the substance. Once water becomes ice, the ice can easily turn back into water.

(B) is incorrect. During a chemical change, the chemical composition of the substance changes and cannot be reversed. Baking a cake is an example of a chemical change.

(C) is incorrect. Rusting is an example of a chemical change.

(D) is incorrect. Setting off fireworks causes a chemical change.

16. (C)

(A) is incorrect. Water can generate hydropower, which is a renewable energy source.

(B) is incorrect. Wind is a renewable energy source.

(C) is correct. Coal is nonrenewable because once coal is burned, it cannot be quickly replaced.

(D) is incorrect. Solar energy is a renewable energy source.

17. (B)

(A) is incorrect. One hour is 1/24 of the time it takes for the earth to rotate on its axis.

(B) is correct. Earth takes approximately twenty-four hours to rotate on its axis.

(C) is incorrect. The moon takes approximately one month to revolve around the earth.

(D) is incorrect. The earth takes approximately one year to revolve around the sun.

18. (D)

(A) is incorrect. Digestion is the process whereby large food particles are broken down into small particles.

(B) is incorrect. A chloroplast is the part of the cell where photosynthesis takes place.

(C) is incorrect. Decomposition is the process where substances are broken down into smaller parts.

(D) is correct. Photosynthesis describes the process by which plants convert the energy of the sun into stored chemical energy (glucose).

19. (D)

(A) is incorrect. In a substitution reaction, a single atom or ion swaps places with another atom or ion.

(B) is incorrect. In an acid-base reaction, an acid and a base react to neutralize each other. This reaction does not include an acid or base.

(C) is incorrect. In a decomposition reaction, a compound breaks down into smaller molecules or compounds.

(D) is correct. Combustion is defined as a reaction in which a hydrocarbon reacts with O_2 to produce CO_2 and H_2O.

20. (C)

(A) is incorrect. Producers are living things, which are biotic factors.

(B) is incorrect. Consumers are living things.

(C) is correct. Nonliving things in an ecosystem, like air and water, are abiotic factors.

(D) is incorrect. Decomposers are living things.

21. (B)

(A) is incorrect. The respiratory system helps create sound, but that is not its primary purpose.

(B) is correct. Oxygen intake and carbon dioxide disposal are the primary functions of the respiratory system.

(C) is incorrect. The circulatory system transports nutrients throughout the body.

(D) is incorrect. While parts of the respiratory system filter out foreign pathogens, this is not the system's primary purpose.

22. (D)

(A) is incorrect. Gene flow is the transfer of alleles from one population to another.

(B) is incorrect. Genetic drift is the increase or decrease in the presence of an allele due to chance.

(C) is incorrect. A mutation is a change in the genetic code that leads to advantageous traits.

(D) is correct. The mechanism of natural selection is rooted in the idea that there is variation in inherited traits among a population of organisms and that there is differential reproduction as a result.

23. (B)

(A) is incorrect. The pharynx connects the mouth to the esophagus and larynx.

(B) is correct. The tongue is the muscle that helps break apart food, mix it with saliva, and direct it toward the esophagus.

(C) is incorrect. The diaphragm is the muscle that moves the lungs.

(D) is incorrect. The stomach receives the bolus that passes through the esophagus from the mouth.

24. (A)

(A) is correct. Strong acids break apart into their constituent ions immediately when placed in water.

(B) is incorrect. Strong acids may donate only one proton.

(C) is incorrect. A substance with a pH of 7 is neutral; a strong acid has a pH close to 1.

(D) is incorrect. A strong acid ionizes easily, releasing protons.

25. (C)

(A) is incorrect. Cave formation is an example of chemical weathering. Chemical weathering involves a chemical change.

(B) is incorrect. Rusting is an example of chemical weathering.

(C) is correct. Mechanical weathering involves breaking a substance down without changing the composition of the substance.

(D) is incorrect. Bananas turning brown is an example of a chemical change.

ARITHMETIC REASONING

1. **(C)**

   Work backwards to find the number of runners in the competition (c) and then the number of runners on the team (r).

   $\frac{2}{c} = \frac{10}{100}$

   $c = 20$

   $\frac{20}{r} = \frac{25}{100}$

   $r = \mathbf{80}$

2. **(D)**

   Multiply by the converstion factor to get from meters to feet.

   $55 \text{ m } (\frac{3.28 \text{ ft.}}{1 \text{ m}}) = \mathbf{180.4 \text{ feet}}$

3. **(D)**

   Write a proportion and then solve for x.

   $\frac{40}{45} = \frac{265}{x}$

   $40x = 11{,}925$

   $x = 298.125 \approx \mathbf{298}$

4. **(B)**

   Find the cost of three burgers.

   Cost of 3 burgers $= 3(6.50) = 19.50$

   Subtract this value from the total costs of the meal to find the cost of the fries.

   $26.50 - 19.50 = 7$

   Divide by 2 to find the cost of one order of fries.

   $7 \div 2 = \mathbf{\$3.50}$

5. **(B)**

   Write a proportion and then solve for x.

   $\frac{15{,}036}{7} = \frac{x}{2}$

   $7x = 30{,}072$

   $x = \mathbf{4{,}296}$

6. **(A)**

   Use the formula for inversely proportional relationships to find k and then solve for s.

   $sn = k$

   $(65)(250) = k$

   $k = 16{,}250$

   $s(325) = 16{,}250$

   $s = \mathbf{50}$

7. **(D)**

   Add the probability of drawing a blue marble and the probability of drawing a red marble to find the probability of drawing either a blue or red marble.

   $\frac{1}{20} + \frac{7}{20} = \frac{8}{20} = \mathbf{\frac{2}{5}}$

8. **(C)**

   Use the formula for percent change.

   $percent\ change = \frac{amount\ of\ change}{original\ amount}$

   $= \frac{(7{,}375 - 7{,}250)}{7{,}250} = 0.017 = \mathbf{1.7\%}$

9. **(A)**

   To calculate the average, add all of the scores and divide by the total number of scores. Use the variable x in place of the missing score.

   $\frac{(100 + 100 + 100 + x)}{4} = 85$

   $\frac{(300 + x)}{4} = 85$

   $(300 + x) = 340$

   $x = \mathbf{40\%}$

10. **(A)**

    Add the fractions and subtract the result from the amount of flour Allison started with.

    $2\frac{1}{2} + \frac{3}{4} = \frac{5}{2} + \frac{3}{4} = \frac{10}{4} + \frac{3}{4} = \frac{13}{4}$

    $4 - \frac{13}{4} = \frac{16}{4} - \frac{13}{4} = \mathbf{\frac{3}{4}}$

11. **(B)**

    Multiply the number of rooms by the cost of each room to find the total.

    $25(4) + 35(2) + 40(1) = \mathbf{\$210}$

12. (A)

Use the equation for percentages.

part = whole × percent =
$9 \times 0.25 = \textbf{2.25}$

13. (A)

Valerie will receive her base pay plus 27.75 for every hour she worked in addition to her 40 hours.

A = base pay + 27.75 × extra hours

$\textbf{A = 740 + 27.75(t − 40)}$

14. (D)

Set up a proportion and solve.

$\frac{AB}{DE} = \frac{3}{4}$

$\frac{12}{DE} = \frac{3}{4}$

$3(DE) = 48$

$\textbf{DE = 16}$

15. (A)

His profit will be his income minus his expenses. He will earn $40 for each lawn, or 40*m*. He pays $35 is expenses each week, or 35*x*.

$\textbf{profit = 40m − 35x}$

16. (C)

$23 \div 4 = 5.75$ pizzas
Round up to **6 pizzas**.

17. (C)

Use the formula for percent change.

percent change $= \frac{amount\ of\ change}{original\ amount}$

$= \frac{680 − 425}{425}$

$= \frac{255}{425} = 0.60 = \textbf{60\%}$

18. (C)

Use the formula for percentages.

whole $= \frac{part}{percent} = \frac{meal + tax}{1 + 0.0825}$

$= \frac{24.65}{1.0825} = \textbf{\$22.77}$

19. (A)

Use the formula for percentages to find the number of games the team won.

part = whole × percent =
$12 \times 0.75 = 9$

Subtract the number of games won from the games played to find the number of games the team lost.

$12 − 9 = \textbf{3}$

20. (D)

Assign variables and write the ratios as fractions. Then, cross-multiply to solve for the number of apples and oranges sold.

x = apples

$\frac{apples}{bananas} = \frac{3}{2} = \frac{x}{20}$

$60 = 2x$

$x = 30$ apples

y = oranges

$\frac{oranges}{bananas} = \frac{1}{2} = \frac{y}{20}$

$2y = 20$

$y = 10$ oranges

To find the total, add the number of apples, oranges, and bananas together. $30 + 20 + 10 = \textbf{60 pieces}$ **of fruit**

21. (D)

To estimate the amount of the change, round the price of each item to the nearest dollar amount and subtract from the total.

$\$50 − (\$13 + \$12 + \$4 + \$6)$

$= \$50 − \$35 = \textbf{\$15}$

22. (D)

Set up an equation to find the number of people wearing neither white nor blue. Subtract the number of people wearing both colors so they are not counted twice.

$21 = 7 + 6 + neither − 5$

neither = **13**

23. (B)

Find the 5th term.

$−9 − (−36) = 27$

$27 \times −3 = −81$

Find the 6th term.

$−36 − (−81) = 45$

$45 \times −3 = \textbf{−135}$

24. **(D)**

Use the formula for the area of a rectangle to find the increase in its size.

$A = lw$

$A = (1.4l)(0.6w)$

$A = 0.84lw$

The new area will be 84% of the original area, a decrease of **16%**.

25. **(C)**

Set up a proportion and solve.

$$\frac{2775 \text{ miles}}{3 \text{ hr}} = \frac{x \text{ miles}}{5 \text{ hr}}$$

$2775(5) = 3x$

$x = 4{,}625$ miles

26. **(D)**

Use the formula for the sum of an arithmetic series.

$S_n = \frac{n}{2}(a_1 + a_n)$

$= \frac{n}{2}[2a_1 + (n-1)d]$

$= \frac{180}{2}[2(10) + (180-1)4]$

$= 66{,}240$ seats

27. **(D)**

Find the time that Erica spends on break and subtract this from her total time at work.

$30 + 2(15) = 1$ hour

$8\frac{1}{2} - 1 = 7\frac{1}{2}$

$= 7$ hours, 30 minutes

28. **(B)**

Multiply the cost per pounds by the number of pounds purchased to find the cost of each fruit.

apples: $2(1.89) = 3.78$

oranges: $1.5(2.19) = 3.285$

$3.78 + 3.285 = 7.065 = $ **$7.07**

29. **(C)**

Multiply the car's speed by the time traveled to find the distance.

$1.5(65) = 97.5$ miles

$2.5(50) = 125$ miles

$97.5 + 125 = $ **222.5 miles**

30. **(B)**

The square root of 169 is **13**.

WORD KNOWLEDGE

1. **(A)**
The word root *pax* means "peace," and the suffix *–ify* means "to cause to become more," and so, to pacify someone means to cause that person to become more peaceful, or to soothe him.

2. **(D)**
The prefix *im–* means "not," and the word root *materialis* means "material, relevant, or important," so *immaterial* means "inconsequential or of no importance."

3. **(B)**
The root word *flagrantem* means "burning, glowing," and the suffix *–ly* means "having the nature or qualities of." Someone who breaks rules and laws flagrantly does so in an open, deliberate manner, with no shame.

4. **(C)**
An indolent person is lazy and avoids activity or exertion.

5. **(A)**
The word root *judicium* means "judgment," and the suffix *–ous* means "possessing or full of." And so, the cat made a decision based on good judgment, wisdom, or practicality.

6. **(C)**
Pragmatic means "related to practical matters." For example, a pragmatic person evaluates the facts and makes a realistic plan before acting.

7. **(D)**
Someone with a smiling countenance has a smile on her face.

8. **(A)**
The word root *kak* means "evil," and the word root *phone* means "sound," so cacophony is the opposite of harmony; it is a combination of harsh, unpleasant noises that sound terrible together.

9. **(D)**
Someone with charisma, or charm, is attractive to others.

10. **(C)**
Capricious means "unpredictable or impulsive," so others cannot rely on a capricious person.

11. **(C)**
To daunt means to intimidate or make someone apprehensive. For example, difficult tests are daunting to most people.

12. **(B)**
The word root *acclamare* in *acclaim* means "to cry out." Over time, this word came to mean "applause or praise."

13. **(A)**
The word root *crēdere* means "to believe," and the suffix *–ous* means "possessing or full of," so a credulous person is naïve enough to believe almost everything he hears or reads.

14. **(B)**
The word root *obsolētus* means "worn out." And so, an obsolete device such as a rotary phone has outlived or worn out its usefulness.

15. **(A)**
A labyrinth is a maze or intricate pathway. Once someone enters a labyrinth, she can find it very difficult to find the way out.

16. (D)

The word root *sacrōsānctus* means "made holy by sacred rites." Related words include *sacred*, *sacrifice*, *sanction*, and *sanctuary*.

17. (B)

Someone with an effervescent personality is animated, charming, and bubbly. The adjective *effervescent* also means "fizzy," so it can be used to describe a carbonated beverage.

18. (B)

Rudimentary means "basic or elementary." For example, familiarity with the alphabet is a rudimentary reading skill that children learn at a young age.

19. (D)

The word root *fervere* means "to boil." And so, someone who is filled with fervor "boils with" passion or eagerness.

20. (A)

To cajole means to wheedle, coax, or entice someone into doing something. For example, a child might cajole her parents into buying her ice cream.

21. (C)

The prefix *im–* means "not," and the word root *parcial* means "biased," so an impartial jury is one whose members are not biased and are therefore able to evaluate evidence in an objective, unprejudiced manner.

22. (C)

The prefix *im–* means "not," and the word root *mutare* means "to change." And so, a mutation is a change, and something immutable is unchangeable.

23. (B)

Reiterate means "to do something over again." For example, when someone reiterates a piece of information, she restates it.

24. (C)

Bombastic language is too flowery, pretentious, and overly fancy for the topic it describes.

25. (D)

The prefix *pre–* means "before," the word root *cede* means "to go," and the suffix *–ent* means "something that," so a precedent is an event or action that comes before another event or action. A model comes first and is used as a plan to make something else.

26. (A)

Prudent means "wise or judicious." For example, a prudent decision is a wise, practical one.

27. (C)

Haphazard means "a lack of planning or order." For example, when a room is arranged haphazardly, it is disorganized, messy, and chaotic.

28. (C)

The word root *figūrāre* means "to shape," and the suffix *–ive* means "indicating a tendency," so a figurative expression, or figure of speech, is shaped or invented rather than based on literal truth.

29. (C)

Innocuous means "harmless or inoffensive." For example, an innocuous substance is not harmful.

30. (D)

The word root *officium* means "service or duty," and the suffix *–ous* means "possessing or full of." And so, Shelby is someone who perhaps takes her leadership duties so seriously that she acts in an overbearing manner.

31. **(C)**

The word root *neglegere* means "to neglect," and the suffix root *–ence* means "the act of," so negligence is the act of neglecting—not paying proper attention to—someone or something.

32. **(D)**

Lax means "loose or open." For example, a lax set of rules would be permissive.

33. **(D)**

To meander means to wander, roam, or amble around on a winding, twisting route.

34. **(D)**

The word root in the nouns *arson* and *ardor* means "to burn," and the suffix *–ent* means "doing a certain action," and so an ardent person burns with passion.

35. **(C)**

To garner things means to gather, acquire, get, or collect them.

PARAGRAPH COMPREHENSION

1. **(A)**

    (A) is correct. The context implies that the fighting was intense and tiring.

    (B) is incorrect. Nothing in the passage addresses the price of the battle.

    (C) is incorrect. The passage indicates nothing about the pattern of fighting.

    (D) is incorrect. The author states that the fighting ultimately led to a US victory.

2. **(B)**

    (A) is incorrect. The author identifies the ideals associated with idealism but does not offer an opinion on or advocate for them.

    (B) is correct. The purpose of the passage is to explain what an idealist believes in. The author does not offer any opinions or try to persuade readers about the importance of certain values.

    (C) is incorrect. The author states that social and political discourse are "permeated with idealism" but does not suggest that this is destructive or wrong.

    (D) is incorrect. The author provides the reader with information but does not seek to change the reader's opinions or behaviors.

3. **(B)**

    (A) is incorrect. The passage states that "vision does not become the dominant sense until around the age of 12 months."

    (B) is correct. The passage states that "infants rely primarily on hearing."

    (C) is incorrect. The sense of touch in not mentioned in the passage.

    (D) is incorrect. The sense of smell is not mentioned in the passage.

4. **(B)**

    (A) is incorrect. While this is stated in the first sentence, it is not the main idea.

    (B) is correct. The passage describes the origin of Yellowstone's geysers.

    (C) is incorrect. While the author states this in the passage, it is not the main idea.

    (D) is incorrect. This is not stated in the passage.

5. **(D)**

    (A) is incorrect. There is no evidence that the protest movement was successful; in fact, the passage implies the opposite.

    (B) is incorrect. While the author states that Western countries observed the events in China, there is no evidence they became involved.

    (C) is incorrect. There is no evidence in the passage that factory workers had any involvement beyond "cheering on" the protestors.

    (D) is correct. The author writes, "it seemed to be the beginning of a political revolution in China, so the world was stunned when, on July 4, Chinese troops and security police stormed the square," stifling any possibility of democratic revolution.

6. **(D)**

    (A) is incorrect. While the text does list several family members of Custer who died in the battle, this is not the main idea.

    (B) is incorrect. The author does not explain why the cavalry was formed.

    (C) is incorrect. The author does not describe the personal relationship between Sitting Bull and Custer.

    (D) is correct. The author writes, "the allied tribes decisively defeated their US foes."

7. **(C)**

    (A) is incorrect. The author writes, "scientists uncovered a 3.2 million-year-old non-human hominid they nicknamed 'Lucy.'"

    (B) is incorrect. The author does not connect Lucy's discovery with the knowledge about the area's past ecosystem.

    (C) is correct. The author writes that before Lucy's discovery, the oldest known fossil from the genus Homo "dated only back to 2.3 million years ago, leaving a 700,000 gap between Lucy's species and the advent of humans."

    (D) is incorrect. The author explains it was the 2013 discovery that narrowed the gap.

8. **(D)**

    (A) is incorrect. In regional studies, geographers "examine the characteristics of a particular place[.]"

    (B) is incorrect. In topical studies, geographers "look at a single physical or human feature that impacts the world[.]"

    (C) is incorrect. In physical studies, geographers "focus on the physical features of Earth[.]"

    (D) is correct. The passage describes human studies as the study of "the relationship between human activity and the environment," which would include farmers interacting with river systems.

9. **(A)**

    (A) is correct. The author writes, "a shoelace knot experiences greater g-force than any rollercoaster can generate," helping the reader understand the strength of the g-force experienced by the knots.

    (B) is incorrect. The author does not describe any actual experiments involving rollercoasters.

    (C) is incorrect. The author does not assess the findings of the experiment.

    (D) is incorrect. The rollercoaster reference is a comparison, not specific evidence.

10. **(B)**

    (A) is incorrect. While the author does describe his memory loss, this is not the main idea of the passage.

    (B) is correct. The author writes, "From this, scientists learned that different types of memory are handled by different parts of the brain."

    (C) is incorrect. The author does explain the differences in long-term and short-term memory formation, but not until the end of the passage.

    (D) is incorrect. While it is implied that memories of physical skills are processed differently than memories of events, this is not the main idea of the passage.

11. **(A)**

    (A) is correct. The author goes on to describe the shared perspectives of these writers.

    (B) is incorrect. The author does not indicate the number of writers.

    (C) is incorrect. The author provides no context that implies they were an organized group, simply that they shared certain traits.

    (D) is incorrect. The author states that they gathered in one place—Paris.

12. **(D)**

    (A) is incorrect. The author writes that the officers, not the volunteers, were veterans.

    (B) is incorrect. There passage does not mention a citizenship requirement.

    (C) is incorrect. While most of the volunteers were indeed from the Southwest, the passage does not say this was a requirement.

    (D) is correct. The author writes, "the army set high standards: all of the recruits had to be skilled on horseback…"

13. **(B)**

(A) is incorrect. The author asserts that, despite the popular narrative, cultural differences were not the cause of the Civil War.

(B) is correct. The author writes, "The Civil War was not a battle of cultural identities—it was a battle about slavery. All other explanations for the war are either a direct consequence of the South's desire for wealth at the expense of her fellow man or a fanciful invention to cover up this sad portion of our nation's history."

(C) is incorrect. The author does not discuss the strengths of the North or provide any reason for why it won the war.

(D) is incorrect. Though the author mentions these cultural beliefs, she does not suggest that these were the reasons the South was defeated.

14. **(B)**

(A) is incorrect. While the author states this, it is not the main idea.

(B) is correct. The author states, "Ignored by the government, an activist group known as Indians of All Tribes sailed to Alcatraz in the early morning hours with eighty-nine men, women, and children." The author goes on to describe the nineteen-month occupation of the island.

(C) is incorrect. The author states that up to 600 people joined the occupation.

(D) is incorrect. The author does not describe any violent action towards protestors.

15. **(D)**

(A) is incorrect. There is no indication that the Bastille was occupied by royalty.

(B) is incorrect. There is no indication that the structure was intended to represent anything.

(C) is incorrect. There is no indication that the Bastille was used for governing.

(D) is correct. The author writes that the Bastille was originally built "to protect the city from English invasion during the Hundred Years' War."

MATH KNOWLEDGE

1. **(D)**

   Simplify using PEMDAS.

   $z^3(z + 2)^2 - 4z^3 + 2$

   $z^3(z^2 + 4z + 4) - 4z^3 + 2$

   $z^5 + 4z^4 + 4z^3 - 4z^3 + 2$

   $\mathbf{z^5 + 4z^4 + 2}$

2. **(B)**

   Use the rules of exponents to simplify the expression.

   $\frac{(3x^2y^2)^2}{3^3x^{-2}y^3} = \frac{3^2x^4y^4}{3^3x^{-2}y^3} = \mathbf{\frac{x^6y}{3}}$

3. **(A)**

   $\left(\frac{1}{2}\right)^3 = \frac{1}{2} \times \frac{1}{2} \times \frac{1}{2} = \mathbf{\frac{1}{8}}$

4. **(C)**

   Use the formula for the area of a cylinder.

   $V = \pi r^2 h$

   $= \pi(4^2)(0.5) = \mathbf{25.12 \ ft^3}$

5. **(A)**

   (A) Corresponding angles in right triangles are not necessarily the same, so they do not have to be similar.

   (B) All spheres are similar.

   (C) Corresponding angles in 30–60–90 triangles are the same, so all 30–60–90 triangles are similar.

   (D) Corresponding angles in a square are all the same (90°), so all squares are similar.

   (E) All corresponding angles in cubes are congruent, so they are all similar.

6. **(B)**

   The slope 0.0293 gives the increase in passenger car miles (in billions) for each year that passes. Muliply this value by 5 to find the increase that occurs over 5 years: 5(0.0293) = **0.1465 billion miles**.

7. **(A)**

   Simplify each root and add.

   $\sqrt[3]{64} = 4$

   $\sqrt[3]{729} = 9$

   $4 + 9 = \mathbf{13}$

8. **(B)**

   Find the highest possible multiple of 4 that is less than or equal to 397, and then subtract to find the remainder.

   $99 \times 4 = 396$

   $397 - 396 = \mathbf{1}$

9. **(C)**

   Find the height of the cylinder using the equation for surface area.

   $SA = 2\pi rh + 2\pi r^2$

   $48\pi = 2\pi(4)h + 2\pi(4)^2$

   $h = 2$

   Find the volume using the volume equation.

   $V = \pi r^2 h$

   $V = \pi(4)^2(2) = \mathbf{32\pi \ ft.^3}$

10. **(D)**

    Use FOIL to multiply the first two terms.

    $(x + 3)(x - 2) = x^2 + 3x - 2x - 6$

    $= x^2 + x - 6$

    Multiply the resulting trinomial by $(x + 4)$.

    $(x^2 + x - 6)(x + 4) =$

    $x^3 + 4x^2 + x^2 + 4x - 6x - 24$

    $= \mathbf{x^3 + 5x^2 - 2x - 24}$

11. **(C)**

    Plug each value into the equation.

    $4(3 + 4)^2 - 4(3)^2 + 20 = 180 \neq 276$

    $4(4 + 4)^2 - 4(3)^2 + 20 = 240 \neq 276$

    $4(6 + 4)^2 - 4(6)^2 + 20 = \mathbf{276}$

    $4(12 + 4)^2 - 4(12)^2 + 20 = 468 \neq 276$

12. **(A)**

    Plug 0 in for y and solve for x.

    $10x + 10y = 10$

    $10x + 10(0) = 10$

    $x = 1$

The x-intercept is at **(1, 0)**.

13. **(C)**

Round each value and add.
$129{,}113 \approx 129{,}000$
$34{,}602 \approx 35{,}000$
$129{,}000 + 35{,}000 = \mathbf{164{,}000}$

14. **(C)**

Factor the trinomial and set each factor equal to 0.
$x^2 - 3x - 18 = 0$
$(x + 3)(x - 6) = 0$
$(x + 3) = 0$
$\mathbf{x = -3}$
$(x - 6) = 0$
$\mathbf{x = 6}$

15. **(A)**

Use the midpoint formula to find point B.
$M_x: \frac{(7 + x)}{2} = -3$
$x = -13$
$M_y: \frac{(12 + y)}{2} = 10$
$y = 8$
$B = \mathbf{(-13, 8)}$

16. **(C)**

Use the triangle inequality theorem to find the possible values for the third side, then calculate the possible perimeters.
$13 - 5 < s < 13 + 5$
$8 < s < 18$

$13 + 5 + 8 < P < 13 + 5 + 18$
$26 < P < 36$
26.5 is the only answer choice in this range.

17. **(D)**

$5 \div 8 = 0.625$
$0.625 \times 100 = \mathbf{62.5\%}$

18. **(D)**

Solve the system using substitution.
$z - 2x = 14 \rightarrow z = 2x + 14$
$2z - 6x = 18$

$2(2x + 14) - 6x = 18$
$4x + 28 - 6x = 18$
$-2x = -10$
$x = 5$

$z - 2(5) = 14$
$\mathbf{z = 24}$

19. **(D)**

Plug $m = 3$ and $n = -4$ into the expression and simplify.
$15m + 2n^2 - 7 =$
$15(3) + 2(-4)^2 - 7 = \mathbf{70}$

20. **(C)**

Write out each number to find the largest.
A. 9299 ones = 9299
B. 903 tens = 9030
C. 93 hundreds = **9300**
D. 9 thousands = 9000
E. 9 thousandths = 0.009

21. **(A)**

Use the points to find the slope.
$m = \frac{y_2 - y_1}{x_2 - x_1} = \frac{-3 - 9}{4 - (-2)} = -2$
Use the point-slope equation to find the equation of the line.
$(y - y_1) = m(x - x_1)$
$y - (-3) = -2(x - 4)$
$\mathbf{y = -2x + 5}$

22. **(D)**

All the points lie on the circle, so each line segment is a radius. The sum of the 4 lines will be 4 times the radius.
$r = \frac{75}{2} = 37.5$
$4r = \mathbf{150}$

23. **(B)**

Add 5 to each side to isolate the variable k.
$10 \leq k - 5$
$15 \leq k$
$\mathbf{k \geq 15}$

24. **(B)**

Calculate the volume of water in tank A.

$V = l \times w \times h$

$5 \times 10 \times 1 = 50 \text{ ft}^3$

Find the height this volume would reach in tank B.

$V = l \times w \times h$

$50 = 5 \times 5 \times h$

$h = \textbf{2 ft}$

25. **(B)**

Plug each set of values into the inequality $2a - 5b > 12$ and simplify.

(A) $2(2) - 5(6) = -26 \not> 12$

(B) $2(1) - 5(-3) = \textbf{17} > \textbf{12}$

(C) $2(-1) - 5(3) = -17 \not> 12$

(D) $2(7) - 5(2) = 4 \not> 12$

ELECTRONICS

1. (C)

(A) is incorrect. An atom with a charge of −17e would have seventeen more electrons than protons.

(B) is incorrect. An atom with a charge of −7e would have seven more electrons than protons.

(C) is correct. This atom has a total charge of −5e + 12e = +7e.

(D) is incorrect. An atom with a charge of +17 would have seventeen more protons than electrons.

2. (A)

(A) is correct. Watts (W) is the unit for power.

(B) is incorrect. Amperes (A) is the unit for current.

(C) is incorrect. Joules (J) is the unit for energy.

(D) is Incorrect. Ohms (Ω) is the unit for resistance.

3. (D)

(A) is incorrect. Positive and negative charge is neither created nor destroyed. No particle can change its charge.

(B) is incorrect. Electrons, not protons, move to create current.

(C) is incorrect. Voltage sources are sources of electric potential. They do not store electrons.

(D) is correct. The valence electrons are the outermost and most loosely held electrons. They are more likely to move in a conducting material.

4. (B)

(A) is incorrect. Conventional current is in the opposite direction of the flow of electrons.

(B) is correct. Conventional current is in the same direction of the flow of holes.

(C) is incorrect. Direct current means current has a constant value.

(D) is incorrect. Alternating current means current alternates direction.

5. (B)

Use Ohm's law.

$V = IR = (5 \ A)(0.5 \ \Omega) = \textbf{2.5 V}$

6. (D)

(A) is incorrect. All power supplies have an EMF.

(B) is incorrect. Mechanical movement provides EMF in an electric generator.

(C) is incorrect. A changing magnetic field creates EMF in a generator, inductor, or transformer.

(D) is correct. Chemical reactions create the EMF in batteries.

7. (A)

(A) is correct. It is usually easy to see if the wire is intact or if it has been destroyed from a blown fuse.

(B) is incorrect. A blown fuse is an open circuit with infinite resistance.

(C) is incorrect. This describes a circuit breaker.

(D) is incorrect. This behavior would occur in a current limiter circuit.

8. (B)

(A) is incorrect. The symbol for a diode is:

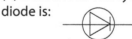

(B) is correct. This is the figure for a switch.

(C) is incorrect. The symbol for a fuse is:

(D) is incorrect. The symbol for a battery is:

9. (D)

Use Ohm's law.

$R = \dfrac{V}{I} = \dfrac{10 \ V}{0.005 \ A} = 2{,}000 \ \Omega = \textbf{2 k}\boldsymbol{\Omega}$

10. **(A)**

Use the equation for equivalent resistance in a parallel circuit.

$$\frac{1}{R_{eq}} = \frac{1}{R_1} + \frac{1}{R_2} + ... + \frac{1}{R_n}$$

$$\frac{1}{R_{eq}} = \frac{1}{1\,k\Omega} + \frac{1}{2\,k\Omega} + \frac{1}{0.5\,k\Omega} = 3.5\frac{1}{k\Omega}$$

$$\frac{1}{R_{eq}} = \mathbf{0.3\ k\Omega}$$

11. **(A)**

(A) is correct. A dimmer needs a variable resistance to raise and lower the amount of voltage and therefore the current through the light bulb.

(B) is incorrect. A regular light switch is simply off and on.

(C) is incorrect. A doorbell button is similar to a switch. No variable resistance is needed.

(D) is incorrect. A key on a keyboard is similar to a switch. No variable resistance is needed.

12. **(B)**

(A) is incorrect. The capacitor does not act as a switch.

(B) is correct. The capacitor stores energy in the electric field.

(C) is incorrect. The diode allows current in only one direction.

(D) is incorrect. The heating element in an oven is a resistor.

13. **(A)**

(A) is correct. The most common use of a transistor is as a switch.

(B) is incorrect. The transistor cannot be used as a capacitor.

(C) is incorrect. The transistor cannot be used as a solenoid.

(D) is incorrect. The transistor cannot be used as a laser.

14. **(C)**

(A) is incorrect. A transformer would be used in this application.

(B) is incorrect. A transformer would be used in this application.

(C) is correct. A rectifier changes AC into DC.

(D) is incorrect. And inverter changes DC into AC.

15. **(C)**

(A) is incorrect. The inductor does not act as an antenna.

(B) is incorrect. Sound is made from vibrations, and the inductor should not vibrate.

(C) is correct. The inductor resists current change due to its self-inductance.

(D) is incorrect. A rectifier converts AC into DC.

16. **(A)**

(A) is correct. Because the power supply and the rotation are at the same frequency, this is a synchronous motor.

(B) is incorrect. An asynchronous motor has different rotation and input power frequencies.

(C) is incorrect. The speed of the motor is not provided in the question.

(D) is incorrect. The torque of the motor is not provided in the question.

17. **(A)**

(A) is correct. The stator field is the magnetic field produced in the stator assembly.

(B) is incorrect. The stator field is a magnetic field.

(C) is incorrect. The stator field is the magnetic field produced in the stator assembly.

(D) is incorrect. The stator field is a magnetic field created in the stator.

18. **(B)**

(A) is incorrect. An alternator produces AC power.

(B) is correct. A transformer converts voltages to different values.

(C) is incorrect. A rectifier converts AC to DC.

(D) is incorrect. A capacitor is an energy storage element in electronic circuits.

19. **(C)**

Use Ohm's law.

$$I = \frac{V}{R} = \frac{120\,V}{15\,\Omega} = \textbf{8 A}$$

20. **(D)**

(A) is incorrect. Capacitors store energy in an electric field.

(B) is incorrect. Batteries store chemical energy.

(C) is incorrect. Inductors store energy in a magnetic field.

(D) is correct. A transformer uses electromagnetic induction to transfer electrical energy between two circuits.

Automotive and Shop Information

1. (C)

(A) is incorrect. An air-fuel mixture must enter the cylinder, then be compressed and then ignited.

(B) is incorrect. The air-fuel mixture must be heated.

(C) is correct. Combustion is the process of a controlled explosion from a burning pressurized air-fuel mixture.

(D) is incorrect. The air-fuel mixture needs to be pressurized then burnt—ignited.

2. (C)

(A) is incorrect. A tape measure is used for linear measurements in construction.

(B) is incorrect. An outside caliper is used only for outside measurements.

(C) is correct. A Vernier caliper is used for both inside and outside measurements.

(D) is incorrect. A level is used to check the level of machinery and framework.

3. (D)

(A) is incorrect. Intake is closed at this time.

(B) is incorrect. Both are closed at this time.

(C) is incorrect. Exhaust is closed at this time.

(D) is correct. Both valves need to be closed for the power stroke to happen.

4. (A)

(A) is correct. A coping saw is used to cut shapes or curves into wood.

(B) is incorrect. A band saw is not a handsaw. With the appropriate blade, it can cut metal.

(C) is incorrect. This saw is used to cut against the grain on wooden boards.

(D) is incorrect. A hacksaw is used to cut metal.

5. (C)

(A) is incorrect. Right-hand bits are used for normal drilling operations.

(B) is incorrect. Left-hand bits rotate counterclockwise to turn the object out of the threads.

(C) is correct. A tap is used to thread holes.

(D) is incorrect. A tap can only thread holes.

6. (A)

(A) is correct. The compression stroke occurs when all valves are closed, and the piston is moving from BDC to TDC to compress the air-fuel mixture.

(B) is incorrect. This is the power stroke.

(C) is incorrect. This is the exhaust stroke.

(D) is incorrect. This is the intake stroke.

7. (C)

(A) is incorrect. This is the four-cycle process.

(B) is incorrect. This allows intake air and exhaust to leave.

(C) is correct. The spark firing is in a defined order: cylinder 1, then 3, then 4, and finally 2.

(D) is incorrect. Camshaft rotation is part of timing.

8. (B)

(A) is incorrect. A nail gun will only drive nails.

(B) is correct. A ball-peen hammer is used with chisels.

(C) is incorrect. A wooden mallet is not used with impact tools.

(D) is incorrect. A claw hammer is used to drive and remove nails.

9. (B)

(A) is incorrect. The cylinder head helps contain the heat and pressure.

(B) is correct. The piston head is exposed.

(C) is incorrect. Air is part of the combustion, but fuel is needed too.

(D) is incorrect. Fuel is part of the combustion, but air is needed too.

10. **(B)**

(A) is incorrect. This fastener has a star hole and rod insert in the head.

(B) is correct. A Torx fastener has a star hole in head.

(C) is incorrect. A Robertson fastener does not have a star hole in the head.

(D) is incorrect. This fastener does not have a star hole in the head.

11. **(B)**

(A) is incorrect. The thermostat is closed at this time.

(B) is correct. The thermostat opens when the engine is hot.

(C) is incorrect. Acceleration does not have anything to do with the thermostat opening or closing.

(D) is incorrect. The thermostat should be closed at start-up. The engine would be cold.

12. **(D)**

(A) is incorrect. Neither a ratchet nor a socket is a wrench.

(B) is incorrect. A ratchet must be used with a socket.

(C) is incorrect. An end wrench does not have a box end.

(D) is correct. A combination wrench has both an open end and a box end.

13. **(C)**

(A) is incorrect. This would be a sign of a major leak in the system.

(B) is incorrect. If the fan was not working, this would indicate another component has failed.

(C) is correct. A weep hole is used to show signs of damaged seals or bearings.

(D) is incorrect. If the bypass tube is leaking, it is either disconnected or cracked.

14. **(C)**

(A) is incorrect. This screw is used for attaching sheet metal to framework.

(B) is incorrect. A self-drilling screw is used for metal and does not need a pilot hole.

(C) is correct. A machine screw is used with a washer and nut combination or with a threaded hole.

(D) is incorrect. This screw is used for wood applications only.

15. **(A)**

(A) is correct. Engine lubrication has these four functions.

(B) is incorrect. Coolant does this.

(C) is incorrect. The valves should never touch.

(D) is incorrect. Coolant or air help remove heat from the cylinder.

16. **(A)**

(A) is correct. Wing nuts are designed to be removed quickly and often.

(B) is incorrect. Standard bolts are designed for permanent installations. Bolts cannot be used with studs.

(C) is incorrect. Lock nuts are designed for permanent installations.

(D) is incorrect. A castle nut is used with a cotter key and is often used in front-end applications.

17. **(B)**

(A) is incorrect. This is used in two-stroke engines.

(B) is correct. Dry sumps use an oil tank to store oil.

(C) is incorrect. This is part of the cooling system.

(D) is incorrect. This is part of the cooling system.

18. **(A)**

(A) is correct. An inside snap ring is used to secure bearings inside a bore.

(B) is incorrect. This is used to secure a bearing to a shaft.

(C) is incorrect. Snap-ring pliers are used to install and remove snap rings.

(D) is incorrect. Locking nuts are on studs or bolts.

19. **(D)**

(A) is incorrect. The compression in a diesel engine is higher than a gasoline engine.

(B) is incorrect. The compression in a diesel engine is higher than a gasoline engine.

(C) is incorrect. The compression in a diesel engine is higher than a gasoline engine.

(D) is correct. The compression in a diesel engine is higher than a gasoline engine.

20. **(D)**

(A) is incorrect. These nails are used in furniture applications.

(B) is incorrect. Framing nails are used to attach boards in construction applications.

(C) is incorrect. These nails are used to attach drywall to wood framing.

(D) is correct. Roofing nails are used to attach shingles to roof boarding.

21. **(C)**

(A) is incorrect. The fuel pump delivers fuel to the fuel system.

(B) is incorrect. Normally a control module will regulate when the injector sprays. Older mechanical systems vary.

(C) is correct. The pressure regulator regulates the fuel pressure to the injectors.

(D) is incorrect. The control module and other components help adjust the air-fuel ratio.

22. **(B)**

(A) is incorrect. A jack plane is used for wood-finishing operations.

(B) is correct. Rivets are used for connecting pieces of metal.

(C) is incorrect. Drill bits bore holes.

(D) is incorrect. Wood screws are used for wood applications.

23. **(A)**

(A) is correct. A lean mixture is 15:1.

(B) is incorrect. This is a rich mixture.

(C) is incorrect. This mixture is optimal for an air-fuel ratio.

(D) is incorrect. This is normally a coolant mixture.

24. **(B)**

(A) is incorrect. A MIG welder uses wire feed.

(B) is correct. An arc welder uses a welding rod.

(C) is incorrect. An oxyacetylene welder uses a fill rod.

(D) is incorrect. A is the only correct answer.

25. **(C)**

(A) is incorrect. Pre-ignition is a symptom, not a part.

(B) is incorrect. Pre-ignition is a symptom, not a part.

(C) is correct. Pre-ignition is when the piston is traveling upward, but the air-fuel mixture ignites before the piston reaches TDC.

(D) is incorrect. Pre-ignition normally happens at TDC.

MECHANICAL COMPREHENSION

1. **(A)**

    Sum the forces to find the net force on the block.

    $F_r - F_l = 300 - 400\ N = \mathbf{-100\ N}$

2. **(C)**

    Use the formula for acceleration.

    $a = \dfrac{\Delta v}{t} = \dfrac{5 - 0\ m}{s/1\ s} = \mathbf{5\ m/s^2}$

3. **(C)**

    The mechanical advantage for a system of pulleys is equal to the number of pulleys. The MA of the system shown is **3**.

4. **(D)**

    (A) is incorrect. A wrench has a small mass compared to the International Space Station, so it would be easier to move.

    (B) is incorrect. While another astronaut has a larger mass than the tools in the other answer choices, a human being is still quite small in mass compared to the International Space Station. This option is incorrect.

    (C) is incorrect. A screwdriver has a small mass compared to the International Space Station, so it would be easier to move.

    (D) is correct. The largest mass will be the hardest to move. The space station has the largest mass.

5. **(A)**

    (A) is correct. This is the proper definition.

    (B) is incorrect. This describes mass.

    (C) is incorrect. This describes the magnitude of the acceleration.

    (D) is incorrect. This defines the term *jerk*.

6. **(D)**

    Use the equation for kinetic friction. In this case, the normal force will equal the weight of the object.

    $f_k = \mu_k N$

    $f_k = 0.5 \times 10\ N = \mathbf{5\ N}$

7. **(A)**

    (A) is correct. The object will gain energy.

    (B) is incorrect. The object will lose energy if negative work is done.

    (C) is incorrect. It is not guaranteed that the temperature will change.

    (D) is incorrect. It is not guaranteed that the temperature will change.

8. **(C)**

    Use the formula for potential energy.

    $PE = Wh = (150\ N)(1\ m) = \mathbf{150\ J}$

9. **(C)**

    Use the formula for mechanical advantage of a ramp.

    $MA = \dfrac{l}{h} = \dfrac{20}{5} = \mathbf{4}$

10. **(A)**

    (A) is correct. Power is measured in watts (W).

    (B) is incorrect. Energy is measured in joules (J).

    (C) is incorrect. Force is measured in newtons (N).

    (D) is incorrect. Electric charge is measured in coulombs (C).

11. **(C)**

    Use the formula for momentum.

    $p = mv = (100\ kg)(2\ m/s)$

    $= \mathbf{200\ kg\ m/s}$

12. **(C)**

    Use the formula for torque.

    $\tau = rF$

    $F = \dfrac{\tau}{r} = \dfrac{100\ Nm}{1\ m} = \mathbf{100\ N}$

13. (D)

The moment of inertia is largest when the mass is large and the distance of the mass from the axis of rotation is large.

14. (A)

(A) is correct. This is the correct explanation of the operation of a pulley.

(B) is incorrect. A pulley does not have a motor.

(C) is incorrect. A pulley does not have an inclined plane.

(D) is incorrect. A torque from friction will lower the effectiveness of the pulley.

15. (C)

The tension will be equal to the weight it supports, **100 N.**

16. (D)

(A) is incorrect. Impulse is *force × time*.

(B) is incorrect. Torque is rotational force.

(C) is incorrect. A wedge is a simple machine.

(D) is correct. Pitch is the distance a screw goes into the wood during one rotation.

17. (B)

(A) is incorrect. The net force on the object will be zero; there is no acceleration.

(B) is correct. The net force on the object will be zero, so the mass is in equilibrium.

(C) is incorrect. The net force on the object will be zero; there is no acceleration.

(D) is incorrect. There is no component of the applied forces in the vertical direction.

18. (C)

Use the formula for center of mass.
$$x_{cm} = \frac{m_1 x_1 + m_2 x_2}{m_1 + m_2} = \frac{0 + (1 \text{ kg})(1 \text{ m})}{1 \text{ kg} + 1 \text{ kg}}$$
$$= \mathbf{0.5 \text{ m}}$$

19. (A)

(A) is correct. The weight of the air in the ball is much less than the same volume of water that was displaced. Therefore, the buoyant upward force is very large.

(B) is incorrect. It was not stated that the ball shrinks, and the ball would still feel a large buoyant force upward.

(C) is incorrect. It was not stated that the ball expands, and the ball would still feel a large buoyant force upward.

(D) is incorrect. It will have a large buoyant force regardless of the temperature.

20. (D)

Use the formula for power.
$$P = \frac{E}{t}$$
$$E = Pt = (60 \text{ W})(100 \text{ s}) = \mathbf{6,000 \text{ J}}$$

21. (D)

Each gear will move in the opposite direction as the gear driving its motion. Because Gear A is moving clockwise, Gear B will move counterclockwise. Gear C will then move clockwise.

22. (B)

(A) is incorrect. The normal force will be perpendicular to the surface of the incline and will point up.

(B) is correct. The arrow *F* represents gravity, which is pulling the box down toward the Earth.

(C) is incorrect. Friction would point parallel to the surface of the incline in a direction opposite to the box's motion.

(D) is incorrect. Tension is created by hanging objects, which do not appear in the diagram.

23. (D)

Weight is directly proportional to mass ($W = mg$), so the largest mass will have the largest weight.

24. (A)

(A) is correct. Mass is a measure of an object's inertia.

(B) is incorrect. Speed is distance over time.

(C) is incorrect. Acceleration is the change of velocity over time.

(D) is incorrect. A force is a push or pull.

25. (B)

(A) is incorrect. As it nears its highest point, the pendulum will have a large amount of potential energy and almost no kinetic energy.

(B) is correct. At the bottom of its swing, the pendulum will have its maximum amount of kinetic energy and no potential energy.

(C) is incorrect. Midway through its swing, the pendulum will have a mix of kinetic and potential energy.

(D) is incorrect. As it nears its highest point, the pendulum will have a large amount of potential energy and almost no kinetic energy.

1. (B)
2. (D)
3. (A)
4. (C)
5. (B)
6. (D)
7. (C)
8. (A)
9. (D)
10. (D)
11. (D)
12. (C)
13. (A)
14. (A)
15. (A)
16. (B)
17. (C)
18. (B)
19. (A)
20. (D)
21. (D)
22. (B)
23. (C)
24. (A)
25. (C)

Follow the link below to take your second ASVAB practice test and to access other online study resources:

www.triviumtestprep.com/asvab-online-resources

CPSIA information can be obtained
at www.ICGtesting.com
Printed in the USA
LVHW051408220121
677114LV00009B/618